Rosabeth Moss Kanter

on the

Frontiers of
Management

Rosabeth Moss Kanter

ON THE

Frontiers of Management

Rosabeth Moss Kanter

A Harvard Business Review Book

Library of Congress Cataloging-in-Publication Data

Kanter, Rosabeth Moss.
    Rosabeth Moss Kanter on the frontiers of management / Rosabeth
Moss Kanter.
        p.   cm. — (A Harvard business review book)
    Includes index.
    ISBN 0-87584-802-8 (alk. paper)
    1. Organizational change.   2. Industrial management.   I. Title.
II. Series : Harvard business review book series.
HD58.8.K364   1997
658.4′06—dc21   97-2747
                                                                      CIP

To Matt, Barry, Vineyard family and friends, Harvard colleagues and students, Goodmeasure collaborators and alumni; to my sorely missed mother and father, Helen and Nelson; and to all those leaders and would-be leaders with whom I have shared the joys and challenges of working on change through the years, I offer some poetic wisdom:

> *Perhaps age has taught me that the earth is still new, molten at the core and still forming, that black leaves in the winter forest will crawl with life in the spring, that our story is ongoing and it is indeed a crime to allow the heart's energies to dissipate with the fading of light on the horizon. I can't be sure. I brood upon it and sleep little. I wait like a denied lover for the blue glow of dawn.*
> —James Lee Burke, *Heaven's Prisoners*

Or, as Nelson used to say, stripping poetry to its essentials, *"Tomorrow is another day."*

Contents

Contents

Preface
Notes from the Frontier

Question: What do shamrocks, symphony orchestras, gazelles, federations, astronauts, atoms and molecules, schools of sharks, virtual networks, whitewater rafting, jazz bands, diamonds, and ant colonies have in common?

Answer: Not much. But all of them have been invoked to describe the properties of a new organizational model that is replacing top-down bureaucratic machines.

The search for excellence on the part of business leaders has triggered a corresponding search for metaphors by business writers. Not to mention a search for screaming headlines for business magazines that think they need new attention-grabbers for sated business audiences.

Sometimes there is no virtue in novelty for its own sake. Sometimes it is more useful to remind people of the wisdom that has already been accumulated, to consolidate the lessons from a period of change. That's why I decided to publish this book. It contains no new metaphors for the organization of the future—just insights that continue to be valid about leadership and strategy, innovation and change.

I wrote the short essays and research articles collected here for the *Harvard Business Review (HBR)* over the past decade-and-a-half, a period of great discovery and change for businesses all over the world. This period of discovery has opened a new frontier in management thinking. I have been an active explorer of that thought frontier, helping managers in business as well as government and health care to understand their roles in organizations undergoing massive change.

This revolution has consisted of an attack on organizational rigidities, boundaries, and top-down traditions. Some of the ideas in this book, now seen as current wisdom, were once considered the ravings of the radical fringe. *Empowerment* was first a political term used by student activists, not a business buzzword; *participative management* and *employee involvement* were peripheral ideas pushed by a small group of idealists. Today, thanks in part to articles such as "Power Failure in Management Circuits" (the first piece I wrote for HBR), ideas about empowering people to create change are part of the conventional repertoire of enlightened managers. And a new view of the corporation has emerged and become accepted as the model—one that is flatter, more focused, speedier, and more customer-service-oriented and that includes more teams and projects, more cross-functional contact, more partnering with customers and suppliers, more strategic alliances, more consciousness of social responsibilities.

But just because the terms have been defined and new models established, we should not imagine that everyone has crossed the frontier into a new way of working. The use of the best management ideas is often an aspiration for companies, not a fait accompli. The destination has not been reached just because the map has been drawn. That is another reason I wanted to produce this book—to keep the momentum going, to encourage more organizational self-scrutiny, to help managers to see that the hard work of improving innovation still lies ahead. The pieces gathered here should remind managers across sectors and countries about their tasks in changing organizations. The first time some of these articles were published, managers reading them learned about new tasks. Now, collected here, they constitute a refresher course for experienced leaders as well as a handbook for new ones, a guide for both on thinking about and performing those tasks into the twenty-first century. Now it is up to managers to complete the job and cross the frontier by acting on the agenda for change.

Managers must pursue the new agenda with balance and judgment, to avoid the excesses that unbridled enthusiasm for change is so likely to produce. That is my third reason for wanting to gather together the enduring lessons learned over the past several years—as a reality check for managers enthralled by the latest fad. New management methods are sometimes flogged as miracle cures and translated into programs followed religiously, to the point that all the other things that make organizations effective are

jeopardized. The advice given to managers often consists of opposing pulls and tugs. The managerial challenge is to perform a
balancing act, to steer a course between opposing pulls—for example, between the tendency to make so many rules that innovation is stifled and the risk of having so few rules that duplication
and wasted effort ensue. Advice-givers best serve managers when
they provide a comprehensive view of all of the factors that produce success. This broad view helps to remind them of the other
end of the pendulum whenever they have swung too far in one
direction: cost-obsessed companies need to be reminded about
quality, but then when they raise quality beyond what the market
will pay for, they must be reminded again about costs. The only
thing wrong with pushing systematic approaches to either Total
Quality or cost management is the premise that only one or the
other is needed, and then life will be perfect. Balance and judgment remain essential skills for leaders.

The articles collected here provide an agenda for managerial
work, whether that work is carried out by those bearing a formal
leadership title or by self-managed teams of professionals. Individually, the articles cover a variety of topics of importance to
managers: strategy, innovation, customer focus, global trends,
planning for change, strategic alliances, compensation systems,
and community responsibility. They roam around the world, using
examples from a range of businesses and industries. But underneath the range and variety is a unity of purpose.

Taken together, the chapters in this book reinforce a single,
timeless message: the importance of providing the tools and conditions that liberate people to use their brainpower to make a
difference in a world of constant challenge and change.

PART

I

Introduction

1

The Imagination to Innovate, the Professionalism to Perform, and the Openness to Collaborate: Leading the Change-Adept Organization

All managers have two jobs—handling today's issues and getting ready for the future. To help themselves get ready, they need to know they can count on their best strategic weapon for the information age: a change-adept organization. A change-adept organization anticipates, creates, and responds effectively to change.

By putting change management at the center of strategy, I am not talking about a twelve-step program for corporate reengineering or proposing another manual for business transformation. What I want managers to learn from this book is how to create the conditions that make productive change a natural way of life. In change-adept organizations people do not always identify what they are doing as "changing": They believe they are simply carrying out current projects. But the impact of those projects goes beyond simple departure from the past (the conventional definition of change) to include increased fitness for the future.

Managers who can embed change capabilities in everyday operations and who empower their people to serve as agents of change are less likely to be blindsided by surprises or to face resistance from the work force. They have less need to foment revolutions in order to achieve business goals. They can steer a course between the equally perilous extremes of denial—not enough change—and of radical upheaval—too much change. Companies cannot avoid change, but neither can they afford endless painful "revolutions."

Change-denial is dangerous. Companies cannot be protected from change, regardless of their size, their resources, or the excellence of their current offerings. But excessive, destabilizing, "revolutionary" change is just as threatening. Companies (and the communities in which they operate) cannot afford to continue paying the costs of wrenching change—job loss and work force churn among them. The *re*'s of revolution—reinvention, reengineering, or restructuring—are ultimately high-cost ways to move a company in a new direction, even when they bring short-term gains in profitability and stock price.

Every major managerial action can be assessed not only for its success at achieving immediate goals but for its impact on the organization's ability to embrace change. Such actions either build key organizational assets necessary for the future or deplete them. We have many ready images to characterize such depletion. When a company's actions today succeed on current terms but undermine long-term capabilities, we say, "They won the battle but lost the war," or "The buildings are intact but the people are gone." The term *burn-out* reflects just this issue: Some periods of productivity can be so extreme that the energy expended can never be recovered.

Engaging people in the search for change not only creates a new way of life, it builds employees' capacity to produce more change, more productively.

Managing change takes place at three levels.

- Change projects: discrete, specific streams of action designed to address a particular problem or need. These can succeed in the short-term, especially if they are focused, results-oriented, and do not depart much from company tradition. But if they are merely discrete, stand-alone projects, they will often have no long-term impact, memory of them will fade, and later generations will rediscover the same need.

- Change programs: interrelated projects designed to have major cumulative organizational impact. Here success often depends less on the quality of the plan or tool itself than on the way each project links to other streams of action in the company. Change programs often fail because they are isolated from ongoing business activities, contain too many projects that don't fit well together, or are carried out by an elite of converts who expect everyone else to stop what they're doing and join the cult.

• Change-adept organizations: investments that create the capability for continuous innovation and improvement, for embracing change as an internally desired opportunity before it becomes an externally driven threat, by mobilizing many people in the organization to contribute. Success with efforts of this kind depends on whether the conditions necessary to make the organization change-friendly exist, so that change can occur continuously and feels natural.

All change involves closing a gap. But too many change projects and programs are just problem-solving or turnarounds attuned to the past, rather than asset-building aimed at the future—the hallmark of the change-adept organization. Restructuring programs are likely to be devised when the organization's performance declines relative to the past—their own or that of competitors. The gap to be closed is that between current performance and expectations based on past experience or on the current industry standard; the goal is getting the organization back on track. This narrow, backward-focused approach reminds me of Marshall McLuhan's famous image of trying to drive a car by looking in the rear-view mirror.

In contrast, leadership in a change-adept organization works on a different kind of gap: that between current performance and the organization's possibilities—its collective hopes, dreams, and aspirations. Change-adept leaders are attuned to the future. As Alan Kay, the inventor of the computer mouse, once said, "The best way to predict the future is to invent it." Without knowing yet what must be, leaders in change-adept organizations consider what can be or might be.

Change-adept organizations are dynamic, open systems with many active pathways for participation and influence, with many people involved in the search for better ideas, and with rapid feedback loops extending within and without the organization. They innovate, stress learning, and collaborate with allies and partners. They produce three intangible assets that help them master change:

• *concepts*, the best and latest ideas and technologies, the result of continuous innovation;

- *competence,* the ability to execute flawlessly and to deliver value to customers with ever higher standards, by investing in work force skills and learning; and

- *connections,* the best partners to extend the company's reach, leverage its offerings, or provide a window on innovations and opportunities. The task of managers is to find, create, build, nurture, monitor, measure, and replenish these assets—the organization's ideas, know-how, and relationships.

Concepts, competence, and connections draw on human talents such as intellectual skills, imagination, courage, creativity, sociability, diplomacy, and trust. The dawning information age values intellectual capital and knowledge work; indeed, it has become fashionable for companies to declare that people are their most important assets. But regardless of the sometimes-questionable sincerity of such statements, they are at best only partial truths. People are perhaps a company's most valuable *raw materials,* but they do not become assets or sources of organizational capital until deployed effectively. Human talents exist only as potential until activated by the organization.

Managers have the fundamental, enduring job of mobilizing and motivating individual human talent in pursuit of collective ends. This encompasses defining and communicating tasks, grouping people and attaching them to their tasks, and ensuring appropriate treatment of people on the job. Managers might start with good raw material in the form of well-trained people, but they must use that raw material to create assets that remain with the organization even after particular people leave. Skandia, a Swedish insurance logistics company that pioneered in the measurement and reporting of its intellectual capital, defines this asset as what is left in the organization beyond what is inside the heads of the people—for example, when an expert's know-how is captured on software that allows others to use the same technique, or a discovery of a better method is taught to others and becomes a routine practice. Great companies make something happen above and beyond what their people contribute as individuals, just as great leaders organize people to accomplish more together than they could individually. The organization is strengthened in the process, and the people have greater opportunities to succeed.

Change-adept organizations cultivate the imagination to innovate, the professionalism to perform, and the openness to collaborate. Their managers lead the fight against complacency, territoriality, and insularity. Their people serve as idea scouts in search of innovation, professionals in pursuit of ever-better skills, and ambassadors to their partners and communities.

The Imagination to Innovate

The best *concepts* are vital in industries demanding constant innovation to hold customers and attract new ones. That truth from high tech holds even in service industries.

Air transportation, for example, could have easily become a commodity, with each carrier offering the same aircraft, seat configurations, pilot training, interline ticketing, and travel bookers. American Airlines broke the mold by developing the first leading computerized reservations system and inventing frequent flyer programs, but fell behind when everyone else grabbed those concepts. American was not the force behind the next stream of innovations. Virgin Atlantic provoked British Airways, for example, to set the pace with concepts such as arrivals lounges with showers for international travelers, new seat designs, and pajamas and quilts for sleepers. Southwest Airlines used creativity to find a niche in low-cost services. Founder Herb Kelleher's idea for a different kind of airline was augmented by a try-anything mandate to staff who then produced numerous small but significant differences. Southwest was the first airline to offer ticketless travel system-wide, and it saved half the cost of the computers by mobilizing employees to assemble the machines themselves out of off-the-shelf components at a beer and pizza party.

The airline industry examples demonstrate a range of concepts, from new ways of thinking about the basic business model (the core concept or theory of the business) to specific products or services (most often considered the locus of innovation) to processes that support delivering value to customers, whether by making products more attractive or making the organization more effective. Industries in the midst of competitive or technological upheaval are characterized by a large number of new core concepts, breakthroughs, or transformational innovations. New core concepts or theories of business often come from entrepreneurs who bypass the established channels dominated by current players. Examples include Dell Computers, which innovated by using retail chains and manufacturers' direct sales forces to offer computers through catalogues; or Salick Health Centers, which started stand-alone, full-service cancer and catastrophic illness treatment centers, contributing one more model—the carve-out—to a conceptual revolution in health care delivery.

New ways of thinking about opportunities and how to address them do not always correlate with the amount or timing of research-and-development expenditures. Nicholas Hayek of Swatch helped save the Swiss watch industry by reconceptualizing watches as casual fashion items and developing a mass market brand name. That core concept was the platform for a proliferation of product design and marketing concepts, including Swatch retail stores, but the genesis was an idea, not the output of research.

New concepts can stem from many functions beyond the R&D department. Consider some of the innovations associated with the American auto industry throughout its history. Product innovations such as the minivan or technology innovations such as airbrakes or power steering are obvious examples. Less obvious are those innovations driven by other functions: marketing-oriented innovations such as exterior colors, which broke through Henry Ford's fiat that customers could have "any color they want as long as it's black," or financial innovations such as consumer credit, which enlarged the market by enabling more people to afford cars. Sometimes an idea stems from significant scientific and technical research, but just as often the need for R&D follows the idea (as in the development of technology that made colored paint stick to metal car bodies). What is always essential, however, is the idea itself: a concept resulting from new thinking.

There are numerous reasons why innovation is difficult, and failures of human imagination are not foremost among them. Organizational structure and culture are often the culprits. In *The Change Masters,* I proposed a list of "Ten Rules for Stifling Innovation," as a parody of corporate values statements. The list starts with "Be suspicious of any new idea from below—because it's new, and because it's from below." I continued with that classic innovation-killer, pitting departments against one another in brutal battles for territory. Other innovation-stiflers include isolation of mavericks, punishment of experiments as mistakes, and starvation—lack of resources and time for anything new.

Bigger, established companies are inherently more conservative than smaller or newer ones—with notable exceptions such as 3M, Rubbermaid, Hewlett-Packard, or Disney, which are widely cited as role models for success through continuous innovation. Established companies want to squeeze profit out of past investments. Sometimes an innovation proposed by one department proves inconvenient for other departments, which have plans of their own. Even when people are encouraged to try new things, some managers let them know that it is best to keep risk-taking to a minimum. One company's informal rule for success is "Stick your neck out just enough to get a haircut, but not enough to get your head cut off."

Innovation requires courage as well as imagination. I have been amused to hear some managers express a desire for innovation, then in the next breath ask me, "Who else is doing it?" Some declare, "We want more innovation, we just don't want to be the first." Leaders must create cultures in which experiments, questions, and challenges are not just for the courageous. The goal should be not to encourage more risk-taking but to make it less risky to create something that departs from convention—to make it an expectation instead. Rubbermaid and 3M make innovation an explicit focus, setting goals and measures for innovation. Other companies offer incentives, such as awarding innovators a percent of revenue from their new products. These goals force people to stretch beyond their current assumptions.

Stretch goals for innovation apply to workers at all levels. Wainwright Industries, a small auto supplier that won the U.S. Malcolm Baldrige National Quality Award in 1995, has made continuous improvement proposals and the recognition accompanying them a way of life; Wainwright averages 1.5 implemented ideas per person per week. Innovating is so engrained in the culture that shop floor workers sometimes implement their ideas but do not bother to submit them for a recognition award.

In change-adept companies, resources are allocated to innovations at several stages of formulation, in amounts appropriate to the stage, from early ideas to sure things with major strategic impact. Think of this resource allocation strategy as a kind of pyramid: a few big bets at the top; a portfolio of promising but not-yet-proven experiments in active-project stage in the middle; and a large base of incremental innovations, continuous improvements, and early-stage new ideas being helped along by small amounts of seed funding. Influence flows both down and up the pyramid. The big bets influence the domain for experimentation and provide structure for the search for incremental contributions. Sometimes modest ideas accumulate into a bigger force that turns into new opportunities reaching bigger bet status. And for companies that encourage cross-fertilization, projects and ideas from one part of the organization stimulate new thinking in another part.

When goals are set and resources are available, imagination can come into play. Managers can engage people in the search for new concepts in various ways.

- People can be idea scouts, looking for ideas outside the job, the company, and the industry. They can go on "far afield trips" to be stimulated by ideas or technologies emerging elsewhere that suggest new opportunities for the company.

- Seed capital funds can offer small grants to potential innovators to develop their proposals and to encourage their managers to support something that cannot be covered by the budget for routine activities.

- Open brainstorming sessions or new idea forums can offer regular occasions for people to discuss possible concepts, as is the practice at the product-development firm IDEO. At one of Ocean Spray's forums a lower-level engineer proposed the packaging innovations that enabled the beverage company to steal a march on its much-larger competitors by being the first American company to adopt the paper bottle.

- People can work with customers and suppliers as co-developers. Users are often the primary stimulus for innovation, an observation supported by decades of research on industrial innovation. For process innovators, customers are often internal users who need better service or product innovators who need new processes to support product change.

- Managers can support "lead sites" or internal new ventures that develop concepts useful in other parts of the company. Bank-Boston's First Community Bank (FCB) was designed as a bank-within-a-bank to serve neglected inner-city constituencies who often had limited experience with banks; to help these customers, FCB developed user-friendly "First Step" savings and lending products that then became desirable bank-wide offerings for many other markets.

To convert imagination into useful ideas requires persistence, which is also helped or hindered by the organization. My favorite maxim of management, if not of life, is "Everything can look like a failure in the middle."

Predictable problems arise in the middle of nearly every attempt to do something new. Almost inevitably, innovation projects encounter shortages of time or resources because forecasts were overly optimistic. Unexpected obstacles have to be removed for the project to proceed. Momentum is lost because of staff turnover. Morale dips because of setbacks or sheer fatigue. Or critics attack because they start to notice the project when it looks like it might succeed. Before that, it was not enough of a threat to arouse antagonism.

Stop a project because of these problems, and, by definition, that project will be a failure. Persist—by solving the problems, pumping up the troops, or dealing with the critics—and, if the signals still indicate the idea is promising, a chance for success remains. Change-adept organizations support projects through their difficult middle periods. Banc One's greenhouse program was designed as a kind of corporate incubator for banking innovations, offering technical assistance, encouragement, and political cover to fledgling concepts.

Since not every idea will pay off, change-adept companies have an experimental attitude. They start many efforts, check them at many stages, channel resources to the most promising, and derive lessons from their experiences with the less promising. The planning director for DuPont's central R&D labs cites research showing that it can take 3000 raw ideas to produce one to two commercial products in DuPont's field. Yes, a tradeoff exists between quantity and quality; every company would like that one big hit, and most lack the resources to chase every idea, no matter how promising. But a large base of experiments and possibilities offers more choices. And a side benefit reinforces the value of being change-adept: When more people in the organization engage in the development of new ideas, however modest the ideas, those people become less resistant to change. They are more receptive even to changes imposed upon them when experimentation becomes the organization's new approach.

Innovation involves an organizational balancing act between the decentralized or spontaneous processes associated with creativity and idea generation and the more centralized or formal processes associated with rapid adoption or effective commercialization. Innovation requires tradeoffs and judgment calls: quantity versus quality, focus on today's work versus time freed for innovation, bottoms-up proliferation of ideas versus top-down dissemination of requirements for selected innovations. Timing issues arise: Companies must decide when a first mover advantage exists in the marketplace and when it is better to be a "fast follower."

Precisely because of the uncertainties associated with innovation, companies must continue to invest in it, and managers must ensure that the stock of concepts is replenished. Innovations produce their own change dynamics, as they migrate from periphery to mainstream. The best concepts become standard practice; success encourages imitators. Change-adept organizations cannot rest on the last great concept; they must engage in the search for the next one.

The Professionalism to Perform

Competence is the second asset built by change-adept organizations. Competence involves more than raw skills; it extends to the organizational routines that permit people to use their skills to execute to high standards and to continuously improve their ability to deliver value to customers. If "do it right the first time" was the mantra of zero defects, then the slogan for the change-adept organization should be "do it better the second time": Spread best practices so that every time a task is done, results get better and better.

Organizational disciplines turn workers with raw talent into professionals who can be trusted to do the right thing when empowered to take action not covered by formal rules. Disciplines convert discovery into routine. They allow good practices to be used regularly without the need to reinvent them for each occasion. Disciplines enable people to benefit from the lessons of experience. Managers who are assured that people will apply appropriate processes and are knowledgeable about appropriate approaches can free those people to use their judgment about how best to get results. Disciplines can provide helpful structure for guiding autonomous decisions; without them, empowerment produces chaos. Common approaches and vocabulary help people from diverse backgrounds or countries to work together smoothly. The tools and methods taught in Xerox's Total Quality program, for example, became standard disciplines throughout the company, providing a common starting point for any team brought together across functions or geographies to tackle a new task.

The professional model fits many of the expectations that enlightened companies now hold for their people. Professionals are characterized by high performance standards, mastery of common ways of doing things that meet those standards, belief in a mission apart from financial success, career progress through an increase in skills and the respect of peers, a shared language and knowledge base, participation in conferences to exchange knowledge, self-management and autonomous decisions on the job, and peer review of performance. Professionals understand what they are doing and why; they are not automatons performing mindless rituals set by their bosses. Professionals often control their own agenda and manage their own time, an issue of particular importance to today's work force, which must juggle family responsibilities in addition to work demands.

To many people, the term *professional* connotes doctors and lawyers, engineers and scientists. But consider the distinction familiar in athletics between amateurs and professionals. Professionals have made a significant commitment to excellence in their sports and constantly train to ensure that they play the game at their peak. Considering the personal commitment of people in this way can elevate the roles of associates in a wide range of jobs. The British retailer British Home Stores (BhS) turned shop floor sales clerks into professionals by sending them to training programs where they could gain skills, tested by national vocational exams, that would give them higher pay and more autonomy for every level of mastery they attained.

To ensure organizational competence, managers must become educators of professionals and be professionals themselves. That means making fewer prohibitions and restrictions, with less over-the-shoulder monitoring, and offering more help in learning how to do the job autonomously, how to exercise judgment, and how to customize solutions for unique customers. In such open-ended environments permitting change, the old rules-bound control system is out. The new control system for professionals includes:

- shared values, standards, and priorities;

- adequate information about how people's tasks fit into the organizational strategy;

- ongoing process measures and feedback given directly to people to help them judge and guide their own performances;

- systematic transfer of best practices to learn from what works elsewhere; and

- rewards, recognition, and future opportunities that build commitment.

The growth of a service economy of knowledge workers makes professionalism a more salient part of business success in more companies—particularly the kind of professionalism familiar in human service occupations. As manufacturing jobs continue to decline and the shift from an industrial to an information economy accelerates, more people hold jobs involving human contact. They must influence, affect, or satisfy other people, often in direct interactions in which they look customers in the eye or listen to their voices. They are performing *emotional work* (in sociologist Arlie Hochschild's phrase), not just technical work. The quality of the emotional experience in these human exchanges often determines organizational success, whether in health care or hotels, as they influence both immediate outcomes and future purchasing decisions. For retailers, frontline service workers are such a vital link that companies like Taco Bell or Wal-Mart consider information technology a support system that allows workers more time with customers. Even in sectors in which technology substitutes for frontline workers (ATMs or automated airline reservation lines), the remaining jobs in those industries tend to involve human contact.

Customer service plays an ever bigger role outside the service sector. In manufacturing companies, Total Quality includes the ways customers are treated. Customers receive extra value through additional services accompanying products, such as convenient delivery, consultations on proper use of products, and quick and gracious resolution of complaints. General Electric wants to grow its service businesses faster than its manufacturing businesses, but as a companion to them; for example, customers buying a CT scanner might be offered training seminars for their health care personnel.

If activating human skills is so essential, why do so many companies still fail to do an adequate job of developing, motivating, and utilizing their people? For all the rhetoric about the manager as coach or servant-leader, human resource development is still too often neglected or left for last, something to be gotten to when there's free time or after completion of the reengineering project. Insensitive managers sometimes fail to see the negative impact they have on people—and how this spills over to customers. For some frontline workers, the Golden Rule of Customer Service is often: "Do unto customers as bosses have just done unto you." The chain of empowerment inside an organization affects customers directly; in bureaucratic cultures, powerlessness, not power, can corrupt, turning the powerless into controlling, petty tyrants who guard their own small patch of turf rather than strive to deliver value for customers.

Performance appraisal and career development are processes too often left to the bureaucracy, involving ritual meetings that cover rote questions and result in filled-out forms that join other forms in file drawers or on disks. Programs adopted by companies to help people cope with their lives and careers are sometimes undermined by managers who lack the skills for dealing with people—from discomfort at giving direct feedback to the inability to identify tricks of the trade that can improve performance. Employee rights that exist on paper cannot always be exercised in practice; managers unable to be flexible can limit the use of flex-time or parental leave. And managers sometimes abuse their power; investigation of allegations of sexual harassment at Astra's American units revealed what journalists called an authoritarian, cult-like environment fostered by management.

Professionalism requires continuous upgrading of skills. It has become fashionable for companies to articulate a desire to become "learning organizations." But sometimes they fail in practice because of underinvestment in occasions for learning and, that other legacy of large bureaucracies, the politics of rank. More senior hierarchical positions often allow managers to surround themselves with sycophants and flatterers or to insulate themselves from challenge and criticism—thereby ensuring that they miss the most vital information for building competence and managing change: knowledge of what's not working. The more senior the person, the greater the need for direct feedback. Powersoft's top executives regularly join on-line forums tearing apart the company's products. The head of ABB's largest American units measures the performance of his managers by the number of customer complaints they uncover and investigate: He wants them to hear more, not fewer.

In the information age, learning takes place in all directions, not just from the top down or from headquarters out. Change-adept organizations recognize that newcomers with knowledge from outside the organization can sometimes add more value than can company veterans. "Kids" can teach their seniors: Distinguished editor Michael Kinsley, for example, unlearned print magazine rules and learned the Internet from Microsoft managers decades younger, as he created the new on-line magazine *Slate*. Useful ideas might come from farflung locations once labelled "backward": Nynex's joint venture in Thailand taught American engineers about telecommunications technology not yet in use in the United States. Rather than holing up in headquarters bunkers, successful CEOs like Gillette's Alfred Zeien are constantly on the road, exchanging ideas face-to-face in the field. Simultaneous dissemination of information means that managers are informed of company decisions at the same time as those who report to them—and, in some cases, later than people below them in official rank.

What role will information and communication technology play in the nurturing of professionals and the development of organizational know-how? This frontier has yet to be fully explored. Information technology can facilitate spontaneous, instantaneous, self-organizing exchanges that bypass formal planning and formal controls. This could be revolutionary in some companies, making social networks a more important factor in business operations and threatening managers not ready for the information age. The conventional wisdom in management theory—before personal computers began to reach every desktop—was that networks were underground rumor mills. They were part of the so-called informal organization that thwarted the bureaucracy, producing illicit understandings about how to break rules or organize workers against management. Now companies encourage networks to form and give them official status, realizing that they perform tasks important to the organization.

Use of networks is especially striking in those organizations whose only product is the knowledge of their professionals, such as consulting firms. Large ones have become heavy utilizers of information systems to help clients in one place tap the total global knowledge of the firm. Knowledge managers assist with documentation (or make sure that busy professionals remember to do so), and knowledge exchange systems become internal tools as well as models touted to clients.

Similar networks are springing up in knowledge-rich functions inside large companies. For DuPont, networks enhance the idea generation process necessary for innovation and the knowledge transfer process necessary to solve problems or to utilize best practices quickly. Its central research lab supports over 400 networks. Combining face-to-face meetings with electronic exchanges, they range from ad hoc discussions aimed at solving a particular problem to ongoing interest groups specializing in technology issues.

Social networks that exchange knowledge—with or without the help of computers—are one building block of the infrastructure for learning that characterizes the change-adept organization. Or perhaps it is more accurate to call it an infrastructure for *teaching* and learning. Change-adept organizations make competence an organizational asset, rather than just an individual attribute, by stressing the need to make tacit knowledge explicit. This will not happen without organizational attention, resources, and events on the calendar. Knowledge exchanges, like synergies, are often considered frosting on the cake, something that busy people will get to someday, when they have time. So change-adept companies create occasions for knowledge exchange, whether informal lunch seminars (Powersoft calls theirs "food for thought"), larger conferences, or internal trade fairs that show off the latest ideas. Classroom-style training courses are sometimes the least important element of the learning infrastructure. Still, education benefits and training programs abound at change-adept companies such as Hewlett-Packard. In addition to more traditional forms of education, some companies are developing new tools to document and pass on the benefit of experience. Skandia created software to codify employee knowledge about opening new offices in new countries, thereby speeding up the country-entry process at least sevenfold.

A downside to professionalism, in the sense the word is being used here, is that professionals sometimes struggle with organizations for ownership of the intellectual assets they produce: They sometimes need to have a financial stake if they are to see their interests as being aligned with that of a company. Professionals in some fields—physicians in health care, for example—want to maintain the right to set all standards and to function without any constraints, becoming arrogant and insular rather than customer-focused. The solution is not to further reduce their autonomy, but to respect their knowledge while creating teams that share a common interest in positive organizational results.

Like innovation, professionalism is a dynamic capability that produces its own demand. Once people have been treated like professionals and have been encouraged to use their judgment, they want more of it. Once people have earned the respect of peers by staying at the cutting edge, they recognize that they must continue to learn as new knowledge accumulates or that respect will erode. Standards thus continue to rise, generating demand for still more knowledge of new developments. Managers need to use this momentum to convert the knowledge gains of individuals into organizational assets by asking people to pass on what they have learned to others or to embed new knowledge in new practices. I have often wondered why companies pay as much as they do to send managers to executive education programs at the Harvard Business School but then fail to debrief those managers when they return or to require them to teach others what they have learned.

Just as individual competence erodes without continuous investment in learning, organizational competence erodes without continuous investment in sharing it.

The Openness to Collaborate

Connections are the third major asset of the change-adept organization. Companies increasingly recognize the strategic importance of their key relationships; who they know can be as important as what they know. Change-adept organizations use their connections to strengthen business processes dependent on input from other organizations, to pursue new opportunities, to listen and learn, and to grow in new directions.

Relationships are such important assets in software companies like Powersoft or Lotus that these companies dedicate senior executives and departments solely to the management of alliances and partnerships. A small Ohio company lists its strategic partners next to the balance sheet in its annual report. Indeed, many companies find boundary-spanning roles increasingly important. Purchasing, for example, has become "global supply chain management." Corporate citizenship strategies increasingly emanate from the boardroom, not from the peripheral corporate foundation.

Jack Welch, CEO of General Electric, coined the term *boundaryless organization* to highlight the value of collaboration across territories, both inside and outside the walls of the company. With increasing frequency, companies express the desire to become more intimate with customers, to turn suppliers into collaborators, and to find venture partners with which to combine offerings or grow markets. Companies may fight fiercely with competitors for market share while collaborating with the same companies for other purposes, such as industry promotion, early-stage scientific research, or joint entry into a new market. These companies have discovered organizational ecology—they participate in a wider business system. How well they choose their partners and how effectively they integrate their activities can determine their

---

survival or extinction. And further outside the boundaries, at the managerial frontier, leaders discover the even wider social system surrounding their businesses—they discover that business is part of society and can derive value from strong ties to the community.

Leveraging connections requires comfort with differences. Never as fast on their feet as small companies, some corporate giants are learning to dance by engaging smaller partners. Both large and small companies recognize that they need each other. Large companies such as Digital Equipment count on technological breakthroughs from tiny, focused partners such as Dragon Systems, a 200-person world leader in voice recognition systems. Dragon, in turn, needs large partners such as Digital to reach international markets.

The tricky step for managers to master is how to dance with dissimilar partners without stepping on any toes. Collaboration requires interpersonal as well as organizational social sensitivity: listening skills, self-awareness, the ability to read others' signals, and a dose of humility. It requires sharing information with partners, networking between the companies at multiple organizational levels, keeping partners' interests in mind when crafting strategies, being willing to learn from those outside the firm's own walls, and respecting differences among companies and cultures.

Globalization intensifies the need for managers to respect differences. Even a decade ago, international strategy was often relegated to separate divisions, afterthoughts in many companies; now it pervades the whole enterprise. Companies in new technology fields such as software, biotechnology, or telecommunications are literally "born global," designing their products with world standards in mind and with worldwide partners in place even before they ship a single item outside their home country market. Managing international alliances makes cultural differences salient. Although such differences need not prevent success, as I found in my research on foreign acquisitions of domestic companies, they cannot be ignored. Some differences involve tastes or views on what is socially acceptable; others involve the social pathways by which purchase decisions are made, licenses granted, or distributors secured. The ability to understand such differences and their implications can determine the fate of international alliances and joint ventures.

Change-adept organizations must work closely with multiple stakeholders, making them allies rather than adversaries. A debate has raged among business leaders in North America and Britain over whose interests should come first—those of shareholders, customers, or employees. Investor capitalism puts shareholders first, assuming that the primary purpose and the only responsibility of a business is to create shareholder value. But some companies make customer interests central, on the premise that the primary mission of an enterprise, the basic test of its effectiveness, and its source of returns for shareholders lies in creating value for customers. Still others—often closely-held companies such as Rosenbluth Travel—argue that employees come first, because their satisfaction ensures the customer satisfaction that ultimately produces profits to ensure shareholder satisfaction. To complicate the matter further, under some circumstances, these three stakeholders are joined in their claims on an enterprise by suppliers, distributors, community members, and government officials. Clearly, a system of institutional relationships enmeshes today's businesses. The primacy and legitimacy of stakeholder interests is determined by social values, which are reflected in laws about how claims are activated, sorted, and prioritized. The answer to the question of which stakeholders come first does not matter much when all are satisfied, but it matters a great deal when one group feels neglected and uses its power to press its claims.

In many parts of the world, claims on business are growing. As governments cut back on funding for social programs, citizens pressure businesses to shoulder greater social burdens. At the same time, some companies find positive financial virtues in social activism. A corporation's image and reputation have economic consequences. Just as public outrage can depress sales, encourage union organizing, or block permits for new facilities, public approval of a company's association with good causes can create consumer goodwill. Adopting a school or sponsoring a prominent charity can bring political benefits, such as helping businesses to impress opinion leaders, court government officials at multiple levels, or gain acceptance by consumers as new market insiders. The economic benefits that flow from these good connections include faster approval of requests, access to information and influence, and even tax breaks. Community service can allay local anxieties about large employers' weaker community roots in a global economy of footloose companies, thereby neutralizing political pressures to re-regulate business.

Community service also benefits employees: It is a form of external collaboration that pleases internal stakeholders. The chance to perform community service through one's company has proven to be among the most appealing employment benefits of the 1990s. It is a source of employee satisfaction; on BankBoston employee surveys, the highest marks go to the company's community partnerships, which offer opportunities for direct involvement in good causes through service days. It can be a recruitment aid; some Timberland employees claim they were attracted to this boot and apparel company because of its active sponsorship of City Year, a national youth service corps that in turn organizes service opportunities for Timberland staff. And it can become an arena for staff development; a division manager at Hoechst Marion Rousell ended a team-building conference for 150 people by involving them in a day of service at the Kansas City Zoo.

How far across the boundaries should change-adept organizations stretch? Business has always been embedded in a social context, enmeshed in multiple relationships with multiple stakeholders whose power and resources can make or break the enterprise. Now societal issues are becoming business issues. Altruism meets self-interest. Strategic social partnerships can represent entrepreneurial growth opportunities for both mainstream businesses and their not-for-profit partners. Timberland teamed with City Year to create City Year Gear, casual clothing carrying messages about the importance of community service and good race relations. Disney partnered with Health Care Forum, a nonprofit association of health care organizations, to improve the attractiveness of its prototype new town of Celebration, Florida, by launching a health-promotion project there; Astra Merck, a pharmaceutical joint venture, joined as a third partner.

Emerging markets with fast-growth potential have often been untapped or underserved because social problems or institutional failings have made them appear less attractive or because governments maintained a monopoly on certain activities. But when growth slows in traditional markets and those markets become saturated, businesses turn to emerging markets, whether in the developing countries of Asia or Latin America, in the underserved inner cities of the United States, or in ethnic or identity niches.

Some of these new business opportunities involve exports and foreign deals, such as those made by numerous real estate developers in Boston who sought properties in former Communist countries during a regional recession. Other companies enter third-world-like domestic markets; some banks and supermarkets, facing saturation in suburban markets, turn to the inner city for growth opportunities. Emerging markets are also found in social or ethnic niches, such as those represented by Hispanics and other language minorities. And still other markets open up because of government privatization, through which major chunks of public services are turned over to private enterprise. Despite the organizational problems inherent in former state agencies never before subject to competition or market demands for value and efficiency, the business prospects are attractive. Anticipating privatization, U.S. regional telephone operating companies scrambled to create alliances with government telecom operations in developing countries, as footholds in enormous "underphoned" markets.

Reaching many of these emerging markets thrusts businesses into new kinds of partnerships, sometimes designed to address the social problems that have kept the markets from full development. Indeed, many of these markets cannot be approached at all without alliances, whether with government, community groups, or non-profit organizations that offer training or technical assistance. Lotus, for example, offered software fellowships to black programmers through village organizations in South Africa, hoping to use the resulting community partnerships to build both a staff and a market. Netas, Nortel's successful (and quality-award–winning) joint venture in Turkey, and Tong Guang Nortel, its joint venture in China, both involve partnerships with national government branches. First Community Bank, BankBoston's inner-city bank-within-a-bank, partnered with a variety of intermediaries to make pools of resources available for inner-city business loans too small to be otherwise profitable for the bank. Private-public partnerships and business-to-business networks comprise what I call an infrastructure for collaboration that helps communities thrive, which in turn increases potential for business success.

As business boundaries continue to expand, and as partnering becomes more common across the supply chain as well as at entrepreneurial frontiers, more people at more levels take on roles new to many of them: as ambassadors and diplomats beyond the walls of the company. They must view differences not as obstacles to getting things done but as opportunities for gaining synergy from complementary resources and skills. They must respect diverse cultural traditions and values. They must deal with fuzzy social variables such as trust and reputation, and they must use soft skills such as empathy and understanding to build mutually beneficial relationships. These fuzzy intangibles are increasingly recognized as having value for economies as well as for businesses. The economic prosperity of nations, regions, and communities benefits from their stocks of social capital (Robert Putnam's term for good working relationships among diverse parts of a community) and from trust among institutions (as Francis Fukuyama argued in a study of national economies).

Some managers will cultivate partnering skills in order to derive value from particular relationships. But a company's engagement in multiple relationships raises additional questions. How many connections can be nurtured in the relationship portfolio? As with innovation, there are quantity and quality tradeoffs; thus, companies often consolidate their supply bases to work more closely with fewer suppliers. Wide networks of relationships tend to serve as listening posts, providing information about opportunities that would not appear in the normal course of business; but to work effectively with partners in an operational sense requires closer integration with fewer of them. When current or potential competitors are involved in a partnership set, or when the strategic interests of partners diverge, issues arise over the free exchange of information versus the need to keep the lines drawn. Companies must also wrestle with questions about when to accede to partner demands and when to do what is in the interest of one's own company. Wainwright Industries, a highly customer-centered company that earned a high proportion of revenues from one automobile company, refused that customer-partner's request that

Wainwright hire its laid-off workers; Wainwright managers felt that such a concession would have undermined the very culture that made Wainwright a desirable supplier.

Relationship dynamics differ by partnership type. Supply-chain partnerships linking suppliers and customers or producers and distributors tend to have more endurance, to involve more commitment, and, often, to create more value than do looser affiliations. Wherever there exists complementarity and mutual dependence for tasks of strategic importance, relationships are more stable. Strategic alliances and joint ventures among similar kinds of partners, in contrast, tend to be unstable. Often they evolve toward closer and deeper ties, such as outright mergers, or they dissolve when they have met—or failed to meet—their goals. Sometimes they constitute disguised sales, with one partner eventually buying out the others. Configurations of alliances shift over time, because each partner has multiple ties and independent interests. Partners might learn enough from the alliance, or benefit sufficiently from the changes that the alliance helps to create, that they no longer need each other in the same way.

And that's how it should be. For the change-adept organization, connections are flexible assets that help open doors to new opportunities. What is important about external relationships is not their permanence but the new possibilities they constantly present leaders, reinforcing a culture open to challenge, learning, and change. Partners need to be brought inside managers' strategic framework, as key organizational assets. Like concepts and competence, connections help create the future.

Toward the Change-Adept Organization

Far from being change-adept, many companies are change-klutzes, making such awkward and ungainly moves under the rubric of large-scale change programs that they throw out numerous promising babies when they drain the bathwater. Consider the increased chances of making mistakes after downsizing. One consumer products company, preoccupied with reengineering, cut its staffs to the bone, only to lose over $30 million to piracy before noticing that products destined for foreign markets were showing up in rebates claimed by domestic retailers. Downsizing had left a void in the control system.

Revolution is in order when an organization has failed to change incrementally and has become ossified, or when it has neglected the interests of a key stakeholder with the power to overthrow the current regime, with activist shareholders playing the agitators' role that unions once did. But companies do not need abrupt, discontinuous change if they have had continuous innovation driven by rapid feedback from internal and external stakeholders. The history of Wainwright Industries reveals a series of projects over many years that embedded continuous improvement within the culture and fabric of the organization. This enhanced Wainwright's ability to adapt quickly to customer changes without radical intervention or revolution. Maybe "slow and steady" does not win the race any longer, but "fast and steady" can.

The context set by managers makes the difference in whether change is traumatic—a terrifying leap into the unknown—or a positive next step in a long sequence of moves. So the best way to lead change is to create conditions that make change natural. That is what managers do in change-adept organizations. They strive to release the potential of their people to create the future—as idea scouts tapping the imagination to innovate, as learning-oriented professionals, and as collaborators maximizing the value of good connections.

The articles that follow can help managers develop insights and skills for creating and leading companies that make change a friend, and make their organization a strategic weapon.

II

Twenty-First Century Management:

Business Strategy and the Tasks of Managers

Overview

Success for companies today comes from the capacity to create change. Today's products and services provide only temporary competitive advantage. Sustainable competitive advantage is based on organizational capabilities to master change. Organizational sources of competitive advantage include core competence, time compression, continuous improvement, and closer relationships to key partners (see "How to Compete"). In short, organizations that are focused, fast-moving, flexible, and "friendly" to key connections are more likely to sustain their ability to weather market shifts and even to create new markets. The strategic logic guiding companies must shift from a producer orientation, which creates bureaucracies stressing conformity and uniformity, to a customer orientation, which entails flexibility, customization, and innovation (see "Think Like the Customer: The Global Business Logic").

As companies move toward flatter, less hierarchical, more flexible and agile change-adept organizations, managers must also change their roles. The business environment of the future requires new kinds of leadership. "The New Managerial Work" describes how the new organizational model affects the work of managers. Command-and-control structures give rise to more active organizations in which cross-functional and cross-company project teams take initiative and exert influence. The new business strategies require managers to find new ways to guide action and motivate people. The old carrots and sticks of pay and promotion are less relevant to the new, flatter organizations. Some managers feel threatened because traditional privileges erode and new skills are required. Managers must become leaders who mobilize people through an inspiring mission and who emphasize learning capabilities. They must use their power to stimulate and steer cross-functional and cross-company teamwork that supports new market-creation strategies.

The new strategic logic gives leaders something to count on, even in times of change (see "Six Certainties for CEOs"). CEOs can be certain that they will have to listen and learn, emphasize their process capabilities and not just their products, value their allies, and be subject to greater scrutiny from all company stakeholders. Complacency will be a trait of losers. In this new environment, the only comfort for CEOs will be comfort with change.

In this new context, managerial work becomes a balancing act (see "The Best of Both Worlds"). Leaders juggle contradictions to secure the best of attractive but opposing alternatives, such as decentralization to respond to local markets or generate new ideas against centralization to improve implementation speed or to procure economies of scale and scope. Order is a temporary illusion. Leaders cannot count on flawless plans to guide action; they must be prepared for constant adjustments. It is difficult to impose authority on a world of constant motion. Leaders can only hope to steer multiple initiatives toward productive ends.

2

How to Compete

New wisdom about how to compete has emerged in recent years. These ideas have the potential to revolutionize organizational life by putting social factors at the forefront of business success.

Companies are shifting away from defining their strategies in terms of the classic sources of competitive advantage—lower costs or differentiated features. In a volatile, intensely competitive world, success comes from the capacity to respond and act—not from characteristics of today's products or markets. Instead, four bases for sustainable competitive advantage guide the actions of successful companies.

1. **Core competence.** Companies compete on the basis of distinctive skill—Honda's knowledge of engines, 3M's competence in adhesives, or Banc One's skills in data processing and retail management. Successful companies remain focused on their core strengths, invest in building a critical mass in them, and de-emphasize activities that do not add value. Defining core competencies and organizing to support and augment them ensure continuing success under changing conditions. DuPont, for example, took its skills in fibers into new fields, opening a market for carpet manufacturers by conceiving of the Stainmaster process.

2. **Time compression.** From first-mover advantages via innovation to faster cycle times for product development to just-in-time deliveries and rapid response to market trends, companies are increasingly competing on time. ABB chose "T50" (cutting in half the time taken to perform any operation), as the central goal of its program to improve global competitiveness. Honda gained competitive advantage from its speedy product innovation, Benetton, from its ability to keep its stores stocked with hot items by

manufacturing goods based on sales data and shipping them within a few days.

3. **Continuous improvement.** "Quality" has come to mean much more than zero defects; the total quality movement now embraces continual upgrading—Japanese *kaizen*—as a central goal. Companies see that such step-by-step product and process improvements based on measures, feedback, and learning are imperative to their ability to compete. PepsiCo, which overtook McDonald's as the largest and fastest growing operator of quick-serve restaurants, constantly modified products, systems, and organization structure to improve every aspect of its operation.

4. **Relationships.** Collaboration across companies, especially supplier-customer partnerships, provides a fourth source of advantage. Companies stretch their own capacity through relationships, adding a partner's competence to their own. Corning derives about half of its profits from joint ventures, and ventures spawn still others (for example, Siecor, a venture of Siemens and Corning, allied with Kaiser Aluminum). NCR's partnership with suppliers like Intel helped cement close ties with customers like Businessland. Throughout the computer industry, tighter relationships, even with competitors, are creating the U.S. equivalent of the Japanese *keiretsu*.

To use these four sources of competitive advantage, companies must pay more attention to human factors. The barriers to effective use of these sources are largely social, not strategic. They stem from rigid distinctions between organizational classes—by level, by function, by division—that interfere with adaptive capability.

Building competitive advantage around a company's core competencies requires spreading and sharing knowledge. Leaders must spend more time actively communicating priorities by translating them into concrete operational terms, ensuring that groups learn from one another, and then personally recognizing achievements that best exemplify these priorities. Key skills must be first in people's minds; people must understand their own work in terms of contributing to or drawing from the pool of shared know-how.

Every company has to see itself as knowledge-based; therefore, the transmission of strategy throughout the ranks—down to the lowest echelon and into the dustiest corner—becomes the leader's central task. Companies cannot maintain distinctions between organizational classes based on individuals' "need to know"; everyone needs to know.

Time-based competition, similarly, requires a more inclusive, less divisive form of organization. Getting more value to customers faster requires more than just excellent service within existing parameters; it requires experimentation and innovation to produce new approaches. To move quickly, companies need a portfolio of new ideas; but unless these are tied to the needs and concerns of existing businesses, they can be worthless. The remote "skunkworks" where mavericks were free to play in the sandbox of their choice without contaminating mainstream activities have produced disappointing overall results, even when they produced viable new ventures. Many prominent corporate venture groups—at Eastman Kodak, Alcan, and Colgate-Palmolive, for example—have been disbanded.

Instead, support for entrepreneurship must occur close to the business core, by seeding numerous small ideas in numerous experiments. Release time and uncommitted resources must be available, and managers must be held accountable for making these investments. This, in turn, requires being open to people's ideas. Status distinctions that exclude some people from the conversation or tell others simply to follow orders stifle innovation. The barriers to innovation in many companies are social as much as they are organizational; whole categories of people are ignored as sources of ideas. In contrast, successful Japanese companies routinely receive large numbers of suggestions from throughout the organization for improving every conceivable aspect of their products and processes.

Social barriers must be breached to get faster cycle time too. Evidence is mounting that the ability to cut product development time or to deliver value to customers faster derives not only from organization—getting the right combination of functions to work together simultaneously rather than sequentially—but also from human considerations. Every organizational barrier establishes a social barrier that can interfere with speed and responsiveness. Computer use did not spread faster among managers when desktop computers were first available because of the reluctance of bosses to learn from (or look like) their secretaries.

Whenever organizational pecking orders establish class systems that assign privilege and attribute superior knowledge to "higher" levels, or whenever walls between departments cause mistrust and rivalries, everything takes longer. Organizing work around flexible project teams with rotating membership and a deemphasis on formal titles can make things go faster.

Many companies that jumped on the quality bandwagon a few years ago have found their efforts stalling at the boundaries between work teams. It has been relatively easy to encourage quality problem solving and other continuous improvement philosophies within existing organizational lines; it has proven much harder to get other departments or areas to adjust, to work out new arrangements that shift territories, or to encourage work groups to accept each other's ideas.

But continuous improvement involves much more than fine-tuning today's practice; it requires the ability to combine existing resources in new ways to tackle new opportunities. Corporate tragedies sometimes stem from the failure to combine existing capacities. When CBS was among the world's largest broadcasters and owned one of the world's largest record companies, why was a rival company rather than CBS able to see the potential in music television? Insiders blamed unbridgeable gaps between business units.

Building the social bonds that overcome organizational divisiveness is an investment well worth making. Depending on corporate culture, these might include standard conferences with spouses and socializing, cross-department councils, Friday afternoon gatherings, or air tours of major facilities. Such events are not frills; they help ensure rapid technology transfer across the business. Banc One pushes travel for face-to-face learning about successful operations, telling newly acquired banks they can expect their travel budgets to double. The head of British-based Castrol stresses use of party-intensive conferences to encourage cross-country collaboration.

Social ties are even more fundamental to sustaining relationship-based competition because partners or allies do not have command rights over each other and negotiation is continual. "Personalities" always play a large role in evolving situations because they are not yet fully routinized or subject to a clear set of procedures and directives—more depends on how the representatives feel about each other. Social compatibilities matter more in situations like joint ventures or supplier-customer partnerships in which the parties involved also maintain independent commitments that pull them in other directions. Rarely do strategic alliances fall apart, of course, simply because the two companies' top managers don't get along; but one Anglo-French partnership dissolved in frustration because top managers didn't like each other enough to stay attuned to the shifting strategic priorities of their ally.

To make cross-company collaborations work, three kinds of links must be maintained: strategic or policy integration by the chief executive; joint project planning by professionals and middle managers; and operational integration to support the ongoing flow of goods or information involved in the alliance (such as direct data integration at the factory level to support JIT relationships with suppliers). At software companies, a product-development team is likely to cross company lines as well as functional lines by including supplier and customer representatives. Both business and social events connect partners and allies.

Acknowledging the centrality of social factors in gearing up for competitive success means considering fundamental organizational and managerial changes: reducing the economic disparity between top and bottom (a 32 to 1 compensation ratio in U.S. auto supply companies compared with 7 to 1 in Japanese counterparts), eliminating status symbols (from office size to carpet thickness), spreading strategic information and soliciting ideas everywhere, rewarding for contribution rather than position, emphasizing flexible project assignments over fixed functional jobs, and bringing outside partners inside the decision-making process.

Competing successfully in the future will depend on bringing together, not separating, the strategic and the social.

3

Think Like the Customer:
The Global Business Logic

Most businesses today say they serve customers. In reality, they serve themselves.

Yet customer power is growing worldwide in industry after industry as the explosion of technology and the globalization of markets increase customers' choices. So to compete effectively, companies must move from thinking like producers to thinking like customers.

The producer logic differs from the customer logic in five fundamental ways.

Producers think they are making products. Customers think they are buying services.

From the customer's standpoint, a product is nothing more than a tangible means for getting a service performed. Is baking soda a cake ingredient or an odor-eater? The answer may be either or both since products derive their meaning and value only from the uses to which customers put them.

Nike does not sell shoes; it offers tools for sports and fitness. The value of these tools to customers is what defines the product—and why chairman and CEO Phil Knight has said that "the product is our most important marketing tool."

Indeed, in a customer-centered world, industries should be defined by consumption or use similarities, not by patterns of production. Visionary companies are reaching across traditional industry lines to define their future technology agendas: C&C (computers and communication) for NEC; IM&M (information movement and management) for AT&T. Already an accounting firm (Arthur Andersen), a hardware manufacturer (IBM), and a software developer (Oracle) can all compete for the same customer.

The Information Age similarly discredits another Industrial Age principle articulated by Karl Marx. Power stems not from control of the "means of production" but from influence over the "means of consumption"—that is, how products can reach customers and be put to use by them. As some European intellectuals have argued, the real test of a capitalist system entering the Information Age lies not in industrial efficiency but in the quality of life it can provide for its people.

Producers worry about visible mistakes. Customers are lost because of invisible mistakes.

Producers want to run their processes smoothly and without errors. Customers want to have their dreams fulfilled.

Some companies worship at the quality altar, hoping that zero defects will produce business salvation. But during the past decade, quality programs have been criticized for being too narrowly producer-oriented, merely focusing on reducing the costs of visible mistakes. Wise executives worry more about invisible mistakes—failing to take risks, failing to innovate to create new value for customers. Research and development needs more attention. It requires ever-higher funding to keep up with the technology explosion—or with the competition. According to Japan expert Robert Cutts, for many Japanese manufacturers, R&D investment is much greater than capital investment.

In a sense, every business is now a "fashion" business. To compete effectively, companies must innovate effectively—and in ever shorter cycles. Keeping customers as well as attracting new ones requires constantly offering new and better products, with design innovations based on new technologies. Nike, facing 50 different competitors in the athletic shoe field, strives to "wake up the consumer" by doing new things, pioneering in shoe R&D.

To be customer-oriented, leaders need to spend more time worrying about what they do not yet see. Ponder this classic Zen lesson about mountain-climbing: to respect what at first we cannot view. What cannot now be seen, can be seen from the other side of the mountain—or by someone else. Companies must attend not only to their current competition but to their "invisible enemies"—unfamiliar companies outside the industry possessing a technological capability that could be a threat if turned to new markets. Companies need a long-term view of how R&D can serve latent demand even when the technology itself is still a dream. The Swiss pharmaceutical companies investing heavily in biotechnology are making this kind of bet.

Producers think their technologies create products. Customers think their desires create products.

Producers think they are market-oriented when they ask customers their opinions of products that already exist. Customers think companies are market-oriented when customers set priorities for design.

Some companies find it hard to take customer desires seriously, even when this is an explicit focus. In a leading computer company trying to move from selling specific products to providing solutions for customer needs, a senior executive was widely quoted as saying, "If customers don't like our solutions, they have the wrong problems."

In contrast, research on industrial innovation has consistently proven that the best innovations are not only user-oriented, they are often user-created. Many successful Japanese technology companies let customer desires drive the R&D agenda. Rather than pushing their own technologies, companies start with a product concept based on market data. They then blend technical improvements from previously separate fields to create products that revolutionize markets, as Sharp did in developing a sleek and powerful electronic calculator.

Phil Knight is candid about Nike's need to shift from producer logic to customer logic. "We used to think that everything started in the lab," he confessed. "Now we realize that everything spins off the consumer. The consumer has to lead innovation. We have to innovate for a specific reason, and that reason comes from the market."

But "the market" is an abstraction; customers are real people who behave like individuals rather than statistics. "Market data" can mask the complexity of customer experiences. So smart companies also stress face-to-face contact with lead users as an innovation engine, converting customer service into the front-line intelligence force for new ideas.

Some companies try to get everyone involved in customer-centered innovation. Because Ocean Spray turned its employees into idea scouts and invited them to regular product development forums, the company scored several important wins with customers; it was the first in the United States to use innovative new packaging technology, the paper bottle. Searching for customer-useful innovation is just another aspect of the job for all employees in Japanese companies; Mitsubishi Materials relied on this almost exclusively to set R&D priorities.

Producers organize for managerial convenience. Customers want their convenience to come first.

In producer logic, managerial considerations are paramount: ease in organizing functions, defining jobs, keeping employees, and controlling the system. What makes a company manageable, however, might detract from serving the customer. For example, from a producer standpoint, uniformity and standardization are easiest to manage. But companies already know that customers have the power to demand variety and customization.

Many quality programs are producer-oriented, not customer-oriented. The idea that every department has an internal customer keeps the focus on the inside rather than the outside. When a company serving the world market from its London headquarters closes the switchboard at five o'clock Greenwich mean time, whose needs are being met, the customers' or the company's?

Bills that are convenient for the billing department but unfathomable for customers are only one impetus for producers to review their entire order management cycle. Because functional areas have conflicting goals, compensation systems, and organizational imperatives, customer needs can be lost in the gaps between departments. Because decision makers lack knowledge of the entire order management cycle, they cannot set appropriate priorities. Customer-focused slogans and posters, even interfunctional problem-solving teams, are not good enough if departments do not share the same priorities or rewards. To make interfunctional cooperation work for the benefit of customers, the entire system must be reviewed and reorganized.

After all, if every product is really a service, then every contact or communication with customers is also the product.

Producers seek a high standard of performance. Customers care about a high standard of living.

Producers want quality goods. Customers want quality of life. And quality of life questions are more political than economic.

For example, debates about U.S. industrial policy have been production-oriented, concerned with whether and how to support manufacturing enterprises. But the most significant problems the United States faces are consumption-oriented, since income inequality exacerbates social and racial tensions.

Similarly, the recent revolutions in Eastern Europe were consumption-driven. They were fueled by people's desire to eat rather than their desire to vote, by dreams of purchasing rather than dreams of participating. In this light, the social choice that many European countries have consciously made to distribute the benefits of capitalist enterprise across all levels of society could provide a model of capitalism well suited to the triumph of customer-think.

Henry Ford recognized almost a century ago that paying his employees high wages could allow them to buy the cars they made, thus treating them like customers from the start. In Europe today, auto workers at Daimler-Benz can often afford to drive the high-priced Mercedes they make.

More and better production will not solve a country's problems. Even developing nations are recognizing that continued economic growth requires spreading prosperity to all segments of the society—in short, ensuring a high standard of living and not just attracting business investment. A new political logic must accompany the new customer-focused business logic.

4

The New Managerial Work

Managerial work is undergoing such enormous and rapid change that many managers are reinventing their profession as they go. With little precedent to guide them, they are watching hierarchy fade away and the clear distinctions of title, task, department, even corporation, blur. Faced with extraordinary levels of complexity and interdependency, they watch traditional sources of power erode and the old motivational tools lose their magic.

The cause stems from the new environment facing organizations. Competitive pressures are forcing corporations to adopt new flexible strategies and structures. Many of these are familiar: acquisitions and divestitures aimed at more focused combinations of business activities, reductions in management staff and levels of hierarchy, increased use of performance-based rewards. Other strategies are less common but have an even more profound effect. In a growing number of companies, for example, horizontal ties between peers are replacing vertical ties as channels of activity and communication. Companies are asking corporate staffs and functional departments to play a more strategic role with greater cross-departmental collaboration. Some organizations are turning themselves nearly inside out—buying formerly internal services from outside suppliers, forming strategic alliances and supplier-customer partnerships that bring external relationships inside where they can influence company policy and practice. These emerging practices involve the application of entrepreneurial creativity and flexibility to established businesses, and they help organizations become change-adept.

Such practices come highly recommended by the experts who urge organizations to become leaner, less bureaucratic, more entrepreneurial. But so far, theorists have given scant attention to the dramatically altered realities of managerial work in these transforming corporations. We don't even have good words to describe the new relationships. "Superiors" and "subordinates" hardly seem accurate, and even "bosses" and "their people" imply more control and ownership than managers today actually possess. "Associates" is the term of preference in many companies instead of "employees," but then, what do we call their managers? On top of it all, career paths are no longer straightforward and predictable but have become idiosyncratic and confusing.

Some managers experience the new managerial work as a loss of power because much of their authority used to come from hierarchical position. Now that everything seems negotiable by everyone, they are confused about how to mobilize and motivate staff. For other managers, the shift in roles and tasks offers greater personal power. The following case histories illustrate the responses of three managers in three different industries to the opportunities and dilemmas of structural change.

Hank was vice president and chief engineer for a leading heavy equipment manufacturer that was moving aggressively against foreign competition. One of the company's top priorities was to increase the speed, quality, and cost-effectiveness of product development. So Hank worked with consultants to improve collaboration between manufacturing and other functions and to create closer alliances between the company and its outside suppliers. Gradually, a highly segmented operation became an integrated process involving project teams drawn from component divisions, functional departments, and external suppliers. But along the way, there were several unusual side effects. Different areas of responsibility overlapped. Some technical and manufacturing people were co-located. Liaisons from functional areas joined the larger development teams. Most unusual of all, project teams had a lot of direct contact with higher levels of the company.

Many of the managers reporting to Hank felt these changes as a loss of power. They didn't always know what their people were doing, but they still believed they ought to know. They no longer had sole input into performance appraisals; other people from other functions had a voice as well, and some of them knew more about employees' project performance. New career paths made it less important to please direct superiors in order to move up the functional line.

Moreover, employees often bypassed Hank's managers and interacted directly with decision makers inside and outside the company. Some of these so-called subordinates had contact with division executives and senior corporate staff, and sometimes they sat in on high-level strategy meetings to which their managers were not invited.

At first Hank thought his managers' resistance to the new process was just the normal noise associated with any change. Then he began to realize that something more profound was going on. The reorganization was challenging traditional notions about the role and power of managers and shaking traditional hierarchy to its roots. And no one could see what was taking its place.

When George became head of a major corporate department in a large bank holding company, he thought he had arrived. His title and rank were unmistakable, and his department was responsible for determining product-line policy for hundreds of bank branches and the virtual clerks—in George's eyes—who managed them. George staffed his department with MBAs and promised them rapid promotion.

Then the sand seemed to shift beneath him. Losing market position for the first time in recent memory, the bank decided to emphasize direct customer service at the branches. The people George considered clerks began to depart from George's standard policies and to tailor their services to local market conditions. In many cases, they actually demanded services and responses from George's staff, and the results of their requests began to figure in performance reviews of George's department. George's people were spending more and more time in the field with branch managers, and the corporate personnel department was even trying to assign some of George's MBAs to branch and regional posts.

To complicate matters, the bank's strategy included a growing role for technology. George felt that because he had no direct control over the information systems department, he should not be held fully accountable for every facet of product design and implementation. But fully accountable he was. He had to deploy people to learn the new technology and figure out how to work with it. Furthermore, the bank was asking product departments like George's to find ways to link existing products or develop new ones that crossed traditional categories. So George's people were often away on cross-departmental teams just when he wanted them for some internal assignment.

Instead of presiding over a tidy empire the way his predecessor had, George encountered what looked to him like chaos. The bank said senior executives should be "leaders, not managers," but George didn't know what that meant, especially since he seemed to have lost control over his subordinates' assignments, activities, rewards, and careers. He resented his perceived loss of status.

The CEO tried to show him that good results achieved the new way would bring great monetary rewards, thanks to a performance-based bonus program that was gradually replacing more modest yearly raises. But the pressures on George were also greater, unlike anything he'd ever experienced.

For Sally, purchasing manager at an innovative computer company, a new organizational strategy was a gain rather than a loss, although it changed her relationship with the people reporting to her. Less than ten years out of college, she was hired as an analyst—a semiprofessional, semiclerical job—then promoted to a purchasing manager's job in a sleepy staff department. She didn't expect to go much further in what was then a well-established hierarchy. But after a shocking downturn, top management encouraged employees to rethink traditional ways of doing things. Sally's boss, the head of purchasing, suggested that "partnerships" with key suppliers might improve quality, speed innovation, and reduce costs.

Soon Sally's backwater was at the center of policy-making, and Sally began to help shape strategy. She organized meetings between her company's senior executives and supplier CEOs. She sent her staff to contribute supplier intelligence at company seminars on technical innovation, and she spent more of her own time with product designers and manufacturing planners. She led senior executives on a tour of supplier facilities, traveling with them in the corporate jet.

Because some suppliers were also important customers, Sally's staff began meeting frequently with marketing managers to share information and address joint problems. Sally and her group were now also acting as internal advocates for major suppliers. Furthermore, many of these external companies now contributed performance appraisals of Sally and her team, and their opinions weighed almost as heavily as those of her superiors.

As a result of the company's new direction, Sally felt more personal power and influence, and her ties to peers in other areas and to top management were stronger. But she no longer felt like a manager directing subordinates. Her staff had become a pool of resources deployed by many others besides Sally. She was exhilarated by her personal opportunities but not quite sure the people she managed should have the same freedom to choose their own assignments. After all, wasn't that a manager's prerogative?

Hank's, George's, and Sally's very different stories say much about the changing nature of managerial work. However hard it is for managers at the very top to remake strategy and structure, they themselves will probably retain their identity, status, and control. For the managers below them, structural change is often much harder. As work units become more participative and team oriented, and as professionals and knowledge workers become more prominent, the distinction between manager and nonmanager begins to erode.

The New Managerial Quandaries

■ At American Express, the CEO instituted a program called "One Enterprise" to encourage collaboration between different lines of business. One Enterprise has led to a range of projects where peers from different divisions work together on such synergistic ventures as cross-marketing, joint purchasing, and cooperative product and market innovation. Employees' rewards are tied to their One Enterprise efforts. Executives set goals and can earn bonuses for their contributions to results in other divisions.
□ But how do department managers control their people when they're working on cross-departmental teams? And

who determines the size of the rewards when the interests
of more than one area are involved?

■ At Security Pacific National Bank, internal departments became forces in the external marketplace. For example, the
bank developed a joint venture with local auto dealers to
sell fast financing for car purchases, involving the information technology department in work with outside partners.
The department is now a profit center selling its services inside and outside the bank.

☐ But what is the role of bank managers accountable for the
success of such entrepreneurial ventures? And how do they
shift their orientation from the role of boss in a chain of
command to the role of the customer?

■ At Digital Equipment Corporation, emphasis on supplier
partnerships to improve quality and innovation multiplied
the need for cross-functional as well as cross-company collaboration. Key suppliers were included on product planning teams with engineering, manufacturing, and purchasing staff. Digital used its human resources staff to train and
do performance appraisals of its suppliers, as if they were
part of the company. In cases where suppliers were also customers, purchasing and marketing departments had to start
exchanging information and working collaboratively.

☐ But how do managers learn enough about other functions
to be credible, let alone influential, members of such teams?
How do they maintain adequate communication externally
while staying on top of what their own departments are doing? And how do they handle the extra work of responding
to projects initiated by other areas?

■ At Banc One, a growing reliance on project teams spanning more than 70 affiliated banks led the CEO to propose
eliminating officer titles because of the lack of correlation
between status as measured by title and status within the
collaborative team.

☐ But then what do "rank" and "hierarchy" mean anymore,
especially for people whose careers consist of a sequence of
projects rather than a sequence of promotions? What does
"career" mean? Does it have a shape? Is there a ladder?

■ At Alcan, the search for new uses and applications for its
core product, aluminum, led to an experiment with a new
venture process. Managers and professionals from line divisions formed screening teams to consider and refine new-

venture proposals coming from inside and outside the company. A venture manager, chosen from the screening team, took charge of concepts that pass muster, drawing on Alcan's worldwide resources to build the new business. In one case of global synergy, Alcan created a new product for the Japanese market using Swedish American technology and Canadian manufacturing capacity.

□ But why should senior managers release staff to serve on screening and project teams for new businesses when their own businesses are making do with fewer and fewer people? How do functionally oriented managers learn enough about worldwide developments to know when they might have something of value to offer someplace else? And how do the managers of these new ventures ever go back to the conventional line organization as middle managers once their venture has been folded into an established division?

■ At IBM, an emphasis on customer partnerships to rebuild market share led to practices that reversed tradition. IBM formed joint development teams with customers, where engineers from both companies share proprietary data. The company moved from merely selling equipment to actually managing a customer's management information system. Eastman Kodak handed its U.S. data center operations to IBM to consolidate and manage, which meant lower fixed costs for Kodak and greater ability to focus on its core businesses rather than on ancillary services. Some 300 former Kodak people switched to filling Kodak's needs as IBM employees, while committees of IBM and Kodak managers oversaw the partnership.

□ But who exactly do the people in such arrangements work for? Who is in charge? And how do traditional notions of managerial authority square with such a complicated set of relationships?

———————————

To understand what managers must do to achieve results in the change-adept corporation, we need to look at the changing picture of how such companies operate. The picture has five elements:

1. There are a greater number and variety of channels for taking action and exerting influence.

2. Relationships of influence are shifting from the vertical to the horizontal, from chain of command to peer networks.

3. The distinction between managers and those managed is diminishing, especially in terms of information, control over assignments, and access to external relationships.

4. External relationships are increasingly important as sources of internal power and influence, even of career development.

5. As a result of the first four changes, career development has become less intelligible but also less circumscribed. There are fewer assured routes to success, which produces anxiety. At the same time, career paths are more open to innovation, which produces opportunity.

To help companies implement their competitive organizational strategies, managers must learn new ways to manage, confronting changes in their own bases of power and recognizing the need for new ways to motivate people.

The Bases of Power

The changes I've described can be scary for people like George and the managers reporting to Hank, who were trained to know their place, to follow orders, to let the company take care of their careers, to do things by the book. Now the book is gone. In the new corporation, managers have only themselves to count on for success. They must learn to operate without the crutch of hierarchy. Position, title, and authority are no longer adequate tools, not in a world where subordinates are encouraged to think for themselves and where managers have to work synergistically with other departments and even other companies. Success depends increasingly on tapping into sources of good ideas, on figuring out whose collaboration is needed to act on those ideas, on working with both to produce results. In short, the new managerial work implies very different ways of obtaining and using power.

The emerging, more entrepreneurial corporation is not only leaner and flatter, it also has many more channels for action. Cross-functional projects, business-unit joint ventures, labor-management forums, innovation funds that spawn activities outside mainstream budgets and reporting lines, strategic partnerships with suppliers or customers—these are all overlays on the traditional organization chart, strategic pathways that ignore the chain of command.

Their existence has several important implications. For one thing, they create more potential centers of power. As the ways to combine resources increase, the ability to command diminishes. Alternative paths of communication, resource access, and execution erode the authority of those in the nominal chain of command. In other words, the opportunity for greater speed and flexibility undermines hierarchy. As more and more strategic action takes place in these channels, the jobs that focus inward on particular departments decline in power.

As a result, the ability of managers to get things done depends more on the number of networks in which they're centrally involved than on their height in a hierarchy. Of course, power in any organization always has a network component, but rank and formal structure used to be more limiting. For example, access to information and the ability to get informal backing were often confined to the few officially sanctioned contact points between departments or between the company and its vendors or customers. Today these official barriers are disappearing, while so-called informal networks grow in importance.

In the change-adept organization, managers add value by deal making, by brokering at interfaces, rather than by presiding over their individual empires. It was traditionally the job of top executives or specialists to scan the business environment for new ideas, opportunities, and resources. This kind of environmental scanning is now an important part of a manager's job at every level and in every function. And the environment to be scanned includes various company divisions, many potential outside partners, and large parts of the world. At the same time, people are encouraged to think about what they know that might have value elsewhere. An engineer designing windshield wipers, for example, might discover properties of rubber adhesion to glass that could be useful in other manufacturing areas.

Every manager must think cross-functionally because every department has to play a strategic role, understanding and contributing to other facets of the business. In Hank's company, the technical managers and staff working on design engineering used to concentrate only on their own areas of expertise. Under the new system, they have to keep in mind what manufacturing does and how it does it. They need to visit plants and build relationships so they can ask informed questions.

One multinational corporation, eager to extend the uses of its core product, put its R&D staff and laboratory personnel in direct contact with marketing experts to discuss lines of research. Similarly, the superior economic track record of Raytheon's New Products Center—dozens of new products and patents yielding profits many times their development costs—derived from the connections it builds between its inventors and the engineering and marketing staffs of the business units it serves.

This strategic and collaborative role is particularly important for the managers and professionals on corporate staffs. They need to serve as integrators and facilitators, not as watchdogs and interventionists. They need to sell their services, justify themselves to the business units they serve, literally compete with outside suppliers. Some large companies have put overhead charges for corporate staff services on a pay-as-you-use basis. Formerly, these charges were either assigned uniformly to users and nonusers alike, or the services were mandatory. Product managers sometimes had to work through as many as eight layers of management and corporate staff to get business plans approved. Now these staffs must prove to the satisfaction of their internal customers that their services add value.

By contrast, some banks still have corporate training departments that do very little except get in the way. They do no actual training, for example, yet they still exercise veto power over urgent divisional training decisions and consultant contracts. Such roadblock departments are the first targeted for extinction, as traditional banking evolves into a highly competitive information-technology-rich financial services industry requiring business units to act fast and find whatever resources and services they need quickly—inside or outside the company.

As managers and professionals spend more time working across boundaries with peers and partners over whom they have no direct control, their negotiating skills become essential assets. Alliances and partnerships transform impersonal, arm's-length contracts into relationships involving joint planning and joint decision making. Internal competitors and adversaries become allies on whom managers depend for their own success. At the same time, more managers at more levels are active in the kind of external diplomacy that only the CEO or selected staffs used to conduct.

In the collaborative forums that result, managers are more personally exposed. It is trust that makes partnerships work. Since collaborative ventures often bring together groups with different methods, cultures, symbols, even languages, good deal making depends on empathy—the ability to step into other people's shoes and appreciate their goals. This applies not only to intricate global joint ventures but also to the efforts of engineering and manufacturing to work together more effectively. Effective communication in a cooperative effort rests on more than a simple exchange of information; people must be adept at anticipating the responses of other groups. "Before I get too excited about our department's design ideas," an engineering manager told me, "I'm learning to ask myself, 'What's the marketing position on this? What will manufacturing say?' That sometimes forces me to make changes before I even talk to them."

An increase in the number of channels for strategic contact within the change-adept organization means more opportunities for people with ideas or information to trigger action: salespeople encouraging account managers to build strategic partnerships with customers, for example, or technicians searching for ways to tap new-venture funds to develop software. Moreover, top executives who have to spend more time on cross-boundary relationships are forced to delegate more responsibility to lower level managers. Delegation is one more blow to hierarchy, of course, since subordinates with greater responsibility are bolder about speaking up, challenging authority, and charting their own course.

For example, it is common for new-venture teams to complain publicly about corporate support departments and to reject their use in favor of external service providers, often to the consternation of more orthodox superiors. A more startling example occurred in a health care company where members of a task force charged with finding synergies among three lines of business shocked corporate executives by criticizing upper management behavior in their report. Service on the task force had created collective awareness of a shared problem and had given people the courage to confront it.

The search for internal synergies, the development of strategic alliances, and the push for new ventures all emphasize the political side of a leader's work. Executives must be able to juggle a set of constituencies rather than control a set of subordinates. They have to bargain, negotiate, and sell instead of making unilateral decisions and issuing commands. The leader's task, as Chester Barnard recognized long ago, is to develop a network of cooperative relationships among all the people, groups, and organizations that have something to contribute to an economic enterprise. More entrepreneurial change-oriented strategies magnify the complexity of this task. After leading Teknowledge, a producer of expert systems software, through development alliances with six corporations including General Motors and Procter & Gamble, company chairman Lee Hecht said he felt like the mayor of a small city. "I have a constituency that won't quit. It takes a hell of a lot of balancing." The kind of power achieved through a network of stakeholders is very different from the kind of power managers wield in a traditional bureaucracy. The new way gets more done, but it also takes more time. And it creates an illusion about freedom and security.

The absence of day-to-day constraints, the admonition to assume responsibility, the pretense of equality, the elimination of visible status markers, the prevalence of candid dialogues across hierarchical levels—these can give employees a false sense that all hierarchy is a thing of the past. Yet at the same time, employees still count on hierarchy to shield them when things go wrong. This combination would create the perfect marriage of freedom and support—freedom when people want to take risks, support when the risks don't work out.

In reality, less benevolent combinations are also possible, combinations not of freedom and support but of insecurity and loss of control. There is often a pretense in change-oriented companies that status differences have nothing to do with power, that the deference paid to top executives derives from their superior qualifications rather than from the power they have over the fates of others. But the people at the top of the organization chart still wield power—and sometimes in ways that managers below them experience as arbitrary. Unprecedented individual freedom also applies to top managers, who are now free to make previously unimaginable deals, order unimaginable cuts, or launch unimaginable takeovers. The reorganizations that companies undertake in their search for new synergies can uncover the potential unpredictability and capriciousness of corporate careers. A man whose company was undergoing drastic restructuring told me, "For all of my ownership share and strategic centrality and voice in decisions, I can still be faced with a shift in direction not of my own making. I can still be reorganized into a corner. I can still be relocated into oblivion. I can still be reviewed out of my special project budget."

These realities of power, change, and job security are important because they affect the way people view their leaders. When the illusion of simultaneous freedom and protection fades, the result can be a loss of motivation.

Sources of Motivation

One of the essential, unchanging tasks of leaders is to motivate and guide performance. But motivational tools are changing fast. More and more businesses are doing away with the old bureaucratic incentives and using entrepreneurial opportunity to attract the best talent. Managers must exercise more leadership even as they watch their bureaucratic power slip away. Leadership, in short, is more difficult yet more critical than ever.

Because of the unpredictability of even the most benign restructuring, managers are less able to guarantee a particular job—or any job at all—no matter what a subordinate's performance level. The reduction in hierarchical levels curtails a manager's ability to promise promotion. New compensation systems that make bonuses and raises dependent on objective performance measures and on team appraisals deprive managers of their role as the sole arbiter of higher pay. Cross-functional and cross-company teams can rob managers of their right to direct or even understand the work their so-called subordinates do. In any case, the shift from routine work, which was amenable to oversight, to "knowledge" work, which often is not, erodes a manager's claim to superior expertise. And partnerships and ventures that put lower level people in direct contact with each other across departmental and company boundaries cut heavily into the managerial monopoly on information. At a consumer packaged-goods manufacturer that replaced several levels of hierarchy with teams, plant team members in direct contact with the sales force often had data on product ordering trends before the higher level brand managers who set product policy.

As if the loss of carrots and sticks was not enough, many managers can no longer even give their people clear job standards and easily mastered procedural rules. Change-adept corporations seek problem-solving, initiative-taking employees who will go the unexpected extra mile for the customer. To complicate the situation further still, the complexities of work in the new organization—projects and relationships clamoring for attention in every direction—exacerbate the feeling of overload.

With the old motivational tool kit depleted, leaders need new and more effective incentives to encourage high performance and build commitment. There are five new tools:

Mission. Helping people believe in the importance of their work is essential, especially when other forms of certainty and security have disappeared. Good leaders can inspire others with the power and excitement of their vision and give people a sense of purpose and pride in their work. Pride is often a better source of motivation than the traditional corporate career ladder and the promotion-based reward system. Technical professionals, for example, are often motivated most effectively by the desire to see their work contribute to an excellent final product.

Agenda Control. As career paths lose their certainty and companies' futures grow less predictable, people can at least be in charge of their own professional lives. More and more professionals are passing up jobs with glamour and prestige in favor of jobs that give them greater control over their own activities and direction. Leaders give their subordinates this opportunity when they give them release time to work on pet projects, when they emphasize results instead of procedures, and when they delegate work and the decisions about how to do it. Choice of their next project is a potent reward for people who perform well.

Share of Value Creation. Entrepreneurial incentives that give teams a piece of the action are highly appropriate in collaborative companies. Because extra rewards are based only on measurable results, this approach also conserves resources. Innovative companies are experimenting with incentives like phantom stock for development of new ventures and other strategic achievements, equity participation in project returns, and bonuses pegged to key performance targets. Given the cross-functional nature of many projects today, rewards of this kind must sometimes be system-wide, but individual managers can also ask for a bonus pool for their own areas, contingent, of course, on meeting performance goals. And everyone can share the kinds of rewards that are abundant and free—awards and recognition.

Learning. The chance to learn new skills or apply them in new arenas is an important motivator in a turbulent environment because it's oriented toward securing the future. "The learning organization" promises to become a 1990s business buzzword as companies seek to learn more systematically from their experience and to encourage continuous learning for their people. In the world of high technology, where people understand uncertainty, the attractiveness of any company often lies in its capacity to provide learning and experience. By this calculus, access to training, mentors, and challenging projects is more important than pay or benefits. Some prominent companies—General Electric, for example—have always been able to attract top talent, even when they could not promise upward mobility, because people see them as a training ground, a good place to learn, and a valuable addition to a resume.

Reputation. Reputation is a key resource in professional careers, and the chance to enhance it can be an outstanding motivator. The professional's reliance on reputation stands in marked contrast to the bureaucrat's anonymity. Professionals have to make a name for themselves, while traditional corporate managers and employees stayed behind the scenes. Indeed, the accumulation of reputational "capital" provides not only an immediate ego boost but also the kind of publicity that can bring other rewards, even other job offers. Managers can enhance reputation—and improve motivation—by creating stars, by providing abundant public recognition and visible awards, by crediting the authors of innovation, by publicizing people outside their own departments, and by plugging people into organizational and professional networks.

The change-adept organization is predicated on a logic of flexible work assignments, not of fixed job responsibilities. To promote innovation and responsiveness, two of today's competitive imperatives, managers need to see this new organization as a cluster of activity sets, not as a rigid structure. The work of leadership in this new corporation will be to organize both sequential and synchronous projects of varying length and breadth, through which varying combinations of people will move, depending on the tasks, challenges, and opportunities facing the area and its partners at any given moment.

Leaders need to carve out projects with tangible accomplishments, milestones, and completion dates and then delegate responsibility for these projects to the people who flesh them out. Clearly delimited projects can counter overload by focusing effort and can provide short-term motivation when the fate of the long-term mission is uncertain. Project responsibility leads to ownership of the results and sometimes substitutes for other forms of reward. In companies where product development teams define and run their own projects, members commonly say that the greatest compensation they get is seeing the advertisements for their products. "Hey, that's mine! I did that!" one engineer told me he trumpeted to his family the first time he saw a commercial for his group's innovation.

This sense of ownership, along with a definite time frame, can spur higher levels of effort. Whenever people are engaged in creative or problem-solving projects that will have tangible results by deadline dates, they tend to come in at all hours, to think about the project in their spare time, to invest in it vast sums of physical and emotional energy. Knowing that the project will end and that completion will be an occasion for reward and recognition makes it possible to work much harder.

Leaders in the new organization do not lack motivational tools, but the tools are different from those of traditional corporate bureaucrats. The new rewards are based not on status but on contribution, and they consist not of regular promotion and automatic pay raises but of excitement about mission and a share of the glory and the gains of success. The new security is not employment security (a guaranteed job no matter what) but employability security—increased value in the internal and external labor markets. Commitment to the organization still matters, but today managers build commitment by offering project opportunities. The new loyalty is not to the boss or to the company but to projects that actualize a mission and offer challenge, growth, and credit for results.

The old bases of managerial authority are eroding, and new tools of leadership are taking their place. Managers whose power derived from hierarchy and who were accustomed to a limited area of personal control are learning to shift their perspectives and widen their horizons. The new managerial work consists of looking outside a defined area of responsibility to sense opportunities and of forming project teams drawn from any relevant sphere to address them. It involves communication and collaboration across functions, across divisions, and across companies whose activities and resources overlap. Thus rank, title, or official charter will be less important factors in success at the new managerial work than having the knowledge, skills, and sensitivity to mobilize people and motivate them to do their best.

5

Six Certainties for CEOs

Everyone knows that uncertainty abounds. Political or economic developments surprise us daily. Competitive conditions and product generations change so fast in some industries that the value of tangible assets (inventory or real estate) can erode overnight. A "long-range plan" is filling next week's calendar.

In a world of uncertainty and surprises, what can we count on? In 1789, Benjamin Franklin found only two things certain: death and taxes. Today, medical advances and government waffling make even those two less certain.

Business leaders must find new sources of certainty that encompass volatility. The new certainties involve *skills* and *capabilities*— the capacity to change.

1. Leading through Learning. Leaders create the future by emphasizing what the company's people must learn, not by reinforcing what they already know. What CEOs choose to learn themselves, on their own, sends a powerful signal about the skills others should acquire. Arnold Hiatt, former chairman of Stride Rite, a shoe company, learned by looking at people's feet. Flying from Korea to Hong Kong, for example, he noticed a tab on a toddler's shoe that allowed her to put the shoe on by herself. A creative new product idea followed. Could any Stride Rite people miss the message?

CEOs can be more powerful role models when they learn rather than when they teach. David Dworkin, when head of British retailer BhS, made numerous speeches about the importance of technology on the selling floor to help sales associates serve customers. The message was received when he and his top staff trained on new sales registers.

2. Process Capabilities. Focusing on processes is as important as focusing on products. Processes not only create today's efficiencies but also ensure the future via skills that extend to new products.

Consider a comparison of Japanese and U.S. R&D expenditures by Harvard's Kennedy School of Government professor Lewis Branscomb. Japanese companies invested 70% of their R&D funds in *process* innovations; U.S. companies invested 70% of their R&D funds in *product* innovations. Japanese companies also emphasized innovations for low-end products first so they can offer high quality and low cost simultaneously—a pairing sure to win market dominance.

Major new products may satisfy a CEO's ego, but spending too much to chase them is not the best way to build a company's future. Rapid process innovation, in contrast, can result in strengthened process capabilities that permit new products to be developed faster. Well-chosen incremental innovations can lead to major breakthroughs. Variety within a common product framework enables the framework itself to change.

3. Absolute Excellence, Not Relative Quality. With global competition intensifying, it is more important to meet the highest standards than to hope for lowest common denominator solutions. CEOs build company capabilities by reaching for absolute excellence instead of merely trying to beat today's competition or meet today's regulatory standards. One Japanese quality secret is to seek perfection, not to do one notch better than competitors. Though more costly initially, this philosophy is ultimately more sustainable.

"Green" issues are one area in which absolute excellence is sensible. Consider the politics involved in Europe's attempt to harmonize environmental standards. Even if the European Union agrees on lower standards, countries that set higher than minimum standards can offer advantages to their own companies in their home markets. And if those home markets are large, as in Germany, the result can be protectionist.

Some pharmaceutical companies, facing different regulatory standards around the world, choose the most stringent ones to guide every new offering. Hewlett-Packard tries to produce to the world's highest standard, redesigning office machine packages worldwide to conform to German environmental standards. This approach reinforces a reputation for quality everywhere.

4. Politics and Scrutiny. As CEOs open their minds to learning, they must also open their doors to more constituencies.

Running a business is no longer a commercial act between consenting adults behind closed doors. More company and competitive information is more readily available to more people. Hungry journalists search for the inside story, so CEOs are scrutinized. Companies lurch, so CEOs are attacked.

Deregulation in many countries has not depoliticized corporate life—just the opposite. Consider former American President George Bush's January 1992 trip to Japan with auto industry leaders, which put CEO pay on the U.S political agenda. Will another kind of politics—debates between shareholders and managers over company direction—replace takeovers as the defining tool for corporate governance challenges? Such debates could be heated and bitter—unless companies invite constituencies inside, as Avon does in its regular meetings between directors, investors, and management.

In the past, CEOs insulated themselves more easily than they can today. They could surround themselves with courtiers who told them what they wanted to hear. They could refuse to talk to the press. They could avoid the inconveniences of ordinary people by using such perks as private transportation systems—like the corporate jet that shoe executive Arnold Hiatt once likened to "riding in Lenin's sealed train." But senior management is more accessible today, physically as well as in other ways. The hushed, chapel-like executive floor is giving way to offices with open doors in the middle of operations.

Effective CEOs even see themselves as "politicians" who must put their plans in front of company constituencies for review and support. The 5-person Executive Committee is becoming the 500-person Strategy Conference. In a large French company, 500 managers determined strategy by voting on proposals. A Canadian CEO called his road shows to talk with employees a "campaign" in which he must win their support.

5. Interdependence and Intercompany Relationships. External constituencies are vital allies in mastering change.

One of Wal-Mart's primary capabilities is working closely with suppliers to reduce inventory costs and speed delivery times. The retailer and manufacturer partners share data electronically; manufacturing schedules reflect consumer demand. Whirlpool, which has had a long-term partnership with Sears in the United States, developed similar relationships in Europe.

Managing intercompany relationships occupies more and more CEO time. Such relationships involve multiple links between the organizations: systems experts planning data-interchange compatibility; marketers and manufacturing specialists agreeing on quality standards; finance people arranging billing (for example, Whirlpool Europe financing some of its retailers' stock). A U.S. CEO jokes that he used to have only one extra chair in his office; for any decision today, his office is crowded—with "outsiders" included.

A partnership orientation requires respect for the other company and a willingness to invest for the long term. At Stride Rite, Arnold Hiatt emphasized close connections with dealers and made long-term commitments to Asian manufacturers, which were unusual in the industry at that time. He looked for companies whose culture was compatible with that of Stride Rite.

Relationships of trust occur through people. Partnerships develop because CEOs feel comfortable working together, as do the people down the line. Among the lessons from successful German companies committed to serving foreign markets: continuity of people makes relationships work.

6. Rising Discomfort Levels. The emotional temperature inside organizations is rising.

All of the first five certainties mean that leaders increasingly have to deal with differences—cultural and political differences between countries, between companies, and between parts of their own work force. Differences, and the conflicts that can flow from them, reduce people's comfort level.

Traditional companies minimized differences among employees to ensure ease of communication and high comfort. This was especially true in top ranks, where remarkable ethnic and social homogeneity often prevailed. But companies can no longer afford the costs of segregation—for example, treating female employees like deadweight. The possibility of sexual harassment creates discomfort perhaps more than any other issue besides race. It forces uncomfortable discussions of behavior and practices once ignored or let go with a wink. Contentious diversity issues have hit U.S. companies first, but they are also becoming salient in Europe and Asia. The ability to confront them spurs improvement in many human resource areas.

Leaders should *promote* discomfort. Feeling comfortable can create false security. Self-infatuation with past successes and elegant mission statements distracted Mentor Graphics, to pick one example, from seeing changes in the competitive environment during a turbulent period in its development. Managers make themselves comfortable by disposing of problems quickly, before they understand their full implications. Leaders, in contrast, create challenging workplaces with highly charged emotional peaks and valleys.

Underlying the six certainties is a seventh: the desirability of change. A leader's vision is an imperfect moving target. And it should be. To preserve the best of what a company can accomplish, leaders have to change with the times. *That's certain.*

6

The Best of Both Worlds

To managers today, chaos is not just a scientific theory. It is a daily experience. Maintaining the same structure for long—let alone getting organized at all—can seem miraculous.

From computer companies to consumer goods corporations, constant surprises, be they slipped schedules or unexpected moves by competitors, are now more the norm than the exception. The need to scramble makes a mockery of traditional planning tools such as forecasts by the numbers. Actions to solve one problem produce new problems elsewhere. Answers, however good, are never simple. Consider the dilemma Tom Chapman faced as CEO of Greater Southeast Community Hospital in Washington, D.C.: while investments in disease prevention reduce hospital costs, they also reduce the hospital's revenues.

Flawless plans, unvarying rules, strategies launched without mid-course corrections—"absolutes" such as these have little to do with the task of managing. Now, more than ever, management is a balancing act—the juggling of contradictions to try to get the best of attractive but opposing alternatives. Order is a temporary illusion, strategy a moving target. Leaders cannot impose authority on a world of constant motion; they can only hope to steer some of that action toward productive ends.

Irish poet William Butler Yeats said it best: "The center cannot hold." In every sphere, "centers" are being discredited—from the decline of the superpowers to mistrust of national governments to attacks on non-value-adding corporate headquarters. Traditional banking centers can no longer manage the international monetary system. Technology enables entrepreneurs of every kind to leapfrog established channels. Engineers at a U.S. computer maker can address everyone in the company through the e-mail system.

Businesspeople in Eastern Europe can sidestep obsolete national telephone systems—and censors—by making international calls from their car phones, tapping into a global satellite network.

But chaos need not mean action without guidance or limits. New organizational models offer the best of both worlds—enough structure for continuity, but not so much that creative responses to chaos are stifled.

Federalist principles, which treat a corporation as an alliance of quasi-independent states, allow both flexibility and direction—the freedom of local entrepreneurship without the fragmentation. Instead of command centers, there are communication and coordination vehicles. Instead of single centers of authority, there are multiple centers of expertise. Instead of all-powerful CEOs, there are executive teams that represent independent power bases. "Integration" replaces the old either-or thinking of "centralization versus decentralization."

The new corporate federalism, which seeks the best of both autonomy and authority, has much to teach governments. Many business executives criticize the European Union's Eurofederalism for not striking the appropriate balance between central coordination and local control. At a private meeting, the CEO of a British-Dutch transnational company complained, "centralized bureaucracies were eliminated in Eastern Europe only to be recreated in Brussels." If unity implies old-fashioned centralization and the imposition of uniformity, it is not surprising that nations defend their home markets and methods. In Europe and elsewhere, nineteenth-century models cannot produce twenty-first century cooperation.

The same principle applies to companies. Clinging to outmoded practices and models impedes progress by narrowing options. One result is economically irrational behavior: for example, the decision to keep parts manufacturing in-house even when outsourcing offers both financial and technological benefits. Alas, it is hard to give up the illusion of control that comes from guarding turf.

In contrast, the new federalist thinking supports cooperation across boundaries, a kind of voluntary control through relationships among equals. It also puts the emphasis on multiple small initiatives rather than large uniform programs directed from the center. As chaos theory proposes, small actions can lead to big changes. Bootstrapping entrepreneurs look for small breaks. Change agents look for a series of small quick wins to transform a corporate culture.

Making such changes requires constant learning, since it is detailed knowledge of changes in a business and its context that provokes strategic thinking—and rethinking. Manufacturing managers cannot make sound sourcing decisions without a careful breakdown of their company's parts portfolio. Senior managers cannot bring into being the new "learning organization" without understanding their enterprise's system dynamics. For example, by watching what happened before patients got to his hospital and after they left, Tom Chapman realized that the key to containing costs at Greater Southeast was to improve the community's well-being.

"Real planning is a learning process, not a means of control, and it is more anecdotal than numerical" was the conclusion of re-formed numbers-cruncher Ken Veit, an entrepreneur whose store start-up taught him the wisdom of the truism that retail is detail, often based on imaginative response to circumstances. Organizations must be able to capture and transmit anecdotal experience-based knowledge from the small local actions that can influence the whole system. And so networks, alliances, partnerships, and federations with multiple centers of expertise emerge to replace centralized bureaucracies.

P A R T

III

Leading Change:

Innovation and Transformation

Overview

Certain kinds of change appear to come easily—bold strokes by leaders that turn the world upside down, such as the decision to buy or sell a business, open a market, or close a facility. But transforming the way an organization operates and how its people work is a long march, requiring many individuals to change their behavior over a long period of time. Change is full of false starts, messy mistakes, and controversial experiments involving the participation and guidance of many people. Even bold strokes are merely announcements of intention whose success will depend on the longer march of implementation. It is tempting for leaders to try to transform their organizations by throwing everything out and starting over again, but it is more effective to nurture changes already developing within the organization. That is why constant innovation—new concepts in processes as well as products—makes change smoother and more continuous.

Change is often said to begin with a "vision," but it often works best when it begins with a careful diagnosis of both strengths and weaknesses (see "Change: Where to Begin"). Awareness of strengths in an organization's current business model and in the concepts it already has under development helps the company avoid abrupt discontinuities that can cause the costly waste of energy, talent, time, and resources. Businesses cannot turn themselves overnight into something entirely different. They must turn existing platforms into springboards from which to leap further, faster—even, perhaps, to new platforms. And they should encourage constant experimentation from many inside innovators and change leaders to help anticipate the possibilities of the future before radical change is forced upon them.

Business change and culture change go hand in hand. "Championing Change" describes the systematic approach taken by Bell Atlantic over several years to transform itself from regulated monopoly to feisty competitor in the rapidly evolving telecommunications industry. CEO Ray Smith made structural changes, such as cutting out layers of management and reducing rules, but most of the change process involved values and behavior—the culture. Smith wanted people to work differently, to be more accountable, and to feel empowered to innovate. Change started with senior managers, who had to develop and model a new style of leadership. Then followed programs to create a more entrepreneurial environment that encouraged further change. Each department was challenged to retool its processes and to work more collaboratively with other departments. Corporate staffs were put in a market-like situation, in which their budgets depended on selling their services to users, thus provoking an internal-customer orientation. The Champion program provided seed money, guidance, and training to inside entrepreneurs with big new product ideas. Anyone could submit a proposal, and then, if the project proceeded, proposers could invest up to 10% of their base salaries for three years, earning 5% of the project's net revenue on their investment.

"The Manager as Innovator" could serve as a how-to guide for all corporate entrepreneurs and change agents. Successful innovations are led by people who are comfortable with ambiguity. Leaders of change are willing to commit to long-term goals and to persist in achieving them, and they are participative and inclusive in their management styles. They bring skills to every stage of the change drama. In the first phase, they translate vague assignments into salable projects by tuning in to their environment, challenging assumptions, and crafting a vision. Next, using diplomatic skills to get favorable responses, they build coalitions of backers and supporters willing to invest in the effort and to help it over the hurdles. Finally, they manage the project well and keep the action moving forward by handling interference, maintaining momentum, and incorporating emergent developments into new designs, never losing sight of the overall goal.

A change-adept organizational culture supports the work of change leaders. Bell Atlantic, for example, aspires to such a culture. More ideas are generated and more new concepts emerge in environments in which information circulates freely, people communicate across boundaries, job descriptions are broad and encourage initiative, and rewards are oriented toward future opportunities, not just offered in payment for past services.

Change must cut through mental as well as organizational barriers. Innovations grow out of unexpected, surprising, and even irreverent mental connections that create new concepts. Companies now say they want "out-of-the-box" thinking. But try the familiar puzzle in "Thinking Across Boundaries" to see if you can come up with any novel solutions. Even tools designed to stimulate innovation can turn into tried-and-true formulas.

Concept-rich, change-adept companies need constant external challenge and stimulation to avoid the tendency to fall into ruts. They should take better advantage of a company's best change ally: its customers (see "Even Closer to the Customer"). Customers should become members, real to all employees, and companies should be willing to act on the information customers provide to champion change. Both disgruntled and loyal customers have something to offer.

Finally, companies should recognize the importance of persistence in making new ideas succeed. The work is not done when the Big Idea is hatched (see "Follow-Up and Follow-Through"). True change requires many small steps toward operational excellence.

7

Change: Where to Begin

Fine-tuning is no longer enough, business leaders are told. Nothing short of transformation will do.

Business survival today depends on courage and imagination—the courage to challenge prevailing business models and the imagination to invent new markets.

Rosenbluth Travel, for example, faced with the turmoil of airline deregulation in the 1980s, shifted its product mix from 75% leisure to 92% business travel, inventing new processes to enable the new strategy to take hold. Similarly, future success in competitive industries like computers requires rethinking where value is added for customers and what alliances are necessary to deliver that value. Competitive success in the 1990s will belong to companies that escape the tyranny of their served markets to create new ones, as Gary Hamel and C. K. Prahalad have proposed.

Equally sweeping challenges to obsolete assumptions are advocated by experts examining other aspects of business. Be suspicious of quick fixes that paper over fundamental weaknesses. Improvement in profitability, for example, requires reexamining and reinventing the underlying business system rather than mechanistically cutting costs.

Increasingly, leaders do not question whether to change, but they want to know *how*. Where, they wonder, does a company begin to transform its culture?

Lessons from disappointments, stalled efforts, and outright failures make clear how *not* to begin. Not with a Master Plan crafted at the top and a Total Program worked out in bureaucratic detail and staffed by dozens of complex self-perpetuating task forces. Not by trying to start at the *end* of the change process, when the shape of the new markets or the details of the new practices are understood and can be communicated and institutionalized. And not by emulating the current practices of companies that successfully transformed their businesses while ignoring all the false starts, messy mistakes, and controversial experiments that got them there.

Change looks revolutionary only in retrospect. The connotation of change—an abrupt disjunction, a clean break—does not always match the reality of change.

Most of us begin recording events at the moment we become conscious of our own strategic actions, neglecting the groundwork that has already been laid. Popular models of planned change, like the strategic planning frameworks from which they derive, start when leaders make an explicit decision to seek a well-constructed new course of action. Such models reflect a bias toward official history and suggest that only leadership actions count.

Generally, however, by the time high-level organizational odometers are set at zero to record a change process, many less perfect and less public events that set the stage for the official decision process have already occurred—such as a series of intriguing grass-roots innovations that depart from organizational tradition. Lack of awareness of this "prehistory" of change makes any conclusions about how a particular organization managed a change suspect—and perhaps impossible to replicate.

Xerox, Motorola, and Corning are considered exemplars of U.S. companies that have rethought their business models and renewed their organizations. Generally neglected in the accounts of successful change processes, however, is just how long it took each company to hit upon its approach and how much trial and error was involved. Corning began its partnerships five decades ago; Motorola had a participative management program in the 1970s; Xerox's companywide quality effort grew out of shaky and controversial attempts to promote employee involvement and benchmarking in the early 1980s.

Predictably, retrospective accounts of change processes often distort the real story. Early events and people recede in importance as later events and people take center stage. Conflict disappears into consensus. Equally plausible alternatives disappear into obvious choices. Accidents, uncertainties, and confusions disappear into clear-sighted strategies. Multiple activities disappear into single thematic events. The fragility of change disappears into a public image of solidity and full actuality.

Organizations seeking total transformation cannot avoid the messy, mistake-ridden muddling stage. This is when people get comfortable with change, tailor it to their circumstances, and take charge of the process. And the full direction of change becomes clear only after action is under way. Companies embracing a Total Transformation Master Plan without laying the groundwork are merely postponing confrontation with messy reality.

So where should change begin?

1. *Begin with use-directed, action-oriented information.* Improve the quality of information about the realities of customers' and employees' situations. Discover what people actually *do;* assess how processes actually work. The best part of the Malcolm Baldrige National Quality Award in the United States is that it gives companies a checklist of items to use for self-assessment; the worst part is that it encourages some companies to mount a Total Program to Fix Problems before they have even discovered a direction for change. Similarly, a "green" transformation begins not with a glamorous product that capitalizes on the environmental bandwagon, but by providing better information, such as how production processes affect the environment.

In addition to collecting concrete information about today's realities, tune in to unmet needs. Explore customers' and employees' hopes and dreams. At the heart of market shifts in any industry is the changing nature of value as defined by customers. There are no products anymore, in the narrow sense, only services. Even manufacturing companies should be thinking about the services their products offer, not the products themselves. "Functionality" or "utility" convey a similar idea—how customers can use what a company produces is what creates a market for it.

2. *Be willing to build on the platforms already in place.* Begin by stepping back to define strengths and potentialities in existing resources, experiences, and bases. Volkswagen's former chairman, Carl Hahn, created a European platform for global competition. Volkswagen may or may not be correct in some ultimate planning-analytic way that a strong European base is an excellent

vehicle for global success, but that's what VW's got, and it might as well make the most of it. VW could no more will itself into another kind of company overnight than Rochester, New York could wish itself on the prosperous Spanish Riviera. Rochester, like VW, is constructing its changes out of existing capabilities. Those capabilities do not have to be geographic—and indeed, VW has more freedom of action in a global economy than does Rochester. But even cities and regions are developing a view of their existing assets, such as industry clusters or work force skills, that provide the platform from which any new strategies should spring.

Every company, regardless of its difficulties, has some positive innovations to build on, some seeds of the future already blossoming. Even in troubled industries, some companies do well—for example, Dillard Department Stores during a period of crisis in U.S. retailing. Even in troubled companies, some departments do well, providing a platform for growth—for example, the crafts department in another, more distressed retail chain.

Moreover, it is important not to insult people by assuming that the organization has no experience with the new phenomenon, as some companies do when they launch Total Quality Programs with the implicit message that no one has focused on quality until then.

3. *Encourage incremental experimentation that departs from tradition without totally destroying it.* Many companies begin Major Change Programs with training when they should really begin with doing. Experimentation produces options, opportunities, and learning—and training can be provided to the innovating teams. A proliferation of modest experiments provides the organization's own experience with elements of many different business models.

Grass-roots innovation can occur through "expeditionary marketing" (trials of lots of different options in the marketplace), localized problem solving, a commitment to continual experimentation, or by taking new risks, such as challenging team norms.

A rapid succession of experiments from an existing platform resolves an important dilemma surrounding the very idea of corporate transformation. A company cannot neglect existing businesses while leaping into new ones. It cannot shut down one day and become something totally different the next.

Experimentation both requires and builds confidence. It permits a company to write its own case studies of successful change and to learn from its own experience. Large numbers of small experiments reduce risks while providing alternatives. The best can then be chosen for dissemination. Internal benchmarking is as important as external benchmarking.

Where to begin is a complex determination, requiring organizational self-scrutiny. *When* to begin is simple. Now.

8

Championing Change:
An Interview with Bell Atlantic's CEO
Raymond Smith

Competing in the telecommunications industry is increasingly a world game. Rapid scientific advances are increasing communications speed and blurring the distinction between information technologies and communications technologies—computer companies are in the communications business, and telephone companies are selling systems integration. The old-fashioned Phone Company— once a monopoly in the United States and a government ministry elsewhere—is now subject to forces of competition, through changing regulation or privatization.

Few industries as old have been transformed so dramatically in such a short time, and further transformations are on the horizon. The U.S. edge in the telecommunications sector may well depend on the skill with which change—human, organizational, and technological—is managed.

Bell Atlantic Corporation was formed in 1983, in preparation for the breakup of the Bell System telephone monopoly on January 1, 1984. It was one of seven U.S. regional telecommunications holding companies (sometimes called "baby Bells") created when AT&T was required by judicial decree to divest its local telephone operations, ushering in the era of greater competition.

Bell Atlantic began with a charter to provide local telephone service in six mid-Atlantic states and the District of Columbia. A decade later, Bell Atlantic was introducing new products and services at a rapid clip, starting ventures and forming alliances throughout the world, and pursuing leadership in the information technology industry of the future.

Bell Atlantic's vision centers around the creation of the "Intelligent Network," a computer-driven network capable of transmitting audio, video, and data signals through speedy fiber-optic lines. Calling itself the world's most efficient telephone company, Bell Atlantic had 1996 revenues of over 13 billion dollars and ventures in Mexico, New Zealand, Slovakia, the Czech Republic, and Italy.

Raymond Smith became Bell Atlantic's CEO in January 1989, adding the responsibilities of chairman of the board in July 1989. Earlier in his career, he managed operations, regulatory affairs, engineering, and finance for AT&T, rising to the presidencies of the Pennsylvania and Delaware companies, positions he held when Bell Atlantic was formed. A year after Bell Atlantic's inception, he moved to the corporate team as vice chairman and chief financial officer (1985 to 1987) and then president and chief operating officer (1988). He worked closely with his predecessor Thomas Bolger to shape the business concept and to eliminate vestiges of the traditionally complacent, monopolistic mind-set known as having "Bell-shaped heads."

I spoke with Mr. Smith about the CEO's role in transforming a monopolistic, bureaucratic corporation into one that is both efficient and entrepreneurial, posing questions derived from my models of organizational change.

RMK: How did you view the state of your business when you became Bell Atlantic's chief executive?

Raymond Smith: I saw that the way we had been managing all of these years was going to have to change. The problem was clear. The intrinsic growth of the core business would not sustain the company in the competitive global economy of the twenty-first century.

The difficulty of addressing our basic business problem was complicated by competition on one side and regulation on the other. Even our 3% projected growth rate was subject to considerable, well-financed competition in the most profitable lines. As a regulated company, we owed a subsidy to the local telephone rate-payers, so we were limited in what we could earn in the core business. And the legislation and judicial decree that broke up the Bell System restricted the kinds of businesses we could enter. For example, the Cable Act of 1984 kept Bell Atlantic from competing in the cable television business in our region.

How did you think the company could increase its rate of growth in revenues and earnings?

We identified five initial strategies. Four of them would sound familiar to many businesses: improved efficiency; substantially improved marketing to protect market share; new products and services; and entirely new businesses operating outside of our territory and outside of the United States.

The fifth strategy was one we had to work on right away. It involved regulatory reform that we called "incentive regulation" to allow us to benefit from our own initiatives while protecting the telephone rate-payers. We worked intensively with regulators and crafted social contracts with consumer groups and those most affected by telephone rates, such as senior citizens and people with disabilities.

With incentive regulation accomplished, we could concentrate on the business growth strategies. But none of our strategies could be achieved with the company culture in place after the breakup. So I had to focus on the culture first.

What was wrong with the culture?

The company had grown out of a long-standing monopoly, with the centralized organizational structure and culture of a monopoly. In the old Bell System culture, no operating company could introduce a product of its own. The way a small work center in a small town in Pennsylvania would operate was mandated by the central staff. There was no strategic planning, no product development, no long-range planning in the operating companies. It was all centralized at AT&T.

What was the consequence of that?

The operating companies had an implementation mentality. They did not understand the initiative, innovation, risks, and accountability necessary to meet our business goals. Managers were held accountable for implementation of a process or practice exactly as it was written, not for the end result. Managers simply could not imagine rewriting a process even if they knew a better one. They were maintenance managers, not business managers.

When I told those same managers that we wanted improved marketing, new products, and new business, it was a mental shock. We had no experience to draw on. And the ways we were accustomed to operating impeded our ability to achieve our goals.

How so?

Cross-departmental competition raised costs and prevented new initiatives. This problem was a consequence of our heritage.

The old Bell System was like a great football team with the best athletes and the best equipment. Every Saturday morning, we'd run up and down the football field and win 100 to 0 because there was no one on the other side of the line of scrimmage; we were a monopoly. Being human, the football players found their competition inside the team. This sometimes resulted in lowest common denominator solutions and substantial inefficiency. Despite dedication and hard work, it often took more resources to get things done than were ever really needed.

The conventions of behavior grew out of cross-departmental competition and were very parochial. There was no true unifying concept to rally around. I represented my department, you represented your department, and we behaved as if we were opposing lawyers or political opponents.

When did you begin to see that this kind of behavior had to change?

In the early 1980s, when we began to see real competition. Tom Bolger, my predecessor as CEO, and I agreed that we needed a new culture to support our business strategies.

Where did you start?

We started by articulating the values of the corporation. I was personally involved, with another officer, in the design of seminars in which 1,400 managers spent half a week to think through our values and state them clearly. At the seminars, a draft was handed out for discussion. These managers were actively engaged in editing the document word by word. New categories were suggested; eventually, "teamwork" became "respect and trust." I attended virtually every seminar and met with the participants for five or six hours a week.

Ultimately, we agreed on five values: integrity, respect and trust, excellence, individual fulfillment, and profitable growth, with a paragraph of description explaining each.

What happened when the sessions were completed and the statement of values was published?

Not enough! It became very apparent to me and to the managers involved that we needed to move from general statements of values to concrete behaviors and work practices, or what we called the "conventions" of day-to-day business life. So when I became CEO, I announced a ten-year transition to a new way of working together.

Every corporation today is full of rhetoric like "it's time to change" or "we need a new way" or "we want to get rid of bureaucracy." What did you do to show people that you meant it?

One of the first steps I took was to engage the senior officers in a serious examination of our obligations to the corporation. I personally prepared a list of 12 specific guidelines. In a series of day-long meetings, I suggested to each of the top 50 people in Bell Atlantic that they had broad corporate obligations that went beyond their departmental responsibilities. There were arguments and debates about the obligations, but in the end they stood. It took a year to get the required understanding and commitment.

We made quality a corporate imperative in our 1989 strategic plan, designing a Quality Improvement Process using the Baldrige Award criteria and starting our own Quality Institute. We developed an organized program of internal communications for all employees outlining our obligations to each other, the opportunities ahead, and the need and reasons for change. We called this the Bell Atlantic Way.

What is the Bell Atlantic Way, and why did you think you needed it?

Simply stated, the Bell Atlantic Way is an organized, participative method of working together that allows us to get the most out of our own efforts and maximize our contribution to team goals. The Bell Atlantic Way includes the conventions of daily behavior subscribed to by all of us.

In a large business, the most important determinant of success is the effectiveness of millions of day-to-day interactions between human beings. If those contacts are contentious, turf-oriented, and parochial, the company will flounder, bureaucracies will grow, and internal competition will be rampant. But when employees behave in accountable, team-oriented, and collegial ways, it dramatically improves group effectiveness.

The Bell Atlantic Way isn't limited to a list of dos and don'ts, but it does seem to boil down to a few specific behaviors. For example, the plaque on my desk says, "Be Here Now." That just means that it's important that I listen and be totally involved in any discussion we may have. I'm not looking over my shoulder. I'm not taking phone calls. I'm not doodling or having side conversations while you are making a presentation.

In such a large corporation, how do you get people to operate by these codes of behavior?

With the help of consultants, we designed forums to introduce the Bell Atlantic Way to 20,000 managers. The officer group, roughly 50 people, attended first. Then the officers acted as executives-in-residence at forums for the rest of the managers and supervisors. Most of us have been through the sessions two or three times.

We teach the conventions, we don't just talk about them. Each one is impressed on forum participants in experiential exercises that help us examine ourselves and remind us of our obligations to each other. And our responsibilities don't stop at the end of the forum. I'm spending a great deal of my own time in the field meeting with employees and talking about the Bell Atlantic Way. Each of the officers has developed departmental programs of re-inforcement and support back on the job.

Why is it important for you and the other officers to spend scarce executive time on this, involving yourselves in a personal way?

We must ourselves model what we are asking others to do. We call this "the shadow of the leader." We are asking people to change their behavior, to accept a new set of conventions for working together. And I try to provide reinforcement in every way I can. For example, I always wear my Quality button to impress colleagues with my rabid dedication. It serves to remind us that we have a very special obligation to support those who are sup-porting the corporation.

It took about a year for top management to internalize the con-cepts of this change, to recognize it, and to begin to support it fully. Now changes have started to accelerate. We're seeing as much change every three months as we used to see in three years.

What are some tangible signs of change?

The language is changing. The decision process is changing. People are becoming more accountable, more team-oriented, and more effective. For example, our budget process is no longer bitter and contentious. It's still painful and always difficult, but it's much less of a hassle and never personal.

There has been remarkable improvement among the top 400 people of the company who decide on budgets, projects, priorities, and resource allocation. As corny as it may seem, managers will now open sessions saying, "We've got to break the squares today," referring to one of the Bell Atlantic Way games—meaning we've got to compromise here, break out of thinking about only our own territories. We may know that the corporation has to reduce budgets; so we all must give something up for the good of the whole company.

In the old culture, if I contributed resources for the good of the corporation, I'd lose the support of my own group. Now it is no longer acceptable for someone to say, "I've done my bit. I've met my goal. I'll sit back until you meet yours." It's not acceptable to complain to third parties about the boss or the company or some other department. Someone who does that is likely to be asked, "What did they say when you told them?" One manager said that bitch sessions used to be the social event of the week, but now they're no fun. We expect people to accept accountability for results.

How do you get accountability?

We had to make sure that our reward system encouraged people to focus on results consistent with larger business goals. The first step was to base compensation on corporate and team results as well as individual results. Today the corporate performance award is a much higher percentage of compensation than it was in the past. It used to be zero—or such a tiny percentage that it never meant anything. Now the award has a long-term as well as a short-term component for a growing percentage of managers, and it is worth more than a few bucks. It's also flexible; the definition of team can include local groups as well as the whole corporation.

A significant factor in an individual's performance evaluation is whether they have also contributed to the overall team goals. Our team goals include customer service. We look at the customers' attitudes through telephone surveys—whether or not they feel we are conforming to their requirements 100% of the time. We must

reach a minimum level of performance on customer service measures before there are any corporate incentive awards.

Our reward and appraisal system is not perfect, but at least it is
getting better. However, even the best evaluation system will not
produce the desired behavior unless people understand our business problem and our strategies.

Do your employees get this basic business information?

Now they do, but that was not always the case. As I traveled
throughout our company before becoming CEO, I found that very
few people really knew what we were trying to do as a company.
Sometimes they understood the departmental objectives, and certainly they knew their own objectives, but most people had no idea
how to put their day-to-day work life into a corporate context.
Actions of the corporation such as the purchase of a new business
or the consolidation of an operations center were often a mystery.

How did you clear up the mystery?

My senior officers and I wrote out what we thought was the basic
business problem we were trying to solve. We added the specific
strategies to solve it, the departmental goals, and finally the individual objectives that were the employees' contributions to the
goals. Then we shared it with everyone.

This was somewhat new. The notion of intellectually engaging
all of our employees in the solution of the basic business problem
was so different from the past that we had to communicate clearly
and personally. So we asked the 400 top people in the company,
the key managers and communicators, to understand the overall
strategy totally and fully, internalize it, and go forth and share it
with others. There was a brief hiccup in the company while this
idea was absorbed, but then it took off.

*You were also giving top managers a big kick in the pants. You
were arousing them to action. Shouldn't they have known the strategy and been communicating it all along?*

I don't think of it that way. From my first day on the job, I should
have made sure that we were all on the same wavelength. I didn't
realize that everyone wasn't behaving like a CEO and thinking
about the basic corporate problem all day long. When 99% of
someone's efforts are engaged in getting a departmental job done,
the broad goals of the corporation begin to fade if they are not con-

stantly reinforced. As the head coach and teacher, I hadn't really taught the game plan or the course well enough. So I went on the stump, enlisted the aid of a number of others and spread the word.

Now the top 400 certainly know our business problem. They know our purpose, vision, and strategies, and how they fit together. Because the top 400 talk about this, thousands of other Bell Atlantic employees know it too. They can translate their personal and departmental objectives to those of the company. This makes it easier to deal with the tough realities we face.

What are the tough realities?

We had to eliminate jobs to get our costs in line and reduce wasteful bureaucracy. This is one of the biggest culture shocks we faced. People used to join a Bell System company with the expectation that they'd be taken care of from cradle to grave.

We've tried to do two things to cushion the blow. The first is to level with people. We tell them about the problems in the United States—the troubled companies and the layoffs, plant closings, and ruined careers that come from complacency. We explain that this is the way life is in a competitive world. Wishful thinking won't bring back the old world of no change and total security.

In U.S. business today, the understanding of the real world is vital to survival. In our industry, for example, we have a choice of having a larger number of low-paid employees who will be subject to layoffs, or we can have a smaller group of well-paid, efficient employees with security obtained through hard work and providing customers with more value than they can get elsewhere.

The second thing we do is to try to make stressful changes like downsizing in a participative manner. We eliminated one whole level of management, and we did it by involving the employees in the decision. We had no overall template for the organization, the way the Bell System did in the past. We allowed each organization to eliminate the level it wanted the way it felt was appropriate. After all, almost any organization will succeed if the people feel empowered, are recognized for what they do, and understand the purpose of their jobs.

The idea for this initiative came from New Jersey Bell. The officers thought they could run the business more efficiently if they eliminated a management level, but they wanted to leave the choice of which level to the departments. The departments examined the situation and made the right decision. It worked so well, we made this a Bell Atlantic-wide effort. People in jobs that were about to be eliminated participated in the discussions. Naturally, they were not enthusiastic about cutting their own jobs, so in practice the decision was left to the boss. Still, the "soft" aspects of the organizational change—appreciation, recognition, sharing—were given as much importance as the hard side of reducing the head count.

Was work eliminated along with the level? The criticism of downsizing in many companies is that the people are gone, but the work remains.

Unfortunately, that's true. We saw no way to eliminate all the work first. We reluctantly concluded that we had to reduce the force and then empower the people to eliminate the rest of the work.

On the first day of the new organization, some groups had only eight people to do the workload of ten. But the individual departments were empowered to create the organization they thought would be most efficient. They worked hard to eliminate those activities that were least important. That sort of prioritizing can't be done by some superstaff.

What made you believe that people who had been accustomed to following central mandates would be effective at setting priorities?

People were able to do this because of what they learned from the Bell Atlantic Way. An important part of change is moving from a culture in which people are handed procedures to follow mindlessly to one that helps them make tough choices. This is a difficult process and we're still involved in it. It requires guts and a lot of honest communication.

In the seminars, we play a game with poker chips. The blue chips are valuable; the white chips are practically worthless. Participants learn that it is vital to understand priorities and know what those priorities are based on, such as the goals of the corporation and not just the goals of the subgroup. The blue chips mean First Things First—priorities. I carry one in my wallet as a reminder.

How do people feel about being involved in a tough restructuring process?

In our regular employee survey, workers cited our downsizing as one reason for improved morale. They told us that although resources are very tight, Bell Atlantic is now a much better place to work. They said since some of the disaffected, cynical people have left, there is much less time for bureaucracy.

What else are you doing to reduce bureaucracy?

We are determined to revolutionize staff support, to convert a bureaucratic roadblock into an entrepreneurial force.

Large staffs that are not subject to bottom-line pressure tend to grow and produce services that may be neither wanted nor required, and their allegiances generally lean toward their professional positions rather than toward their clients. We had to do something to change this.

Three years ago, when I was vice chairman and the staffs reported to me, I decided to place the control of discretionary staff and support expenditures in the hands of those people who were paying for them, that is, the profit centers, the bottom-line groups. We also had to eliminate duplicate staff groups at corporate headquarters and in the operating companies.

Our approach was to create small profit centers within the staff groups, called client service groups or CSGs. For example, the training department became the Training and Educational Services CSG. The accounting department formed the Accounting Operations CSG.

How do the client service groups work?

They sell their services both to the corporate headquarters and to the operating companies. Each year, CSGs develop a budget and an array of products or services based on what Bell Atlantic clients have committed to fund, plus approved amounts for ad hoc or unanticipated business. They have to meet market tests, providing the same value as any outside organization. The CSGs' total annual expenses must equal anticipated revenues (billing credits) from customers. The goal is to break even.

CSGs market their services continuously through items in internal publications, CSG newsletters and brochures, 800-number hotlines, and exhibits at trade shows. The Training and Educational Services CSG publishes a 370-page catalog of offerings. The Information Systems Professional Services CSG heralds new software, programming possibilities, and applications in a regular newsletter.

CSG account managers stay in touch with customers to learn about their needs, answer their questions, facilitate provision of services, and forecast demand. Monthly bills from the CSGs to customers itemize specific services and costs in detail, helping clients to understand and control these costs.

The profit-center customers have to follow a few simple rules. They must give the client service group an opportunity to bid on a project, formally or informally. If the internal organization wins the bid, they use the internal organization. If an outside company wins, they can use the outside firm. But they cannot create their own media group or their own business research group. We want no internal competition.

What happened when you introduced this major structural change?

First of all, it was believed that the client service groups wouldn't work. In some quarters it was considered a dingbat idea that would go away. Still, the first year got off to a pretty good start.

The second year brought a budget crunch and nearly destroyed the process. The budgets of the client service groups were cut by the central financial staffs without the clients' agreement. This is absolutely counter to the rules we devised. It wasn't done surreptitiously, just out of misunderstanding, but it happened. The new groups called foul, and we did some damage control to restore their budgets. There were also cases in which individual departments tried to form their own support groups under different labels, under different names.

In the third year, there is no question that the client service groups are working.

What results are you getting?

Market pressures are keeping the client service groups at a reasonable level. Expenditures for discretionary staff services are generally flat, while other corporate expenses have gone up. Because of pent-up demand, some CSGs have seen their budgets increase; for example, internal clients wanted more operations support programming. But the Business Research CSG encountered a substantial decline.

The most important fact is that spending for discretionary staff support activities is now controlled by the clients. That's changed the whole nature of staff groups. Not everyone is totally comfortable with this yet; it is much more fun to set a budget based on your professional opinion and let other people pay for it than to compete for resources. The idea is so different that it is very tender and will require careful cultivation.

I see great progress in attitudes and behavior. We put on one of the largest technical expositions in the United States to let our vendors like AT&T, IBM, and Siemens show us their stuff. Last year as I was walking through it, I was astonished to see the Medical CSG selling its services. I turned the corner, and there was another client service group hawking its wares. Both were selling back to their own company as vigorously as any vendor.

Because they have to do the work of selling their services to their clients and all the additional accounting, the groups are learning to be business managers. They are slowly becoming more entrepreneurial.

Are other people at Bell Atlantic acquiring entrepreneurial skills?

We are committed to identifying potential corporate entrepreneurs, training them, and developing their ideas into new businesses. We do this primarily through our Champion program.

The Champion program arose from one of our companies, Chesapeake & Potomac Telephone, and we spread it across the whole corporation in 1989. The program provides seed money, guidance, and training to potential entrepreneurs who propose new products and services. People at any level can make proposals. If projects are accepted, their proposers can run them. And they can invest a portion of their wages in the project, in exchange for the prospect of a piece of the action when their product has been marketed.

Are you getting results?

In the first year, 36 Champions were accepted into the program. In 1989, 39 were added. By late 1990, there were about 33 products and services in the pipeline, several of them near the commercialization stage. Projects include Creative Connections, a line of designer phone jacks; Emerg-Alert, prerecorded emergency messages targeted to latchkey children and the elderly; CommGuard, a package of backup phone services in case of a system breakdown; local usage information services for all lines in a Centrex system; and a do-not-disturb service.

Champion's most noteworthy success is Thinx, new software so innovative that its creator, Jack Coppley, was one of five finalists for *Discover* magazine's award honoring engineers and scientists making technological breakthroughs. Thinx is an intelligent graphics program integrating data with images to help users explore relationships visually and apply data or calculations automatically.

Jack learned about Champion when he attended a meeting introducing it in 1988. At that time, he was a budget manager for the network services staff, but he was intrigued by the opportunity Champion represented. Some of Jack's initial ideas were rejected, but his software idea was warmly received.

After going through the steps to test the idea and develop the business plan, Jack became head of a 20-member team that worked out software glitches, chose the *Thinx* name, and designed packaging. The product was unveiled at Comdex, a large trade show, in November 1989. Jack came home with triple the number of customer leads he had anticipated. In September 1990, Thinx hit the market and received rave reviews.

Champion has now become an actual revenue source in our strategic planning process. That's the ultimate testimony of importance in a corporation—a business plan with dollars of investment and targeted returns. In five years, we expect annual revenues of over $100 million from Champion projects. My question when I first saw the 1995 projection was, "Is this hope or smoke?" I was told that the figure was conservatively stated!

There are potentially thousands of great, innovative ideas in a company our size. The Champion program encourages people to take responsibility for acting on them.

How do the internal cultural and operational changes you've described translate into advantage in the marketplace?

We were always an efficient company, but our new approaches are breaking new ground. Our management process provides another major differentiation factor in world markets. When you match our track record of efficiency and quality service with a state-of-the-art understanding of how to manage large, technologically complex organizations, you've got a terrific package.

The most efficient communications networks in the world don't come from just modern switching machines but from computer operating systems and skilled technicians that operate them—all working in an empowered, accountable organization.

This forms an excellent launching pad for new businesses. Our systems-integration business, for example, is a natural evolution of that theme. It began as a computer-maintenance business with relatively low margins. But it has evolved into the largest independent field-service business in the country, adding products and services and moving up the value chain to application software, disaster recovery, system operation, consulting, and so on.

You have a very strong vision for what the information system linking the world will be in the future.

It's probably the most important vision in our corporation. I think it is the major contribution that Bell Atlantic will make to the United States. We see the Intelligent Network changing not just our company but changing civilization. The Intelligent Network means virtually unlimited memory and logic, instantaneous transport to anywhere in the world, providing intellectual linkages between human beings. These links are equivalent, in my mind, to the revolution of the printing press or perhaps even writing or speech. In the near future, a telephone conversation could start in English at one end and be heard in French or Japanese at the other. Information will eventually go to wherever a person is—at home, at work, in a car, or strolling in the park.

What steps are you taking to realize this vision?

We are building the Intelligent Network for the service area in the Bell Atlantic regulated territory. We have introduced 30 new technology-based services, more than any other regional company. We are leading in deploying the nervous system of the Intelligent Network, Signaling System 7. We've added massive computer capacity and will have a million miles of fiber-optics transport throughout the territory in the next few years. The computers hold extensive database information about customer needs and wants. Fiber optics allow a signal to travel 10,000 times faster than copper wire.

By being focused in the transport and use of information, we realized the capabilities of the Intelligent Network. Our densely populated territory allowed us to visualize and build these kinds of links easily. We concluded, perhaps before others, that this network architecture was a revolutionary way to provide intelligence. We coined the term "Intelligent Network" and began to sell it to our counterparts. The Intelligent Network is a new notion that came out of our search for distinction, our search for a future. The whole world has now accepted it.

How is Bell Atlantic gaining the resources and capability to realize the Intelligent Network vision worldwide?

We recognized very early on that we needed strategic alliances. We've formed partnerships with Siemens, IBM, NTI, and others, including big companies, small companies, and government ministries.

Partnering is a very serious business in Bell Atlantic. Some companies seek strategic alliances because it seems like a good idea in theory or it looks good to be associated with prestigious partners. But often the overall goal of the alliance is lost in the process. Substantial investments are made by large corporations, but little top management attention is given thereafter. Predictably, the local bureaucracy sets up prickly barriers and mousetraps to prove that the new joint venture partner doesn't really understand the business and is an enemy, not a friend.

We can't afford to make that mistake because alliances are too vital for our growth plans, especially outside of the United States. The international field almost always calls for the formation of consortia because of the scale of investment or the preference of governments for local participation. We had to have partners in every one of our investments.

To make sure we are working with our partners effectively and building on their capabilities, we have had to develop a culture of tolerance, listening, and intellectual curiosity, not intellectual arrogance.

How did you develop that culture?

Once again, we turned to the Bell Atlantic Way. A year or so ago, we gathered together 75 people involved in our international business, from lawyers to salespeople to the head of the international business unit. We included all the officers and me.

We went through experiential training, exploring attitudes, and making behavioral commitments. We identified the real purpose of international expansion, which was not to get things "on the board" or "to score" but to produce solutions to the business problem. We wanted long-term investments in our field that would have acceptable risk profiles and higher growth rates than we had in our core business. We worked on how individuals could commit themselves to assist the new effort, to produce real results, not binders, reports, or smoky projections.

In the past, those kinds of understandings were attempted through a memo or at best a brief meeting. No real interaction, no joint understanding, no commitment, no internalization. New activities were launched without any serious preparation.

In your quest for a more entrepreneurial culture, have you had any personal setbacks?

My biggest personal setback was self-inflicted. In my first year as CEO, I was intensely frustrated because people didn't immediately understand my notions of empowerment, accountability, and teamwork. I finally learned to be less impatient.

How did you come to change your own behavior?

A lot of the impatience was coached out of me. One of the aspects of the Bell Atlantic Way is that everyone has an internal coach; mine is Anton Campanella, our president. Somebody said the reason Campy and I got each other as coaches is that no one else wanted us. There is a certain amount of truth to that.

Coaching is not seen as the least bit corny or unusual in our company. Once a week one of us will ask, "Can I coach you on something?" In the past, I've never been able to do that comfortably. I was never able to do it without it being unnecessarily evasive on the one hand or unnecessarily unpleasant on the other. Now the process is acceptable. It is group sanctioned. It is the way we've decided we're going to work together.

I really know we're doing well when I walk into a room of people and they are discussing a project with tremendous excitement, a project that is going to move our corporation ahead significantly, and I've never heard of it. That is a wonderful feeling.

9

The Manager as Innovator

■ When Steve Talbot, an operations manager, began a staff job reporting to the general manager of a product group, he had no line responsibility, no subordinates or budget of his own, and only a vague mandate to "explore options to improve performance."

To do this, Talbot set about collecting resources by bargaining with product-line managers and sales managers. By promising the product-line managers that he would save them having to negotiate with sales to get top priority for their products, he got a budget from them. Then, because he had the money in hand, Talbot got the sales managers to agree to hire one salesperson per product line, with Talbot permitted to do the hiring.

The next area he tackled was field services. Because the people in this area were conservative and tightfisted, Talbot went to his boss to get support for his recommendations about this area.

With the sales and service functions increasing their market share, it was easy for Talbot to get the product-line managers' backing when he pushed for selling a major new product that he had devised. And, to keep his action team functioning and behind him, Talbot made sure that "everyone became a hero" when the senior vice president of engineering asked him to explain his success to corporate officers.

■ Arthur Drumm, a technical department head of two sections, wanted to develop a new measuring instrument that could dramatically improve the company's product quality. But only Drumm thought this approach would work; those around him were not convinced it was needed or would pay off. After spending months developing data to show that the company needed the instrument, Drumm convinced several of his bosses two levels up to contribute $300,000 to its development. He put together a task force made up of representatives from all the manufacturing sites to advise on the development process and to ensure that the instrument would fit in with operations.

When, early on, one high-level manager opposed the project, Drumm coached two others in preparation for an officer-level meeting at which they were going to present his proposal. And when executives argued about which budget line the money would come from, R&D or engineering, Drumm tried to ease the tension. His persistence netted the company an extremely valuable new technique.

■ When Doris Randall became the head of a backwater purchasing department, one of three departments in her area, she expected the assignment to advance her career. Understandably, she was disappointed at the poor state of the function she had inherited and looked around for ways to make improvements. She first sought information from users of the department's services and, with this information, got her boss to agree to a first wave of changes. No one in her position had ever had such close contacts with users before, and Randall employed her knowledge to reorganize the unit into a cluster of user-oriented specialties (with each staff member concentrating on a particular need).

Once she had the reorganization in place and her function acknowledged as the best purchasing department in the region, Randall wanted to reorganize the other two purchasing departments. Her boss, perhaps out of concern that he would lose his position to Randall if the proposed changes took place, discouraged her. But her credibility was so strong that her boss's boss—who viewed her changes as a model for improvements in other areas—gave Randall the go-ahead to merge the three purchasing departments into one. Greater efficiency, cost savings, and increased user satisfaction resulted.

These three managers are enterprising, innovative corporate entrepreneurs who are part of a group playing a key role in making sure companies can succeed in a world of challenging, fast-moving competition. Their names and that of their companies are disguised, because of the unusual level of access I had to them, but their stories—and the lessons from them—are powerful and real.

Cultivating innovators is one of the most important things companies can do to make sure they lead, not lag behind, change. If that seems like an overly grand statement, consider the basis for American companies' success in the past: innovation in products and advances in management techniques. Product innovation may be the result of breakthroughs in concept or technology supported by large research budgets and from-the-top commitments. But while waiting for the breakthroughs, companies rely on innovators to ensure operational excellence, and when the breakthroughs come, they rely on them for all the micro-innovations required to support transformational change. Thus, mid-level managers and professionals can make pivotal contributions to innovation and change. Top leaders' general directives to open a new market, improve quality, or cut costs could mean nothing without entrepreneurial managers below them able to imagine the future, design the projects and processes, carry them out, and redirect their groups' activities accordingly. Furthermore, these potential innovators have their fingers on the pulse of operations and their ears out to the customers; they can also conceive, suggest, and set in motion new ideas that top managers may not have thought of.

The innovating managers described here are not extraordinary individuals. They do, however, share a number of characteristics:

Comfort with change. They are confident that uncertainties will be clarified. They also have foresight and see unmet needs as opportunities.

Clarity of direction. They select projects carefully and, with their long time horizons, view setbacks as temporary blips in an otherwise straight path to a goal.

Thoroughness. They prepare well for meetings and are professional in making their presentations. They have insight into organizational politics and a sense of whose support can help them at various junctures.

Participative management style. They encourage subordinates to put in maximum effort and to be part of the team, promise them a share of the rewards, and deliver on their promises.

Persuasiveness, persistence, and discretion. They understand that they cannot achieve their ends overnight, so they persevere—using tact—until they do.

What makes it possible for managers to use such skills for the company's benefit? They work in organizations where the culture fosters collaboration and teamwork and where structures encourage people to "do what needs to be done." Moreover, they usually work under leaders who consciously incorporate conditions facilitating innovation and achievement into their companies' structures and operations.

These conclusions come from many years of work with companies undergoing change, supported by a methodology to determine a company's capability to produce innovation (see "The Innovation Audit"). I first developed this diagnostic process through a study of the major accomplishments of 165 effective middle managers in five leading American corporations, designed to determine levels of innovation, the process by which it occurred, forces that supported or hindered it, and the conditions that stimulate innovation. The Innovation Audit helped identify the contribution of corporate entrepreneurs to a company's overall success— both current business results and capabilities for a successful future.

The Innovation Audit

After a pilot project involving 26 effective middle managers from 18 companies, my research team studied, in-depth, 165 middle managers from five major corporations across the United States as a prototypical "Innovation Audit." The 165 were chosen by their companies to participate because of their reputations for effectiveness. We did not want a random sample: we were looking for "the best and the brightest" who could serve as models for others. It turned out, however, that every major function was represented, and roughly in proportion to its importance in the company's success. (For example, there were more innovative sales and marketing managers representing a "market-driven" company and more technical, R&D, and manufacturing managers from a "product-driven" company.)

During interviews spanning many hours, the managers talked about all aspects of a single significant accomplishment, from the glimmering of an idea to the results. We asked them to focus on the most significant of a set of four or five of their accomplishments over the previous two years. We also elicited a chronology of the project as well as responses to a set of open-ended questions about the acquisition of power, the handling of roadblocks, and the doling out of rewards. We supplemented the interviews with discussions about current issues in the five companies with a cross-section of other leaders in each company.

The five companies represented a range of types and industries: from rather traditional, slow-moving, mature companies to fast-changing, newer, high-technology companies. We included both service and manufacturing companies that are from different parts of the country and are at different stages in their development. The one thing that all five have in common is an intense interest in the topic of the study. Facing highly competitive markets (for the manufacturing companies a constant since their founding; for the service companies a newer phenomenon), all of these corporations wanted to encourage their middle managers to be more enterprising and innovative.

Pseudonyms for the companies emphasize a central feature of each:

CHIPCO: manufacturer of computer products

FINCO: insurance and related financial services

MEDCO: manufacturer of large medical equipment

RADCO (for R&D): manufacturer of optical products

UTICO: communications utility

Each of the 165 leaders in the audit—all of whom were deemed "effective" by their companies—told the research team about a particular accomplishment; these covered a wide range. Some of the successes, though impressive, clearly were achieved within the boundaries of established company practice. Others, however, involved innovation: introduction of new methods, structures, or products that increased the company's capacity. All in all, 99 of the

165 accomplishments fell within the definition of an innovative effort. The differences between basic wins and innovations allowed us to identify the characteristics of the projects themselves; the differences between companies in the proportion of the two kinds of results provided comparative benchmarks about a company's innovation capabilities.

Basic accomplishments differ from innovative ones not only in scope and long-run impact but also in what it takes to achieve them. (See "Identifying Innovation" for definitions of *basic* and *innovative* accomplishments.) Basic wins are part of the assigned job and require only routine and readily available means to carry them out. Managers reporting this kind of accomplishment said they were just doing their jobs. Little was problematic—they had an assignment to tackle; they were told, or they already knew, how to go about it; they used existing budget or staff; they didn't need to gather or share much information outside of their units; and they encountered little or no opposition. Managers performing such activities don't generate innovations for their companies; they hold the current system in place, solving today's problems or creating today's revenues without securing the future by improving upon current ways. In contrast, innovative accomplishments are strikingly entrepreneurial. Moreover, they are sometimes highly problematic and generally involve acquiring and using power and influence.

Identifying Innovation

In the Innovation Audit prototype, we categorized the 165 managers' accomplishments according to their primary impact on the company. Many accomplishments had multiple results or multiple components, but it was the breadth of scope of the accomplishment and its future utility for the company that defined its category. Immediate dollar results were *not* the central issue; rather, organizational "learning" or increased future capacity was the key. Thus, improving revenues by cutting costs while changing nothing else would be categorized differently from improving revenues by designing a new production method; only the latter leaves a lasting trace.

The accomplishments fell into two clusters:

Basic. Done solely within the existing framework and not affecting the company's longer-term capacity; 66 of the 165 fall into this category.

Innovative. A new way for the company to use or expand its resources that raises long-term capacity; 99 of the 165 are such achievements.

Basic accomplishments include:

Doing the basic job—simply carrying out adequately a defined assignment within the bounds of one's job (e.g., "fulfilled sales objectives during a reorganization").

Affecting individuals' performance—having an impact on individuals (e.g., "found employee a job in original department after failing to retrain him").

Advancing incrementally—achieving a higher level of performance within the basic job (e.g., "met more production schedules in plant than in past").

Innovative accomplishments include:

Finding a new opportunity—developing an entirely new product or opening a new market (e.g., "sold new product program to higher management and developed staffing for it").

Developing a new policy—creating a change of orientation or direction (e.g., "changed price-setting policy in product line with new model showing cost-quality trade-offs").

Devising a fresh method—introducing a new process, procedure, or technology for continued use (e.g., "designed and implemented new information system for financial results by business sectors").

Designing a new structure—changing the formal structure, reorganizing, or introducing a new structure, or forging a different link among units (e.g., "consolidated three offices into one").

While members of the audit team occasionally argued about the placement of accomplishments in the subcategories, we were almost unanimous as to whether an accom-

---

plishment rated as basic or innovative. Even bringing off a financially significant or flashy increase in performance was considered basic if the accomplishment was well within the manager's assignment and territory, involved no new methods that could be used to repeat the feat elsewhere, opened no opportunities, or had no impact on corporate structure— in other words, reflected little inventiveness. The manager who achieved such a result might have been an excellent manager, but he or she was not an innovative one.

What Drives Innovation: The Role of Power in Enterprise

Because most innovative achievements cut across organizational lines and threaten to disrupt existing arrangements, enterprising managers need tools beyond those that come with the job. Innovations have implications for other functions and areas, and they require data, agreements, and resources of wider scope than routine operations demand. Even R&D managers, who are expected to produce innovations, need more information, support, and resources for major projects than those built into regular R&D functions. They too may need additional data, more money, or agreement from extrafunctional officials that the project is necessary. Only hindsight shows that an innovative project was bound to be successful.

Because of the extra resources they require, entrepreneurial managers need to go beyond the limits of their formal positions. For this, they need power. In large organizations at least, I have observed that powerlessness "corrupts." That is, lack of power (the capacity to mobilize resources and people to get things done) tends to create managers who are more concerned about guarding their territories than about collaborating with others to benefit the organization. At the same time, when managers hoard potential power and don't invest it in productive action, it atrophies and eventually blocks achievements.

Furthermore, when some people have too much unused power and others too little, problems occur. To produce results, power—

----

like money—needs to circulate. To come up with innovations, managers have to be in areas where power circulates, where it can be grabbed and invested. In this sense, organizational power is transactional: it exists as potential until someone makes a bid for it, invests it, and produces results with it.

The overarching condition required for managers to produce innovative achievements is this: they must envision an accomplishment beyond the scope of the job. They cannot alone possess the power to carry their idea out but they must be able to acquire the power they need easily. Thus, creative managers are not empowered simply by a boss or their job; on their own they seek and find the additional strength it takes to carry out major new initiatives. They are indeed corporate entrepreneurs.

Three commodities are necessary for accumulating productive power—information, resources, and support. Managers might find a portion of these within their purview and pour them into a project; managers with something they believe in will eagerly leverage their own staff and budget and even bootleg resources from their subordinates' budgets. But innovations usually require a manager to search for additional supplies elsewhere in the organization. Depending on how easy the organization makes it to tap sources of power and on how technical the project is, acquiring power can be the most time-consuming and difficult part of the process.

Phases of the accomplishment

A prototypical innovation goes through three phases: project definition (acquisition and application of information to shape a manageable, salable project), coalition building (development of a network of backers who agree to provide resources and support), and action (application of the resources, information, and support to the project and mobilization of an action team). Let us examine each of these steps in more detail.

Defining the project.

Before defining a project, managers need to identify the problem. People in an organization may hold many conflicting views about the best method of reaching a goal, and discovering the basis of these conflicting perspectives (while gathering hard data) is critical to a manager's success.

In one case, information circulating freely about the original design of a part was inaccurate. The manager needed to acquire new data to prove that the problem he was about to tackle was not a manufacturing shortcoming but a design flaw. But, as often happens, some people had a stake in the popular view. Even hard-nosed engineers in our study acknowledged that, in the early stages of an entrepreneurial project, managers need political information as much as they do technical data. Without political savvy, say these engineers, no one can get a project beyond the proposal stage.

The culmination of the project definition phase comes when managers sift through the fragments of information from each source and focus on a particular target. Then, despite the fact that managers may initially have been handed a certain area as an assignment, they still have to "sell" the project that evolves. In the innovative efforts I observed, the managers' assignments involved no promises of resources or support required to do anything more than routine activities.

Furthermore, to implement the innovation, a manager has to call on the cooperation of many others besides the boss who assigned the task. Many of these others may be independent actors who are not compelled to cooperate simply because the manager has carved a project out of a general assignment. Even subordinates may not be automatically on board. If they are professionals or managers, they have a number of other tasks and the right to set some of their own priorities; and if they are in a matrix, they may be responsible to other bosses as well.

For example, in her new job as head of a manufacturing planning unit for a computer company, Heidi Wilson's assignment was to improve the cost efficiency of operations and thereby boost the company's price competitiveness. Her boss told her she could spend six months "saying nothing and just observing, getting to know what's really going on." One of the first things she noticed was that the flow of goods through the company was organized in an overly complicated, time-consuming, and expensive fashion.

The assignment gave Wilson the mandate to seek information but not to carry out any particular activities. Wilson set about to gather organizational, technical, and political information in order to translate her ambiguous task into a concrete project. She followed goods through the company to determine what the process was and how it could be changed. She sought ideas and impressions from manufacturing line managers, at the same time learning the location of vested interests and where other patches of organizational quicksand lurked. She compiled data, refined her approach, and packaged and repackaged her ideas until she believed she could "prove to people that I knew more about the company than they did."

Wilson's next step was "to do a number of punchy presentations with pictures and graphs and charts." At the presentations, she got two kinds of response: "Gee, we thought there was a problem but we never saw it outlined like this before" and "Aren't there better things to worry about?" To handle the critics, she "simply came back over and over again with information, more information than anyone else had." When she had gathered the data and received the feedback, Wilson was ready to formulate a project and sell it to her boss. Ultimately, her project was approved, and it netted impressive cost savings.

Thus although innovation may begin with an assignment, it is usually one—like Wilson's—that is couched in general statements of results with the means largely unspecified. Occasionally, managers initiate projects themselves; however, initiation seldom occurs in a vacuum. Creative managers listen to a stream of information from superiors and peers and then identify a perceived need. In the early stages of defining a project, managers may spend more time talking with people outside their own functions than with subordinates or bosses inside.

One R&D manager said he had "hung out" with product designers while trying to get a handle on the best way to formulate a new process-development project. Another R&D manager in our survey got the idea for a new production method from a conversation about problems he had with the head of production. He then convinced his boss to let him determine whether a corrective project could be developed.

Building a coalition.

Next, entrepreneurial managers need to pull in the resources and support to make the project work. For creative accomplishments, these power-related tools do not come through the vertical chain of command but rather from many areas of the organization.

George Putnam's innovation is typical. Putnam was an assistant department manager for product testing in a company that was about to demonstrate a product at a site that attracted a large number of potential buyers. Putnam heard through the grapevine that a decision was imminent about which model to display. The product managers were each lobbying for their own, and the marketing people also had a favorite. Putnam, who was close to the products, thought that the first-choice model had grave defects and so decided to demonstrate to the marketing staff both what the problems with the first one were and the superiority of another model.

Building on a long-term relationship with the people in corporate quality control and a good alliance with his boss, Putnam sought the tools he needed: the blessing of the vice president of engineering (his boss's boss), special materials for testing from the materials division, a budget from corporate quality control, and staff from his own units to carry out the tests. As Putnam put it, this was all done through one-on-one "horse trading"—showing each manager how much the others were chipping in. Then Putnam met informally with the key marketing staffer to learn what it would take to convince him.

As the test results emerged, Putnam took them to his peers in marketing, engineering, and quality control so they could feed them to their superiors. The accumulated support persuaded the decision makers to adopt Putnam's choice of a model; it later became a strong money-maker. In sum, Putnam had completely stepped out of his usual role to build a consensus that shaped a major policy decision.

Thus the most successful innovations derive from situations where a number of people from a number of areas make contributions. They provide a kind of checks-and-balances system to an activity that is otherwise nonroutine and, therefore, is not subject to the usual controls. By building a coalition before extensive project activity gets under way, the manager also ensures the avail-ability of enough support to keep momentum going and to guar-antee implementation.

In one company, the process of lining up peers and stakehold-ers as early supporters is called "making cheerleaders"; in an-other, "preselling." Sometimes managers ask peers for "pledges" of money or staff to be collected later if higher management ap-proves the project and provides overall resources.

After garnering peer support, usually innovators next seek sup-port at much higher levels. While we found surprisingly few in-stances of top management directly sponsoring or championing a project, we did find that a general blessing from the top is clearly necessary to convert potential supporters into a solid team. In one case, top officers simply showed up at a meeting where the pro-posal was being discussed; their presence ensured that other peo-ple couldn't use the "pocket veto" power of headquarters as an excuse to table the issue. Also, the very presence of a key executive at such a meeting is often a signal of the proposal's importance to the rest of the organization.

Enterprising managers learn who at the top-executive level has the power to affect their projects (including material resources or vital initial approval power). Then they negotiate for these execu-tives' support, using polished formal presentations. Whereas man-agers can often sell the project to peers and stakeholders by ap-pealing to these people's self-interests and assuring them they know what they're talking about, managers need to offer top ex-ecutives more guarantees about both the technical and the politi-cal adequacies of projects.

Key executives tend to evaluate a proposal in terms of its sal-ability to their constituencies. Sometimes entrepreneurial manag-ers arm top executives with materials or rehearse them for their own presentations to other people (such as members of an execu-tive committee or the board) who have to approve the project.

Most often, since many of the projects that originate at the middle of a company can be supported at that level and will not tap corporate funds, those at high levels in the organization simply provide a general expression of support. However, the attention top management confers on this activity, many of our interviewees told us, makes it possible to sell their own staffs as well as others.

But once in a while, a presentation to top-level officers results in help in obtaining supplies. Sometimes enterprising managers walk away with the promise of a large capital expenditure or assistance getting staff or space. Sometimes a promise of resources is contingent on getting others on board. "If you can raise the money, go ahead with this," is a frequent directive to an enterprising manager.

In one situation, a service manager approached his boss and his boss's boss for a budget for a college recruitment and training program that he had been supporting on his own with funds bootlegged from his staff. The top executives told him they would grant a large budget if he could get his four peers to support the project. Somewhat to their surprise, he came back with this support. He had taken his peers away from the office for three days for a round of negotiation and planning. In cases like this, top management is not so much hedging its bets as using its ability to secure peer support for what might otherwise be risky projects.

With promises of resources and support in hand, enterprising managers can go back to the immediate boss or bosses to make plans for moving ahead. Usually the bosses are simply waiting for this tangible sign of power to continue authorizing the project. But in other cases the bosses are not fully involved and won't be sold until the manager has higher-level support.

Of course, during the coalition-building phase, the network of supporters does not play a passive role; their comments, criticisms, and objectives help shape the project into one that is more likely to succeed. Another result of the coalition-building phase is, then, a set of reality checks that ensures that projects unlikely to succeed will go no farther.

Moving into action.

The innovator's next step is to mobilize key players to carry out the project. Whether the players are nominal subordinates or a special project group such as a task force, managers forge them into a team. Enterprising managers bring the people involved in the project together, give them briefings and assignments, pump them up for the extra effort needed, seek their ideas and suggestions (both as a way to involve them and to further refine the project), and promise them a share of the rewards. As one manager put it, "It takes more selling than telling." In most of the innovations we observed, the key leader couldn't just order subordinates to get involved. Doing something beyond routine work that involves creativity and cooperation requires the full commitment of subordinates; otherwise the project will not succeed.

During the action phase, innovation leaders have four central organizational tasks. The technical details of the project and the actual work directed toward project goals are now in the hands of the action team. Leaders may contribute ideas or even get involved in hands-on experimentation, but their primary functions are still largely external and organizational, centered around maintaining the boundaries and integrity of the project.

The first task is to **handle interference** or opposition that may jeopardize the project. Corporate entrepreneurs encounter strikingly little overt opposition—perhaps because their success at coalition building determines whether a project gets started in the first place. Resistance takes a more passive form: criticism of the plan's details, foot-dragging, late responses to requests, or arguments over allocation of time and resources among projects.

Managers are sometimes surprised that critics keep so quiet up to this point. One manufacturing manager who was gearing up for production of a new item had approached many executives in other areas while making cost estimates, and these executives had appeared positive about his efforts. But later, when he began organizing the manufacturing process itself, he heard objections from these very people.

During this phase, therefore, innovators may have to spend as much time in meetings, both formal and one-to-one, as they did to get the project launched. They need to prepare thoroughly for these meetings so they can counter skepticism and objections with clear facts, persuasion, and reminders of the benefits that can accrue to managers meeting the project's objectives. In most cases, a clear presentation of facts is enough. But not always: one of our respondents, a high-level champion, had to tell an opponent to back down, that the project was going ahead anyway, and that his carping was annoying.

Whereas innovation leaders need to directly counter open challenges and criticism that might result in the flow of power or sup-

eing cut off, they simply keep other interference outside
undaries of the project. In effect, the entrepreneur-turned-
eader defines a protected area for the group's work. He or
)es outside this area to head off critics and to keep people
or rules imposed by higher management from disrupting project
tasks.

While the team itself is sometimes unaware of the leader's contribution, the leader patrols the boundaries. Acting as interference
filters, managers in my study protected innovative projects by
bending rules, transferring funds "illicitly" from one budget line
to another, developing special reward or incentive systems that
offered bonuses above company pay rates, and ensuring that superiors stayed away unless needed.

The second action-phase task is **maintaining momentum** and
continuity. Here interference comes from internal rather than external sources. Foot-dragging or inactivity is a constant danger,
especially if the creative effort adds to workloads. In our study, enterprising managers as well as team members complained continually about the tendency for routine activities to take precedence over special projects and to consume limited time.

In addition, it is easier for corporate entrepreneurs to whip up
excitement over a vision at start-up than to keep the goal in
people's minds when they face the tedium of the work. Thus,
team-building skills are essential. So the project doesn't lose momentum, managers must sustain the enthusiasm of all—from supporters to suppliers—by being persistent and keeping the team
aware of supportive authorities who are clearly waiting for results.

One manager, who was involved in a full-time project to develop
new and more efficient methods of producing a certain ingredient,
maintained momentum by holding daily meetings with the core
team, getting together often with operations managers and members of a task force he had formed, putting out weekly status
reports, and making frequent presentations to top management.
When foot-dragging occurs, many entrepreneurial managers pull
in high-level supporters—without compromising the autonomy of
the project—to get the team back on board. A letter or a visit from
the big boss can remind everyone just how important the project is.

A third task of innovators in the action phase is to engage in whatever **secondary redesign**—other changes made to support the key change—is necessary to keep the project going. For example, a manager whose team was setting up a computerized information bank held weekly team meetings to define tactics. A fallout of these meetings was a set of new awards and a fresh performance appraisal system for team members and their subordinates.

As necessary, managers introduce new arrangements to conjoin with the core tasks. When it seems that a project is bogging down—that is, when everything possible has been done and no more results are on the horizon—managers often change the structure or approach. Such alterations can cause a redoubling of effort and a renewed attack on the problem. They can also bring the company additional unplanned innovations as a side benefit from the main project.

The fourth task of the action phase, **external communication,** brings the accomplishment full circle. The project begins with gathering information; now it is important to send information out. It is vital to (as several managers put it) "manage the press" so that peers and key supporters have an up-to-date impression of the project and its success. Delivering on promises is also important. As much as possible, innovative managers meet deadlines, deliver early benefits to others, and keep supporters supplied with information. Doing so establishes the credibility of both the project and the manager, even before concrete results can be shown.

Information must be shared with the team and the coalition as well. Good managers periodically remind the team of what they stand to gain from the accomplishment, hold meetings to give feedback and to stimulate pride in the project, and make a point of congratulating each staff member individually. After all, as Steve Talbot (of my first example) said, many people gave this innovation leader power because of a promise that everyone would be a hero.

A Leadership Style for Innovation

Clearly there is a strong association between carrying out an innovative accomplishment and employing a participative-collaborative leadership style. The managers observed reached success by:

- Persuading more than ordering, though they sometimes use pressure as a last resort.

- Building a team, which entails among other things frequent staff meetings and considerable sharing of information.

- Seeking inputs from others—that is, asking for ideas about users' needs, soliciting suggestions from subordinates, welcoming peer review, and so forth.

- Acknowledging others' stake or potential stake in the project—in other words, being politically sensitive.

- Sharing rewards and recognition willingly.

A collaborative style is also useful when carrying out basic accomplishments; however, in such endeavors it is not required. Managers can bring off many basic accomplishments using a traditional, more autocratic style. Because they're doing what is assigned, they don't need external support; because they have all the tools to do it, they don't need to get anyone else involved (they simply direct subordinates to do what is required). But for innovative accomplishments—seeking funds, staff, or information (political as well as technical) from outside the work unit; attending long meetings and presentations; and requiring "above and beyond" effort from staff—a style that revolves around participation, collaboration, and persuasion is essential.

The participative-collaborative style also helps innovation leaders reduce risk because it encourages completion of the assignment. Furthermore, others' involvement serves as a check-and-balance on the project, reshaping it to make it more of a sure thing and putting pressure on people to follow through. The few projects in my study that disintegrated did so because the manager failed to build a coalition of supporters and collaborators.

. . . And Corporate Conditions That Encourage Enterprise

Just as the strategies to develop and implement innovations followed many different patterns, so also the level of enterprise innovators achieved varied strongly across the five companies we studied (see *Table 9-1*). Managers in newer, high-technology companies have a much higher proportion of innovative accomplishments than managers in other industries. At "CHIPCO," a computer parts manufacturer, 71% of all the things effective managers did were innovative; for "UTICO," a communications utility, the number is 33%; for "FINCO," an insurance company, it is 47%.

This difference in levels of innovation correlates with the extent to which these companies' structures and cultures support managers' creativity. Companies producing the most entrepreneurs have cultures that encourage collaboration and teamwork. Moreover, they have complex structures that link people in multiple ways and help them go beyond the confines of their defined jobs to do "what needs to be done."

CHIPCO, which showed the most entrepreneurial activity of any company in our study, was a rapidly growing electronics company with abundant resources. That its culture favored independent action and team effort was communicated quickly and clearly to the newcomer. Sources of support and money were constantly shifting and, as growth occurred, managers rapidly moved on to other positions. But even though people frequently expressed frustration about the shifting approval process, slippage of schedules, and continual entry of new players onto the stage, they did not complain about lost opportunities. For one thing, because coalitions supported the various projects, new project managers feel bound to honor their predecessors' financial commitments.

CHIPCO managers had broad job charters to "do the right thing" in a manner of their own choosing. Lateral relationships were more important than vertical ones. Most functions were in a matrix, and some managers had up to four "bosses." Top management expected ideas to bubble up from lower levels. Senior executives then selected solutions rather than issuing confining directives. In fact, people generally relied on informal face-to-face communication across units to build a consensus. Managers spent a lot of time in meetings; information flowed freely, and reputation among peers—instead of formal authority or title—conveyed credibility and garnered support. Career mobility at CHIPCO was rapid, and people took pride in the company's success.

RADCO, the company with the strongest R&D orientation in the

Table 9-1. Characteristics of the five companies in order of most to least "entrepreneurial"

	CHIPCO	RADCO	MEDCO	FINCO	UTICO
Percent of effective managers with entrepreneurial accomplishments	71%	69%	67%	47%	33%
Current economic trend	Steadily up	Trend up but currently down	Up	Mixed	Down
Current "change issues"	Change "normal"; constant change in product generations; proliferating staff and units.	Change "normal" in products, technologies; recent changeover to second management generation with new focus.	Reorganized about 3–4 years ago to install matrix; "normal" product technology changes.	Change a "shock"; new top management group from outside reorganizing and trying to add competitive market posture.	Change a "shock"; undergoing reorganization to install matrix and add competitive market posture while reducing staff.
Organization structure	Matrix	Matrix in some areas; product lines act as quasi-divisions.	Matrix in some areas.	Divisional; unitary hierarchy within divisions, some central services.	Functional organization; currently overlaying a matrix of regions and markets.
	Decentralized	Mixed	Mixed	Centralized	Centralized

| | Free | Free | Moderately free | Constricted | Constricted |
Information flow / Communication emphasis	Horizontal	Horizontal	Horizontal	Vertical	Vertical
Culture	Clear, consistent; favors individual initiative.	Clear, though in transition from emphasis on invention to emphasis on routinization and systems.	Clear; pride in company, belief that talent will be rewarded.	Idiosyncratic; depends on boss and area.	Clear, but top management would like to change it; favors security, maintenance, protection.
Current "emotional" climate	Pride in company, team feeling, some "burnout."	Uncertainty about changes.	Pride in company, team feeling.	Low trust, high uncertainty.	High certainty, confusion.
Rewards	Abundant. Include visibility, chance to do more challenging work in the future and get bigger budget for projects.	Abundant. Include visibility, chance to do more challenging work in future and get bigger budget for projects.	Moderately abundant. Conventional.	Scarce. Primarily monetary.	Scarce. Promotion, salary freeze; recognition by peers grudging.

study, had many of CHIPCO's qualities but carried the burden of recent changes. RADCO's once-strong culture and its image as a fount of new technology were in flux and eroding. A new top management with new ways of thinking was shifting the orientation of the company, and some people expressed concern about the lack of clear direction and long-range planning. People's faith in RADCO's strategy of technical superiority had weakened, and its traditional orientation toward innovation was giving way to a concern for routinization and production efficiency. This shift resulted in conflict and uncertainty. Where once access to the top was easy, by the time of the study the decentralized matrix structure—with fewer central services—made it difficult.

As at CHIPCO, lateral relationships were important, though top management's presence was felt more. In the partial matrix, some managers had as many as four "bosses." A middle manager's boss or someone in higher management was likely to give general support to projects as long as peers (within and across functions) got on board. And peers often worked decisions up the organization through their own hierarchies.

Procedures at RADCO were both informal and formal: much happened at meetings and presentations and through persuasion, plus the company's long-term employment and well-established working relationships encouraged lateral communication. But managers also used task forces and steering committees. Projects often lasted for years, sustained by the company's image as a leader in treating employees well.

MEDCO manufactured and marketed advanced medical equipment, often applying ideas developed elsewhere. Although MEDCO produced a high proportion of innovative accomplishments, it had a greater degree of central planning and routinization than either CHIPCO or RADCO. Despite headquarters' strong role, heads of functions and product managers could vary their approaches. Employers believed that MEDCO's complex matrix system allowed autonomy and created opportunities but was also time wasting because clear accountability was lacking.

Teamwork and competition coexisted at MEDCO. Although top management officially encouraged teamwork and the matrix produced a tendency for trades and selling to go on within the organization, interdepartmental and interproduct rivalries sometimes got in the way. Rewards, especially promotions, were available, but they often came late and even then were not always clear or consistent. Because many employees had been with MEDCO for a long time, both job mobility and job security were high. Finally, managers saw the company as a leader in its approach to management and as a technological follower in all areas but one.

The last two companies in the study, FINCO (insurance) and UTICO (communications), showed the lowest proportion of innovative achievements. Many of the completed projects seemed to be successful *despite* the system. They are instructive as how-*not*-to-do-it examples.

FINCO had an idiosyncratic and inconsistent culture: employees did not have a clear image of the company, its style, or its direction. How managers were treated depends very much on one's boss—one-to-one relationships and private deals carried a great deal of weight. Though the atmosphere of uncertainty created opportunities for a few, it generally limited risk taking. Moreover, reorganizations, a top-management shake-up, and shuffling of personnel fostered insecurity and suspicion. It was difficult for managers to get commitment from their subordinates because they questioned the manager's tenure. Managers spent much time and energy coping with change, reassuring subordinates, and orienting new staff instead of developing future-oriented projects. Still, because the uncertainty created a vacuum, a few managers in powerful positions (many of whom were brought in to initiate change) did benefit.

Unlike the innovation-producing companies, FINCO featured a reliance on vertical relationships. With little encouragement to collaborate, managers seldom made contact across functions or worked in teams. Managers often saw formal structures and systems as constraints rather than as supports. Rewards were scarce, and occasionally a manager broke a promise about them. Seeing the company as a follower, not a leader, the managers at FINCO sometimes made unfavorable comparisons between it and other companies in the industry. Furthermore, they resented the fact that FINCO's top management brought in so many executives from outside; they saw those external searches as an insult.

UTICO was a very good company in many ways; it was well regarded by its employees and is considered progressive for its industry. However, despite the strong need for UTICO to be more creative and thus more competitive and despite movement toward a matrix structure, UTICO's people were not very innovative. UTICO's culture was changing—from being based on security and maintenance to being based on flexibility and competition—but the atmosphere of uncertainty frustrated achievers. Moreover, UTICO remained very centralized. Top management largely directed searches for new systems and methods through formal mechanisms whose ponderousness sometimes discouraged innovation. Tight budgetary constraints made it difficult for middle managers to tap funds; carefully measured duties discouraged risk takers; and a lockstep chain of command made it dangerous for managers to bypass their bosses.

Information flowed vertically and sluggishly. Because of limited cooperation among work units, even technical data could be hard to get. Weak-spot management meant that problems, not successes, got attention. Jealousy and competition over turf killed praise from peers and sometimes from bosses. Managers' image of the company was mixed: they saw it as leading its market segments but behind newer, faster-growing competitors in rate of change.

Organizational Supports for Creativity

Examination of the differences in organization, culture, and practices in these five companies makes clear the circumstances under which innovation can flourish. To tackle and solve tricky problems, people need both the opportunities and the incentives to reach beyond their formal jobs and combine organizational resources in new ways. The following create these opportunities:

- Multiple reporting relationships and overlapping territories. These force potential innovators to carve out their own ideas about appropriate action and to sell peers in neighboring areas or convince more than one boss.

- A free and somewhat random flow of information. Data flow of this kind prods people to find ideas in unexpected places and pushes them to combine fragments of information.

- Many centers of power with some budgetary flexibility. If such centers are easily accessible to middle managers and people through the ranks, they will be encouraged to make proposals and acquire resources.

- A high proportion of managers in loosely defined positions or with ambiguous assignments. Those without subordinates or line responsibilities who are told to "solve problems" must argue for a budget or develop their own constituency.

- Frequent and smooth cross-functional contact, a tradition of working in teams and sharing credit widely, and emphasis on lateral rather than vertical relationships as a source of resources, information, and support. These circumstances require managers to get peer support for their projects before top officers approve.

- A reward system that emphasizes investment in people and projects rather than payment for past services. Such a system encourages people to move into challenging jobs, gives them budgets to tackle projects, and rewards them after their accomplishments with the chance to take on even bigger projects in the future.

Some of these conditions seem to go hand in hand with newer companies in not-yet-mature markets. But top decision makers in older, traditional companies can design these conditions into their organizations. They would be wise to do so because, if empowered, innovative managers and other corporate entrepreneurs can be a potent weapon in today's and tomorrow's competitive contests.

10

Thinking Across Boundaries

It was a meeting of the minds at a crossroads of world trade.

In a Singapore ballroom, the British oil company head was about to reveal to managers from 37 countries the characteristics necessary for success in their global company. The audience squirmed in anticipation of the usual list of sensible-but-bland clichés about biases for action and putting people first.

"Brains," he said. "You need *brains."* And sat down.

How unexpected. How refreshing. How appropriate.

Mental agility is essential when business itself is at a crossroads. Ideas and events are reshaping social and economic institutions. Globalizing markets challenge the concept of the nation-state. Industries are being redefined through the power of information technology. Closer relationships between suppliers and customers blur the operational distinctions between legally separate organizations. New workplace realities and work force demographics are changing the implicit contract about what employers and employees owe to each other. The dependence of business on an adequate supply of natural and human resources puts "external" environmental, educational, and family problems on the company's internal agenda.

In every sphere, it seems, received wisdom about categories, distinctions, and groupings is being challenged. Trying to conduct business while the system itself is being redefined puts a premium on brains—to imagine possibilities outside of conventional categories, to envision actions that cross traditional boundaries, to anticipate repercussions and take advantage of interdependencies, to make new connections or invent new combinations. Those who lack the mental flexibility to think across boundaries will find it harder and harder to hold their own, let alone prosper.

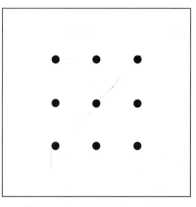

**Figure 10-1. Problem: Connect all 9 dots using no more than 4
straight lines.**

Consider this familiar brainteaser *(Figure 10-1)*. Nine dots are
arranged in three rows and three columns. Try to connect all the
dots with four lines.

If you stay within the boundaries defined by the dots, as most
people assume they must, the task cannot be done. A solution is
found only by going outside the apparent boundaries *(Figure 10-2)*.

Now try using just three lines to connect the dots. Impossible,
you say? Not if you challenge another apparent constraint. Enlarge
the dots enough *(Figure 10-3)*, and the puzzle is solved.

Thinking across boundaries, or integrative thinking, is the ultimate entrepreneurial act. Call it business creativity. Call it holistic
thinking. To see problems and opportunities integratively is to see
them as wholes related to larger wholes, rather than dividing
information and experience into discrete bits assigned to distinct,
separate categories that never touch one another. Blurring the
boundaries and challenging the categories permits new possibilities to emerge, like twisting a kaleidoscope to see the endless
patterns that can be created from the same set of fragments.
Harvard psychologist Ellen Langer coined the term "mindfulness"
for the ability to make aware choices, to pay attention to the
essence and potential of things rather than to be blinded and
inhibited by the categories applied to them. Research has associated integrative thinking with higher levels of organizational innovation, personal creativity, and even longer life.

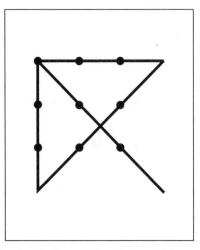

Figure 10-2. Standard solution: Using 4 straight connecting lines, go outside the "boundaries."

The ability to rethink categories and transcend boundaries is essential for every aspect of business practice today. To start with, many firms desperately need a new concept of the business defined across rather than within industries and markets.

In order to survive, a hospital group has to think beyond the bricks-and-mortar limits of hospital buildings to create new relationships among health-care providers dispersed across many places. A computer giant is being nibbled to death on one side by low-cost competition for its commodity products and on the other side by consulting firms grabbing the high-end systems integration business. But bound by a rigid conception of its industry and organized to fit that conception, the company seems unable to reinvent itself. A major bank, in contrast, is prospering by thinking beyond industry boundaries. By redefining its branch banks as "stores," it can sell many additional products through its branches. If Sears can be in financial services, Banc One can be in retailing.

Product integrity, a root cause of Japanese success in the world auto industry, is the result of thinking across boundaries—having an overarching concept for the product that guides the work of diverse specialists. The concept integrates features that might otherwise be perceived by customers as disconnected fragments. It may even challenge conventional mental boundaries by its meta-

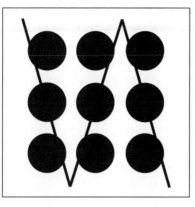

Figure 10-3. Entrepreneurial solution: Enlarge the dots and use 3 straight lines.

phorical quality—e.g., the Honda Accord as "a rugby player in a business suit." Each functional group contributing to the project thinks across boundaries as it listens to and integrates into its own work the results of the others' efforts. A strong product champion patrols the boundaries, protects the integrity of the whole, and prevents the effort from fragmenting.

Generating new ideas is itself boundary-challenging. Innovations grow out of unexpected, surprising, and even irreverent mental connections. To develop them requires collaborations and adjustments by many parts of the organization. Entrepreneurial opportunities do not respect territories; they rarely present themselves to companies in the boxes established on the organizational chart. But the more rigid the walls between functions or between divisions, the less likely that people will venture out of their boxes to try something new.

Even entrepreneurial companies suffer from "localitis." A fast-growing technology pioneer realizes it needs to move beyond local entrepreneurial thinking in order to gain global strength. People must be willing to transfer technology rapidly from one part of the world to another to work on projects in which countries and divisions combine forces. Already the company has an exciting new market opportunity from a joint chemical division/equipment division project.

Leadership also involves thinking across boundaries. Leaders need to incorporate and integrate the perspectives of others. Effective negotiation—the art of "getting to yes"—depends on the ability to understand others' goals and see the situation from their vantage point. Successful business leaders in new sectors thrive on their willingness to be inclusive, to share information with their associates, and to learn from them. There is a similar empathic ability in the leadership of large, complex product development teams. Being organizationally "multilingual" helps members see the perspective of other stakeholders.

Boundaries are sometimes a mental imposition—a decision to divide the world a certain way. They become real when social patterns come to enforce the imaginary walls and when once-deliberate choices become mindless habits. Of course, some barriers are more concrete than others—such as soldiers with machine guns on the Berlin Wall or regulations barring U.S. telephone operating companies from manufacturing. But history teaches us not to assume their permanence. For every barrier, there seems to be a patient entrepreneur who eventually finds a way around it—and then tries to erect a new one to defend his or her position.

Developing skill at thinking across boundaries should not be equated with narcissistic navel-gazing, however. New Age gurus are jumping into the brains-improvement business with today's versions of the power of positive thinking. Transcendental meditation is sweeping Swedish industry. British creativity experts are stars on the European seminar circuit. But when a service group in a company spends a good part of meetings with eyes closed in a "visualization" exercise or when bank managers struggle to take notes using a "whole brain mapping" process, skeptics challenge the business value received.

Under the guise of mental liberation, people can be lulled into another kind of mindless conformity. People's attention may turn inward to themselves when attention should be focused outward on markets or customers. Programs that begin with a desire to change individual attitudes rather than solve tangible problems often fail. Such preoccupation with individual psychology is a particular problem for U.S companies. Throughout U.S. history, attempts to solve economic and social problems have often evolved into individual self-help cults. Westerners should be careful about

mental exercises that are devoid of content. Some Japanese executives may meditate, but they also know their math and markets.

What matters most today is the ability to think *together,* not
alone. To think imaginatively about matters of substance, incorporating many perspectives and reaching beyond conventional categories. To create new concepts that make new connections.

A bias for action is important in a fast-paced world of flux and
change. But even higher on the priority list should be a bias for
brains.

11

Even Closer to the Customer

The Customer Service Revolution involves more than its limited warranties and smile training.

Meeting customer requirements and fixing problems—the *delivery* and *recovery* sides of service—are just the first, familiar steps. Now innovation must also be added to the service mix—how customers change the business itself.

With the help of computer technology, customers are entering the internal business process in unprecedented ways. Customer choices direct production. Customer feedback drives product development. Customer communication creates membership groups.

How can companies find opportunities to get even closer to their customers? Meet these challenges.

Challenge 1—Understanding Who Is the Customer

The basic question is still the most difficult.

A shouting match once broke out at a small computer company over whether it was better to incorporate the perspective of the individual user, the office manager, the purchaser, or the computer store manager in the design process. But why choose only one?

Leave aside for a moment the niche issue—many differentiated customers in many potential specialty markets combining products and services in highly individualized ways. Even in a single market segment, the existence of intermediaries and multiple users makes the customer question complex.

Managers have long differentiated between categories of recipients—the "consumer" versus "customer" (distributor, retailer) distinction in the packaged goods industry, for example. Traditionally, companies have favored one of their key relationships. Some food companies have used advertising to speak directly to consumers, expecting a strong consumer franchise to force retailers to stock their products. Pharmaceutical companies have focused on physicians, ignoring consumers.

Now all relationships are important simultaneously; each influences the others. Innovation affects a network of ties; involving one group in the process without involving the others could bring disaster. A British beverage company, for example, recognized consumer interest in beverages that are sold cold. But placing vending machines (unusual in the U.K.) and refrigerator cases to satisfy consumer demand required redefining many other customer relationships. A customer-oriented company must understand and involve the whole customer system.

Challenge 2—Turning Customers into Members

Involving customers in innovation requires forums for continuing communication with the company. Membership groups of frequent users serve as idea sources and test sites. For those who sell to anonymous consumers in mass markets, "clubs" help identify the most dedicated consumers. They help re-create product loyalty.

In the past, user groups often began in self-defense. They offered mutual education or protection against the company's power—consumer unions, for example, like the French telephone users' association that flourished before that system was transformed, or auto dealers' associations in the United States that bargained with the auto companies for better terms. User groups were common in the computer industry because members could not count on the producers to answer their questions. Clubs helped members make connections with one another for shared problem solving. (Now the companies work closely with these clubs as one of their best forms of customer outreach.)

Industries from toys to banking are creating members. Denmark's Lego developed the Lego Builders Club; Germany's Playmobil offers special sets and newsletters for its fan club; Japan's Nintendo has a telephone hot line, game counselors, and a magazine. The Harley-Davidson motorcycle owners group has over 100,000 members. A Finnish bank created a club for older customers with discounts on many companies' products. Bookstores have frequent reader programs.

Connecting customers as members can bring benefits to all sides—if the company really listens.

Challenge 3—Making Customers Real to All Employees

Despite frequent mention of "the customer" in quality programs in Europe and North America, customers are largely an abstraction to employees whose jobs do not involve direct contact. Ray Smith, CEO of Bell Atlantic, points out that too often quality measures focus employees on numerical scores rather than on outcomes customers care about.

Years of research on industrial innovation have consistently confirmed the importance of direct observation of users. Yet in many manufacturing companies, the only group regularly in contact with customers—the field sales force—has been segregated like a breed apart, with its own compensation plans, its own pep rallies, and little if any input into product design. Some Japanese companies, in contrast, include direct selling as part of the induction process for management trainees. When employees are users, the innovation process is facilitated. According to its knowledge guru at Xerox Parc, John Seely Brown, employees at Xerox stand in for customers. The research department studies the internal work process and involves the rest of the company in testing innovations.

Under other circumstances, making customers real to behind-the-scenes employees requires new forms of contact. Workers in an engine factory meet with truck drivers. Customers of a building components company regularly observe the plant's manufacturing process; workers like the fact that customers are interested. The idea that corporate staffs have internal customers became real at Bell Atlantic through the Client Service group structure in which corporate staffs had to sell their services to line managers who were free to purchase them internally or externally.

Challenge 4—Using Customer Data to Benefit Customers

Consider what the computer brings to marketing: Customization. Supplier-customer dialogues. Feedback loops from sales data to product designers. And this is only the beginning.

The potential exists for collecting, analyzing, and using data to meet customer needs not just once but over and over again—to serve the customer without having to ask. Bell Atlantic's "Intelligent Network" strategy for basic telephone service, for example, involves storing customer preference information and automatically customizing the kind of local service the customer receives (such as no rings between certain hours). For other companies, patterns of use data can be a potent guide for innovation.

How many companies take full advantage of what they know about their customers? To some, customer data means having a mailing list to sell. For others, a customer is just an "account"; there may be as many account records as there are separate transactions with that customer.

At best, unintegrated, unanalyzed data represent lost potential to woo customers. (A Hong Kong hotel, not missing any use of information, uses the birthdate on foreign customers' passports to send a birthday card every year.) At worst, ill-used data make a mockery out of service claims. A widely touted personal banker system failed when personal bankers could not find mortgage account information on their terminals because it was stored in a different computer system. Yet customers commonly tell companies they want a single contact who can answer any question about their relationship. And they want innovations to fit their specific needs.

Challenge 5—Keeping Promises by Championing Change

Company promises are enticing. To customize. To offer education, special delivery, follow-up calls. To solve problems even by providing another company's products.

Such pledges are dynamite—in both the positive and negative senses. If they work, they solidify the bond to the customer. But many companies have not linked their service guarantees to other aspects of their strategies. They leap into "service wars"—besting their competitors' last promise without being sure they can make good on promises or the costs of keeping them. One company hell-bent on customization treated every order as unique, whether or not customers cared. With 40,000 parts numbers for 1,000 products, costs jeopardized business health.

Some promises are relatively easy to keep, as British Airways found when it gained market share after training its crews to be nicer to customers. Other, loftier promises require long-term, fundamental changes in how the business operates. Those are the dangerous ones.

Consider this situation. After years of product leadership, a major computer company recognizes that its products are commodities, so it announces a service orientation: to find the best systems for customer needs regardless of who makes them. How does the company keep that promise? By offering competitors' components. But how are sales reps rewarded? For selling the company's machines. And do any field sales managers want their areas to lag in selling the company's products? Of course not. So they deny that the company has changed its orientation. They reinforce the old view of the customer as a source of orders for what the company already makes.

In the new marketing environment, companies must prove that the ways they operate guarantee their ability to keep promises. Perhaps this is why a new kind of corporate advertising is emerging, one that describes the company's internal management processes (3M about its innovation process, Ford about its quality techniques, Motorola about participative management). But more than advertising a process, companies must mean what they say. As Ray Smith recognized at Bell Atlantic, changing relationships to customers begins with changing internal culture and structure.

Despite the recent media coronation of King Customer, many customers will remain commoners. Inevitably, company strategy favors the most active and involved customers. Attention goes to those who specify their requirements clearly, spend the time to offer feedback, and promise a continuing relationship. Designing products and services with these "good customers" in mind keeps them satisfied and loyal. A close relationship is reinforced.

The trend is clear. Suppliers and customers, sellers and buyers, producers and consumers are forging closer connections. This has been called "the new intimacy." But before companies are seduced by it, they should test their readiness to go beyond just flirting.

12

Follow-Up and Follow-Through

American business has become obsessed with heroes, enamored of bold moves, and addicted to high drama. Mere improvement is not good enough; only "transformation" will do. Incremental innovations are not worth bothering with; instead, companies urge "breakthroughs." Rather than fixing operations, some managers prefer the do-it-from-the-top visibility of asset shuffling. Marketing anything from soap to ideas requires declaring New! Different! Forget the Last Thing and Go on to the Next! Increasing competition inevitably leads to increasing hype.

Some of this is a response to the times. Nimble entrepreneurial startups with true breakthrough concepts have challenged the dominance of corporate giants and created new competitive conditions, as have effective Asian entrants. Capital market pressures have forced reexamination of corporate portfolios, ownership, and governance. Events of sweeping historical scope, such as the political changes in Eastern Europe, dominate the news. Macrophenomena seem more important than microphenomena. Nothing less than a "paradigm shift"—a grandiose phrase for the search for the next Big Idea—will do.

Yet it is just such times of change that demand even more attention to the nitty-gritty of execution. Change of any sort carries with it the added costs of confusion and the dangers of slippage. A good new idea means little—except risk—without follow-up and follow-through. Some of the upstarts and foreign companies changing the terms of competition succeed precisely *because* they concentrate on excellence in execution from the quality of products, to speed in developing new ones, to responsiveness in customer service.

Overvaluing "strategy" (by which many companies mean Big Ideas and Big Decisions) and undervaluing execution lead not only to implementation shortfalls but also to misinterpreting the reasons for success or failure. After a large bank holding company suffered massive losses, the board declared that the problem stemmed from a portfolio of questionable real estate loans—the Big Decisions. Yet employees' conversations revealed execution failures in virtually every aspect of the bank's operations. Bills for safe deposit boxes were mailed three months late. Branches in residential neighborhoods were closed the Saturday before Christmas. Continuing acremony between the bank's management and that of a key acquisition prevented the consolidation of systems. Each problem was small and not very costly, but together they were potentially as responsible for the red ink as the bad loans were. Yet top management refused to look anywhere but at its major lending policies to explain its problems.

Even in the best-run companies, it is too easy to feel that the work is done when the Big Idea is hatched. A prominent packaged goods company was notoriously behind the competition in commercializing its innovations, losing the battle for shelf space because of execution shortfalls. Follow-up was valued so little that the typical tenure of a manager responsible for new products was shorter than the average time it took to bring a new product to market.

It is also too easy for managers to give up when the Big Idea does not produce results quickly enough—and to move on to the next potential blockbuster. Yet the difference between success and failure is often just a matter of time: staying with the project long enough to overcome the unexpected developments, politcal problems, or fatigue that can come between a great-sounding plan and actual results. A basic truth of management—if not of life—is that nearly everything looks like a failure in the middle. At the same time, of course, the next project always looks more attractive (because it is all promise, fresh and untried).

None of this should be surprising. Persistent, consistent execution is unglamorous, time-consuming, and sometimes boring. Ford's turnaround was a matter of taking many small steps toward operational excellence rather than counting on big, bold new directions as competitors did. Former Chairman Donald Petersen's leadership secret was little more than unrelenting emphasis on getting the parts of the organization to work well together. "I made teamwork a daily part of the conversation," he said. Other leaders call the same thing nagging.

IV

Managing People:

Motivating, Empowering, Rewarding

Overview

A change-adept organization begins and ends with its people and their capacity to act. Individual competence translates into organizational competence when people have the tools and channels to make good decisions and to take productive actions. They must want to act, have the power to act, and feel rewarded for their performance—which reinforces their desire to act, thus completing a virtuous circle of higher and higher achievement.

The power to act makes things happen; the absence of power not only constrains action but can poison the whole system. One of the diseases of bureaucracy is its tendency to limit and constrain action, hemming people in with mindless routines and weighing them down with mindless rules. In "Power Failure in Management Circuits" I argue that *powerlessness corrupts.* Power, the ability to mobilize resources to get something done, derives from lines of supply, information, and support from bosses, peers, and subordinates. Those who lack the tools of power and who thus come to feel powerless stifle innovation, over-control others, emphasize rules, and behave punitively. This describes those hemmed in by their formal positions, such as first-line supervisors and backwater staff professionals, but it sometimes extends even to chief executives; it also accounts for the glass ceilings encountered by some women managers. In contrast, those who feel powerful are more likely to empower others. Organizational power grows when it is shared.

Empowerment does not mean throwing all controls to the wind

and allowing people to do whatever they please. Productive empowerment requires discipline and professionalism among staff members, who can be entrusted with greater capacity to act because they have shown they will handle power responsibly. Managers can risk delegating power when they have the confidence that their people are committed to a common set of high professional standards. When organizations have shared methodologies for approaching tasks and shared values guiding decisions, they can afford more empowerment (see "Discipline!").

The need for a common vocabulary and common understanding of how to approach tasks and problems becomes clear when you consider how often people in organizations talk past one another (see "A Walk on the Soft Side"). Managers need soft skills, such as interpersonal sensitivities, that help them to understand the varied reactions and perceptions of people in a diverse work force. Understanding interpersonal differences can help managers transcend them by developing common disciplines well understood by all.

When people are empowered to contribute, they want to be rewarded specifically for their results (see "The Attack on Pay"). Busting bureaucracy and creating change-adept organizations requires new compensation systems that forge closer links to performance and allow more flexibility in pay, bonuses, and recognition. And companies increasingly want to turn people into entrepreneurs and innovators, to focus them on appropriate targets, and to encourage them to behave as professionals. To do so, they must uncouple rewards from formal status or rank, getting rid of the hierarchical principle that higher position means higher rewards and reassessing rewards in terms of the value derived from performance—even in low-ranked jobs.

This is especially important in a service economy (see "Service Quality: You Get What You Pay For"). Many services are inherently local; the quality of their delivery and their impact on customers is shaped by frontline workers who can make or break service strategies. Consider how many service workers are package deliverers, receptionists, sales clerks, or flight attendants making low pay and having little voice in their organizations. Encouraging competence in the performance of service jobs might be a matter of raising pay, using technology to empower people instead of reducing their options, and cutting unnecessary corporate bureaucracy.

Even if people are rewarded for short-term contributions, they can be distressed by the absence of long-term employment security when companies downsize, reengineer, and reduce the guarantees they give their employees. Companies face a major human resource policy issue in determining what will replace lost employment security (see "A New Human Resources Agenda").

"Employability security" has become a catch phrase at some companies. Sometimes it is used to mask brutal intentions, such as preserving the right to cut employment at any moment with little notice. But done correctly, with the right values and intentions, employability security can actually enhance long-term loyalty. By offering ongoing learning to upgrade skills and by spreading the power to innovate, companies help employees to perform better, which allows the companies to perform better, which preserves and expands jobs. Such practices also ensure that current employees continue to be important contributors who are valued by their employers and offered opportunities to continue to grow. The suggested "employability security contract" in "A New Human Resources Agenda" will help employers assess and improve their policies.

13

Power Failure in Management Circuits

Power is one of the last dirty words. It is easier to talk about money—and much easier to talk about sex—than it is to talk about power. People who have it deny it; people who want it do not want to appear to hunger for it; and people who engage in its machinations do so secretly.

Yet, because it turns out to be a critical element in effective managerial behavior, power should come out from undercover. Having searched for years for those styles or skills that would identify capable organization leaders, many analysts, like myself, are rejecting individual traits or situational appropriateness as key and finding the sources of a leader's real power.

Access to resources and information and the ability to act quickly make it possible to accomplish more and to pass on more resources and information to subordinates. For this reason, people tend to prefer bosses with "clout." When employees perceive their manager as influential upward and outward, their status is enhanced by association and they generally have high morale and feel less critical or resistant to their boss. More powerful leaders are also more likely to delegate (they are too busy to do it all themselves), to reward talent, and to build a team that places subordinates in significant positions.

Powerlessness, in contrast, tends to breed bossiness rather than true leadership. In large organizations, at least, it is powerlessness that often creates ineffective, desultory management and petty, dictatorial, rules-minded managerial styles. Accountability without power—responsibility for results without the resources to get them—creates frustration and failure. People who see themselves as weak and powerless and find their subordinates resisting or discounting them tend to use more punishing forms of influence. If organizational power can "ennoble," then, recent research shows, organizational powerlessness can (with apologies to Lord Acton) "corrupt."

So perhaps power, in the organization at least, does not deserve such a bad reputation. Rather than connoting only dominance, control, and oppression, power can mean efficacy and capacity—something managers and executives need to move the organization toward its goals. Power in organizations is analogous in simple terms to physical power: it is the ability to mobilize resources (human and material) to get things done. The true sign of power, then, is accomplishment—not fear, terror, or tyranny. Where the power is "on," the system can be productive; where the power is "off," the system bogs down.

But saying that people need power to be effective in organizations does not tell us where it comes from or why some people, in some jobs, systematically seem to have more of it than others. To discover the real sources of productive power, we have to look not at the person—as conventional classifications of effective managers and employees do—but at the position the person occupies in the organization.

Where Does Power Come From?

The effectiveness that power brings evolves from two kinds of capacities: first, access to the resources, information, and support necessary to carry out a task; and, second, ability to get cooperation in doing what is necessary. (*Table 13-1* identifies some symbols of an individual manager's power.)

Both capacities derive not so much from a leader's style and skill as from his or her location in the formal and informal systems of the organization—in both job definition and connection to other important people in the company. Even the ability to get cooperation from subordinates is strongly defined by the manager's clout outward. People are more responsive to bosses who look as if they can get more for them from the organization.

We can regard the uniquely organizational sources of power as consisting of three "lines":

1. *Lines of supply.* Influence outward, over the environment,

Table 13-1. Some common symbols of a manager's organizational power (influence upward and outward)

To what extent a manger can—

Intercede favorably on behalf of someone in trouble with the organization

Get a desirable placement for a talented subordinate

Get approval for expenditures beyond the budget

Get above-average salary increases for subordinates

Get items on the agenda at policy meetings

Get fast access to top decision makers

Get regular, frequent access to top decision makers

Get early information about decisions and policy shifts

---

means that managers have the capacity to bring in the things that their own organizational domain needs—materials, money, resources to distribute as rewards, and perhaps even prestige.

2. *Lines of information.* To be effective, managers need to be "in the know" in both the formal and the informal sense.

3. *Lines of support.* In a formal framework, a manager's job parameters need to allow for nonordinary action, for a show of discretion or exercise of judgment. Thus managers need to know that they can assume innovative, risk-taking activities without having to go through a stifling multilayered approval process. And, informally, managers need the backing of other important figures in the organization whose tacit approval becomes another resource they bring to their own work unit as well as a sign of the manager's being "in."

Note that productive power has to do with *connections* with other parts of a system. Such systemic aspects of power derive from two sources—job activities and political alliances:

1. Power is most easily accumulated when one has a job that is designed and located to allow *discretion* (nonroutinized action permitting flexible, adaptive, and creative contributions), *recognition* (visibility and notice), and *relevance* (being central to pressing organizational problems).

2. Power also comes when one has relatively close contact with

sponsors (higher-level people who confer approval, prestige, or backing), *peer networks* (circles of acquaintanceship that provide reputation and information, the grapevine often being faster than formal communication channels), and *subordinates* (who can be developed to relieve managers of some of their burdens and to represent the manager's point of view).

When managers are in powerful situations, it is easier for them to accomplish more. Because the tools are there, they are likely to be highly motivated and, in turn, to be able to motivate subordinates. Their activities are more likely to be on target and to net them successes. They can flexibly interpret or shape policy to meet the needs of particular areas, emergent situations, or sudden environmental shifts. They gain the respect and cooperation that attributed power brings. Subordinates' talents are resources rather than threats. And, because powerful managers have so many lines of connection and thus are oriented outward, they tend to let go of control downward, developing more independently functioning lieutenants.

The powerless live in a different world. Lacking the supplies, information, or support to make things happen easily, they may turn instead to the ultimate weapon of those who lack productive power—oppressive power: holding others back and punishing with whatever threats they can muster.

Table 13-2 summarizes some of the major ways in which variables in the organization and in job design contribute to either power or powerlessness.

Positions of Powerlessness

Understanding what it takes to have power and recognizing the classic behavior of the powerless can immediately help managers make sense out of a number of familiar organizational problems that are usually attributed to inadequate people:

- The ineffectiveness of first-line supervisors.
- The petty interest protection and conservatism of staff professionals.
- The crises of leadership at the top.

Table 13-2. Ways organizational factors contribute to power or powerlessness

Factors	Generates power when factor is	Generates powerlessness when factor is
Rules inherent in the job	few	many
Predecessors in the job	few	many
Established routines	few	many
Task variety	high	low
Rewards for reliability/predictability	few	many
Rewards for unusual performance/ innovation	many	few
Flexibility around use of people	high	low
Approvals needed for nonroutine decisions	few	many
Physical location	central	distant
Publicity about job activities	high	low
Relation of tasks to current problem areas	central	peripheral
Focus of tasks	outside work unit	inside work unit
Interpersonal contact in the job	high	low
Contact with senior officials	high	low
Participation in programs, conferences, meetings	high	low
Participation in problem-solving task forces	high	low
Advancement prospects of subordinates	high	low

Instead of blaming the individuals involved in organizational problems, let us look at the positions people occupy. Of course, power or powerlessness in a position may not be all of the problem. Sometimes incapable people *are* at fault and need to be retrained or replaced. (See "When Women Managers Experience Power Failures" for a discussion of another special case, women.) But where patterns emerge, where the troubles associated with some units persist, organizational power failures could be the reason. Then we should treat the powerless not as "villains" causing headaches for everyone else but as "victims."

When Women Managers Experience Power Failures

The traditional problems of women in management are illustrative of how formal and informal practices can combine to engender powerlessness. Historically, women in management have found their opportunities in more routine, low-profile jobs. In staff positions, where they serve in support capacities to line managers but have no line responsibilities of their own, or in supervisory jobs managing "stuck" subordinates, they are not in a position either to take the kinds of risks that build credibility or to develop their own team by pushing bright subordinates.

Such jobs, which have few favors to trade, tend to keep women out of the mainstream of the organization. This lack of clout, coupled with the greater difficulty anyone who is "different" has in getting into the information and support networks, has meant that merely by organizational situation women in management have been more likely than men to be rendered structurally powerless. This is one reason those women who have achieved power have often had family connections that put them in the mainstream of the organization's social circles.

A disproportionate number of women managers are found among first-line supervisors or staff professionals; and they, like men in those circumstances, are likely to be organizationally powerless. But the behavior of other managers can contribute to the powerlessness of women in management in a number of less obvious ways.

One way other managers can make a woman powerless is by patronizingly overprotecting her: putting her in "a safe job," not giving her enough to do to prove herself, and not suggesting her for high-risk, visible assignments. This protectiveness is sometimes born of "good" intentions to give her every chance to succeed (why stack the deck against her?). Out of managerial concerns, out of awareness that a woman may be up against situations that men simply do not have to face, some very well-meaning managers protect their female managers ("It's a jungle, so why send her into it?").

Overprotectiveness can also mask a manager's fear of association with a woman should she fail. One senior bank official at a level below vice president told me about his concerns with respect to a high-performing, financially experienced woman reporting to him. Despite *his* overwhelmingly positive work experiences with her, he was still afraid to recommend her for other assignments because he felt it was a personal risk. "What if other managers are not as accepting of women as I am?" he asked. "I know I'd be sticking my neck out; they would take her more because of my endorsement than her qualifications. And what if she doesn't make it? My judgment will be on the line."

Overprotection is relatively benign compared with rendering a person powerless by providing obvious signs of lack of managerial support. For example, allowing someone supposedly in authority to be bypassed easily means that no one else has to take him or her seriously. If a woman's immediate supervisor or other managers listen willingly to criticism of her and show they are concerned every time a negative comment comes up and that they assume she must be at fault, then they are helping to undercut her. If managers let other people know that they have concerns about this person or that they are testing her to see how she does, then they are inviting other people to look for signs of inadequacy or failure.

Furthermore, people assume they can afford to bypass women because they "must be uninformed" or "don't know the ropes." Even though women may be respected for their competence or expertise, they are not necessarily seen as being informed beyond the technical requirements of the job. There may be a grain of historical truth in this. Many women come to senior management positions as "outsiders" rather than up through the usual channels.

Also, because until very recently men have not felt comfortable seeing women as businesspeople (business clubs have traditionally excluded women), they have tended to seek each other out for informal socializing. Anyone, male or female, seen as organizationally naive and lacking sources of "inside dope" will find his or her own lines of information limited.

Finally, even when women are able to achieve some power on their own, they have not necessarily been able to translate such personal credibility into an organizational power base. To create a network of supporters out of individual clout requires that a person pass on and share power, that subordinates and peers be empowered by virtue of their connection with that person. Traditionally, neither men nor women have seen women as capable of sponsoring others, even though they may be capable of achieving and succeeding on their own. Women have been viewed as the *recipients* of sponsorship rather than as the sponsors themselves.

As more women prove their competence and strive to bring along young people, this situation may change. However, I still hear many more questions from women managers about how they can benefit from mentors, sponsors, or peer networks than about how they themselves can start to pass on favors and make use of their own resources to benefit others.

Viewing managers in terms of power and powerlessness helps explain two familiar stereotypes about women and leadership in organizations: that no one wants a woman boss (although studies show that anyone who has ever had a woman boss is likely to have had a positive experience), and that the reason no one wants a woman boss is that women are "too controlling, rules-minded, and petty."

The first stereotype simply makes clear that power is important to leadership. Underneath the preference for men is the assumption that, given the current distribution of people in organizational leadership positions, men are more likely than women to be in positions to achieve power and, therefore, to share their power with others. Similarly, the "bossy

woman boss" stereotype is a perfect picture of powerlessness. All of those traits are just as characteristic of men who
are powerless, but women are slightly more likely, because
of circumstances I have mentioned, to find themselves powerless than are men. Women with power in the organization
are just as effective—and preferred—as men.

Recent interviews conducted with about 600 bank managers show that, when a woman exhibits the petty traits of
powerlessness, people assume that she does so "because
she is a woman." A striking difference is that, when a man
engages in the same behavior, people assume the behavior
is a matter of his own individual style and characteristics
and do not conclude that it reflects on the suitability of men
for management.

First-line supervisors

Because an employee's most important work relationship is with
his or her supervisor, when many of them talk about "the company," they mean their immediate boss. Thus a supervisor's behavior is an important determinant of the average employee's relationship to work and is in itself a critical link in the production
chain.

Yet it is hard to find companies entirely satisfied with the performance of its supervisors. Most see them as supervising too
closely and not training their people. In one manufacturing company where direct laborers were asked on a survey how they
learned their job, on a list of seven possibilities, "from my supervisor" ranked next to last. (Only company training programs had
a lower score.) Also, it is said that supervisors do not translate
company policies into practice—for instance, that they do not carry
out the right of every employee to frequent performance reviews
or to career counseling.

In court cases charging race or sex discrimination, first-line
supervisors are frequently cited as the "discriminating official."
And, in studies of innovative work redesign, they often appear as
the implied villains; they are the ones who are said to undermine

---

the program or interfere with its effectiveness. In short, they are often seen as "not sufficiently managerial."

The problem affects white-collar as well as blue-collar supervisors. In one large government agency, supervisors in field offices were seen as the source of problems concerning morale and the flow of information to and from headquarters. "Their attitudes are negative," said a senior official. "They turn people against the agency; they put down senior management. They build themselves up by always complaining about headquarters, but prevent their staff from getting any information directly. We can't afford to have such attitudes communicated to field staff."

Is the problem that supervisors need more management training programs or that incompetent people are invariably attracted to the job? Neither explanation suffices. A large part of the problem lies in the position itself—one that almost universally creates powerlessness.

First-line supervisors are "people in the middle," and that has been seen as the source of many of their problems. But by recognizing that first-line supervisors are caught between higher management and workers, we only begin to skim the surface of the problem. There is practically no other organizational category as subject to powerlessness.

First, these supervisors may be at a virtual dead end in their careers. Even in companies where the job used to be a stepping stone to higher-level management jobs, it is now common practice to recruit externally for people with specialized skills for upper ranks. Thus, moving from the ranks of direct labor into supervision may mean, essentially, getting "stuck" rather than moving upward. Because employees do not perceive supervisors as eventually joining the leadership circles of the organization, they may see them as lacking the high-level contacts needed to have clout. Indeed, sometimes turnover among supervisors is so high that workers feel they can outwait—and outwit—any boss.

Second, although they lack clout, with little in the way of support from above, supervisors are forced to administer programs or explain policies that they have no hand in shaping. In one company, as part of a new human resources program supervisors were required to conduct counseling interviews with employees. But supervisors were not trained to do this and were given no incentives to get involved. Counseling was just another obligation. Then managers suddenly encouraged the workers to bypass their supervisors or to put pressure on them. The human resources staff brought them together and told them to demand such interviews as a basic right. If supervisors had not felt powerless before, they did after that squeeze from below, engineered from above.

The people they supervise can also make life hard for them in numerous ways. This often happens when a supervisor has himself or herself risen up from the ranks. Peers that have not made it are resentful or derisive of their former colleague, whom they now see as trying to lord it over them. Often it is easy for workers to break rules and let a lot of things slip.

Yet first-line supervisors are frequently judged according to rules and regulations while being limited by other regulations in what disciplinary actions they can take. They often lack the resources to influence or reward people; after all, workers are guaranteed their pay and benefits by someone other than their supervisors. Supervisors cannot easily control events; rather, they must react to them. In one factory, for instance, supervisors complained that performance of their job was out of their control: they could fill production quotas only if they had the supplies, but they had no way to influence the people controlling supplies.

The lack of support for many first-line managers, particularly in large organizations, was made dramatically clear in another company. When asked if contact with executives higher in the organization who had the potential for offering support, information, and alliances diminished their own feelings of career vulnerability and the number of headaches they experienced on the job, supervisors in five out of seven work units responded positively. For them, contact was indeed related to a greater feeling of acceptance at work and membership in the organization.

But in the two other work units where there was greater contact, people perceived more, not less, career vulnerability. Further investigation showed that supervisors in these business units got attention only when they were in trouble. Otherwise, no one bothered to talk to them. To these particular supervisors, hearing from a higher-level manager was a sign not of recognition or potential support but of danger.

It is not surprising, then, that supervisors frequently manifest symptoms of powerlessness: overly close supervision, rules-mindedness, and a tendency to do the job themselves rather than to train their people (since job skills may be one of the few remaining things they feel good about). Perhaps this is why they sometimes stand as roadblocks between their subordinates and the higher reaches of the company.

Staff professionals

Also working under conditions that can lead to organizational powerlessness are the staff specialists. As advisers behind the scenes, staff people must sell their programs and bargain for resources, but unless they get themselves entrenched in organizational power networks, they have little in the way of favors to exchange. They are seen as useful adjuncts to the primary tasks of the organization but inessential in a day-to-day operating sense. This disenfranchisement occurs particularly when staff jobs consist of easily routinized administrative functions which are out of the mainstream of the currently relevant areas and involve little innovative decision making.

Furthermore, in some organizations, unless they have had previous line experience, staff people tend to be limited in the number of jobs into which they can move. Specialists' ladders are often very short, and professionals are just as likely to get "stuck" in such jobs as people are in less prestigious clerical or factory positions.

Staff people, unlike those who are being groomed for important line positions, may be hired because of a special expertise or particular background. But management rarely pays any attention to developing them into more general organizational resources. Lacking growth prospects themselves and working alone or in very small teams, they are not in a position to develop others or pass on power to them. They miss out on an important way that power can be accumulated.

Sometimes staff specialists, such as strategic planners, accountants, in-house legal counsel, communications professionals, or management trainers, find their work outsourced to external firms, or the "best" challenges turned over to outside consultants. Management considers their staff departments fine for the routine work, but the minute the activities involve risk or something problematic, they bring in outside experts. This treatment says something not only about their expertise but also about the status of their function. Since the company can always hire talent on a temporary basis, it is unclear that the management really needs to have or considers important its own staff for these functions.

And, because staff professionals are often seen as adjuncts to primary tasks, their effectiveness and therefore their contribution to the organization are often hard to measure. Thus visibility and recognition, as well as risk taking and relevance, may be denied to people in staff jobs.

Staff people tend to act out their powerlessness by becoming turf-minded. They create islands within the organization. They set themselves up as the only ones who can control professional standards and judge their own work. They create sometimes false distinctions between themselves as experts (no one else could possibly do what they do) and lay people. But this continues to keep them out of the mainstream.

One form such distinctions take is a combination of disdain when line managers attempt to act in areas the professionals think are their preserve and of subtle refusal to support the managers' efforts. Or staff groups battle with each other for control of new "problem areas," with the result that no one really handles the issue at all. To cope with their essential powerlessness, staff groups may try to elevate their own status and draw boundaries between themselves and others.

When staff jobs are treated as final resting places for people who have reached their level of competence in the organization—a good shelf on which to dump managers who are too old to go anywhere but too young to retire—then staff groups can also become pockets of conservatism, resistant to change. Their own exclusion from the risk-taking action may make them resist *anyone's* innovative proposals. In the past, personnel departments, for example, have sometimes been the last in their organization to know about innovations in human resource development or to be interested in applying them.

Top executives

Despite the great resources and responsibilities concentrated at the top of an organization, leaders can be powerless for reasons that are not very different from those that affect staff and supervisors: lack of supplies, information, and support.

We have faith in leaders because of their ability to make things happen in the larger world, to create possibilities for everyone else, and to attract resources to the organization. These are their supplies. But influence outward—the source of much credibility downward—can diminish as environments change, setting terms and conditions out of the control of the leaders. Regardless of top management's grand plans for the organization, the environment presses. At the very least, things going on outside the organization can deflect a leader's attention and drain energy. And, more detrimental, decisions made elsewhere can have severe consequences for the organization and affect top management's sense of power and thus its operating style inside.

Consider the changes in the role of CEOs in the United States over the last decades. In the expanding economy of the 1960s and 1970s, for example, when American technology still dominated world markets, nearly every major corporation officer or head of a large organization could look—and therefore feel—successful. In Europe, national champions dominated protected country markets. Easy success gave such leaders a great deal of credibility inside the organization, which in turn gave them the power to put new things in motion.

In more recent decades, industry turmoil and challenging global competition has reduced the power of top management in traditional industries undergoing massive change. The capacity of many organization leaders to influence the external environment has created new limits. A changing set of "new " players have flexed their power muscles: the Arab oil bloc, Japanese manufacturing giants, institutional investors and corporate raiders, government regulators opening up markets to competition, or congressional investigating committees. And managing declining or saturated markets is quite different from managing growth. It is no accident that when top leaders personally feel out of control, the control function in corporations grows.

As powerlessness in lower levels of organizations can manifest itself in overly routinized jobs where performance measures are oriented to rules and absence of change, so it can at upper levels as well. Routine work often drives out nonroutine work. Accomplishment becomes a question of nailing down details. It appears easier to slash costs or announce a downsizing than to make strategic moves to grow revenues; top managers can command cost-reduction, but they cannot command customers to buy their products. Short-term results provide immediate gratifications and satisfy stockholders or other constituencies with limited interests.

It takes a powerful leader to be willing to risk short-term deprivations in order to bring about desired long-term outcomes. Much as first-line supervisors are tempted to focus on daily adherence to rules, leaders are tempted to focus on short-term fluctuations and lose sight of long-term objectives. They are tempted to jump in themselves to solve problems, like the CEO of a consumer goods company who decided that he personally was the only one who could rescue a failing division, so he immersed himself in operating details—which grabbed power from the managers with the expertise to work on the problem. The dynamics of such a situation are self-reinforcing. The more the long-term goals go unattended, the more a leader feels powerless and the greater the scramble to prove that he or she is in control of daily events at least. The more he is involved in the organization as a short-term Mr. Fix-it, the more out of control of long-term objectives he is, and the more ultimately powerless he is likely to be.

Credibility for top executives often comes from doing the extraordinary: exercising discretion, creating, inventing, planning, and acting in nonroutine ways. But since routine problems look easier and more manageable, require less change and consent on the part of anyone else, and lend themselves to instant solutions that can make any leader look good temporarily, leaders may avoid the risky by taking over what their subordinates should be doing. Ultimately, a leader may succeed in getting all the trivial problems dumped on his or her desk. This can establish expectations even for leaders attempting more challenging tasks. When Warren Bennis was president of the University of Cincinnati, a professor called him because the heat was off in a classroom. In writing about this incident, Bennis commented, "I suppose he expected me to grab a wrench and fix it."

People at the top need to insulate themselves from the routine operations of the organization in order to develop and exercise power. But this very insulation can lead to another source of powerlessness—lack of information. In one multinational corporation, top executives who are sealed off in a large, distant office, flattered and virtually babied by aides, are frustrated by their distance from the real action.

At the top, the concern for secrecy and privacy is mixed with real loneliness. In one bank, organization members were so accustomed to never seeing the top leaders that when a new senior vice president went to the branch offices to look around, they had suspicion, even fear, about his intentions.

Thus leaders who are cut out of an organization's information networks understand neither what is really going on at lower levels nor that their own isolation may be having negative effects. All too often top executives design "beneficial" new employee programs or declare a new humanitarian policy (e.g., "Participatory management is now our style") only to find the policy ignored or mistrusted because it is perceived as coming from uncaring bosses.

The information gap has more serious consequences when executives are so insulated from the rest of the organization or from other decision makers that they fail to see their own impending downfall—a tragedy of political leaders as well. Such insulation is partly a matter of organizational position and, in some cases, of executive style.

For example, leaders may create closed inner circles consisting of "doppelgängers," people just like themselves, who are their principal sources of organizational information and tell them only what they want to know. The reasons for the distortions are varied: key aides want to relieve the leader of burdens, they think just like the leader, they want to protect their own positions of power, or the familiar "kill the messenger" syndrome makes people close to top executives reluctant to be the bearers of bad news.

Finally, just as supervisors and lower-level managers need their supporters in order to be and feel powerful, so do top executives. But for them sponsorship may not be so much a matter of individual endorsement as an issue of support by larger sources of legitimacy in the society. For top executives the problem is not to fit in among peers; rather, the question is whether the public at large and other organization members perceive a common interest which they see the executives as promoting. If, however, public sources of support are withdrawn and leaders are open to public attack or if inside constituencies fragment and employees see their interests better aligned with pressure groups than with organizational leadership, then powerlessness begins to set in.

When common purpose is lost, the system's own politics may reduce the capacity of those at the top to act. Just as managing decline seems to create a much more passive and reactive stance than managing growth, so does mediating among conflicting interests. When what is happening outside and inside their organizations is out of their control, many people at the top turn into decline managers and dispute mediators. Neither is a particularly empowering role.

Thus when top executives lose their own lines of supply, lines of information, and lines of support, they too suffer from a kind of powerlessness. The temptation for them then is to pull in every shred of power they can and to decrease the power available to other people to act. Innovation loses out in favor of control. Limits rather than targets are set. Financial goals are met by reducing "overhead" (people) rather than by giving people the tools and discretion to increase their own productive capacity. Dictatorial statements come down from the top, spreading the mentality of powerlessness farther until the whole organization becomes sluggish and people concentrate on protecting what they have rather than on producing what they can.

When everyone is playing "king of the mountain," guarding his or her turf jealously, then king of the mountain becomes the only game in town.

To Expand Power, Share it

In no case am I saying that people in the three hierarchical levels described are always powerless, but they are susceptible to common conditions that can contribute to powerlessness. *Table 13-3* summarizes the most common symptoms of powerlessness for each level and some typical sources of that behavior.

I am also distinguishing the tremendous concentration of economic and political power in large corporations themselves from the powerlessness that can beset individuals even in the highest positions in such organizations. What grows with organizational position in hierarchical levels is not necessarily the power to accomplish—productive power—but the power to punish, to prevent, to sell off, to reduce, to fire, all without appropriate concern for consequences. It is that kind of power—oppressive power—that we often say corrupts.

The absence of ways to prevent individual and social harm causes the polity to feel it must surround people in power with constraints, regulations, and laws that limit the arbitrary use of their authority. But if oppressive power corrupts, then so does the absence of productive power. In large organizations, powerlessness can be a bigger problem than power.

In a classic and still-timely book, *Power: The Inner Experience,* psychologist David C. McClelland made a similar distinction between oppressive and productive power:

> The negative . . . face of power is characterized by the dominance-submission mode: if I win, you lose. . . . It leads to simple and direct means of feeling powerful [such as being aggressive]. It does not often lead to effective social leadership for the reason that such a person tends to treat other people as pawns. People who feel they are pawns tend to be passive and useless to the leader who gets his satisfaction from dominating them. Slaves are the most inefficient form of labor ever devised by man. If a leader wants to have far-reaching influence, he must make his followers feel powerful and able to accomplish things on their own. . . . Even the most dictatorial leader does not succeed if he has not instilled in at least some of his followers a sense of power and the strength to pursue the goals he has set.

Table 13-3. Common symptoms and sources of powerlessness for three key organizational positions

Position	Symptoms	Sources
First-line supervisors	Close, rules-minded supervision	Routine, rules-minded jobs with little control over lines of supply
	Tendency to do things oneself, blocking of subordinates' development and information	Limited lines of information
	Resistant, underproducing subordinates	Limited advancement or involvement prospects for oneself/subordinates
Staff professionals	Turf protection, information control	Routine tasks seen as peripheral to "real tasks" of line organization
	Retreat into professionalism	Blocked careers
	Conservative resistance to change	Easy replacement by outside experts
Top executives	Focus on internal cutting, short-term results, "punishing"	Uncontrollable lines of supply because of environmental changes
	Dictatorial top-down communications	Limited or blocked lines of information about lower levels of organization
	Retreat to comfort of like-minded lieutenants	Diminished lines of support because of challenges to legitimacy (e.g., from the public or special interest groups)

Organizational power can grow, in part, by being shared. We do not yet know enough about new organizational forms to say whether productive power is infinitely expandable or where we reach the point of diminishing returns. But we do know that sharing power is different from giving or throwing it away. Delegation does not mean abdication.

Some basic lessons could be translated from the field of economics to the realm of organizations and management. Capital investment in plants and equipment is not the only key to productivity. The productive capacity of nations, like organizations, grows if the skill base is upgraded. People with the tools, information, and support to make more informed decisions and act more quickly can often accomplish more. By empowering others, a leader does not decrease his power; instead he may increase it—especially if the whole organization performs better.

This analysis leads to some counterintuitive conclusions. In a certain tautological sense, the principal problem of the powerless is that they lack power. Powerless people are usually the last ones to whom anyone wants to entrust more power, for fear of its dissipation or abuse. But those people are precisely the ones who might benefit most from an injection of power and whose behavior is likely to change as new options open up to them.

Also, if the powerless bosses could be encouraged to share some of the power they do have, their power would grow. Yet, of course, only those leaders who feel secure about their own power outward—their lines of supply, information, and support—can see empowering subordinates as a gain rather than a loss. The two sides of power (getting it and giving it) are closely connected.

There are important lessons here for both subordinates and those who want to change organizations, whether executives or change agents. Instead of resisting or criticizing a powerless boss, which only increases the boss's feeling of powerlessness and need to control, subordinates instead might concentrate on helping the boss become more powerful. Managers might make pockets of ineffectiveness in the organization more productive not by training or replacing individuals but by structural solutions such as opening supply and support lines.

Similarly, organizational change agents who want a new program or policy to succeed should make sure that the change itself does not render any other level of the organization powerless. In making changes, it is wise to make sure that the key people in the level or two directly above and in neighboring functions are sufficiently involved, informed, and taken into account, so that the program can be used to build their own sense of power also. If such involvement is impossible, then it is better to move these people out of the territory altogether than to leave behind a group from whom some power has been removed and who might resist and undercut the program.

In part, of course, spreading power means educating people to this new definition of it. But words alone will not make the difference; managers will need the real experience of a new way of managing.

Here is how the associate director of a large corporate professional department phrased the lessons that he learned in the transition to a team-oriented, participatory, power-sharing management process.

"Get in the habit of involving your own managers in decision making and approvals. But don't abdicate! Tell them what you want and where you're coming from. Don't go for a one-boss grass roots 'democracy.' Make the management hierarchy work for you in participation.

"Hang in there, baby, and don't give up. Try not to 'revert' just because everything seems to go sour on a particular day. Open up—talk to people and tell them how you feel. They'll want to get you back on track and will do things to make that happen—because they don't really want to go back to the way it was. Subordinates will push you to 'act more like a boss,' but their interest is usually more in seeing someone else brought to heel than getting bossed themselves."

Naturally, people need to have power before they can learn to share it. Exhorting managers to change their leadership styles is rarely useful by itself. In one large plant of a major electronics company, firstline production supervisors were the source of numerous complaints from managers who saw them as major roadblocks to overall plant productivity and as insufficiently skilled supervisors. So the plant personnel staff undertook two pilot programs to increase the supervisors' effectiveness. The first program was based on a traditional competency and training model aimed at teaching the specific skills of successful supervisors. The second program, in contrast, was designed to empower the supervisors by directly affecting their flexibility, access to resources, connections with higher-level officials, and control over working conditions.

After an initial gathering of data from supervisors and their subordinates, the change team held meetings where all the supervisors were given tools for developing action plans for sharing the data with their people and collaborating on solutions to perceived problems. But then, in a departure from common practice in this organization, task forces of supervisors were formed to develop new systems for handling job and career issues common to them and their people. These task forces were given budgets, consultants, representation on a plantwide project steering committee alongside managers at much higher levels, and wide latitude in defining the nature and scope of the changes they wished to make. In short, lines of supply, information, and support were opened to them.

As the task forces progressed in their activities, it became clear to the plant management that the hoped-for changes in supervisory effectiveness were taking place much more rapidly through these structural changes in power than through conventional management training; so the conventional training was dropped. Not only did the pilot groups design useful new procedures for the plant, astonishing senior management in several cases with their knowledge and capabilities, but also, significantly, they learned to manage their own people better.

Several groups decided to involve shop-floor workers in their task forces; they could now see from their own experience the benefits of involving subordinates in solving job-related problems. Other supervisors began to experiment with ways to implement "participatory management" by giving subordinates more control and influence without relinquishing their own authority.

Soon the "problem supervisors" in the "most troubled plant in the company" were getting the highest possible performance ratings and were considered models for direct production management. The sharing of organizational power from the top made possible the productive use of power below.

One might wonder why more organizations do not adopt such empowering strategies. There are standard answers: that giving up control is threatening to people who have fought for every shred of it; that people do not want to share power with those they look down on; that managers fear losing their own place and special privileges in the system; that "predictability" often rates higher than "flexibility" as an organizational value; and so forth.

But I would also put skepticism about employee abilities high on the list. Many modern bureaucratic systems are designed to minimize dependence on individual intelligence by making routine as many decisions as possible. So it often comes as a genuine surprise to top executives that people doing the more routine jobs could, indeed, make sophisticated decisions or use resources entrusted to them in intelligent ways.

In the same electronics company just mentioned, at the end of a quarter the pilot supervisory task forces were asked to report results and plans to senior management in order to have their new budget requests approved. The task forces made sure they were well prepared, and the high-level executives were duly impressed. In fact, they were so impressed that they kept interrupting the presentations with compliments, remarking that the supervisors could easily be doing sophisticated personnel work.

At first the supervisors were flattered. Such praise from upper management could only be taken well. But when the first glow wore off, several of them became very angry. They saw the excessive praise as patronizing and insulting. "Didn't they think we could think? Didn't they imagine we were capable of doing this kind of work?" one asked. "They must have seen us as just a bunch of animals. No wonder they gave us such limited jobs."

As far as these supervisors were concerned, their abilities had always been there, in latent form perhaps, but still there. They as individuals had not changed—just their organizational power.

14

Discipline!

In the Western calendar, January is the month of the diet. Throughout diverse cultures in Europe and North America, New Year's resolutions inevitably contain a common element. After a period of holiday gluttony, people vow that *this* year they will get disciplined—and skinnier.

For business, the 1990s has seemed like the decade of the diet. First worldwide recession, then more intense global competition made controlling costs and raising quality more essential than ever. Financial institutions and other businesses that gorged in the 1980s—gobbling up acquisitions or running up debt—are faced in the 1990s with a choice between dieting or disappearing.

Dieting requires discipline, or as the French say, *le régime.* Consistently successful companies such as Emerson Electric are often characterized by consistently practiced regimens involving collective disciplines—shared approaches to problems and decisions. Indeed, to use some of the newest ideas in management (total quality, work force empowerment, or team self-management), businesses must first return to one of the oldest: the discipline of common methodologies and measures throughout the organization.

Capitalist systems are sometimes praised for their tapping the power of self-interest—the desire of people to improve their lot, as well as to leave the world a better place. British privatization has been touted for strengthening the services provided to the public by more efficient companies. Herbert Henzler, an expert at McKinsey in Europe, argued that the creative pressure of the free market that has now moved from western to eastern Germany will help individuals earn high rewards that coincide with benefits to society. In Japan, SOFTBANK's Masayoshi Son represents the new breed of entrepreneurs who succeed through self-interest and single-minded persistence.

But self-interest alone does not produce effective organizations, even when it is balanced by self-restraint. Empowerment cannot mean setting everyone loose to do whatever they want, however they want to do it. Organizations must also solve the control problem: how to get guidance and coherence in light of complex activities, diverse people and the need for speed and innovation.

One solution is to encourage professionalism at every level by teaching common disciplines. Professionals, whether physicians, chefs, or engineers, share a knowledge base, methodology, and standards of excellence that characterize a community of practitioners. Elaborate training, peer review, and ethical codes encourage application of knowledge to high standards with minimal supervision. Furthermore, professionals generally advance in their careers by adding knowledge, not by climbing a job ladder. Professional disciplines ensure control and coherence without elaborate hierarchies of supervision.

Business disciplines have the same effect. Planning processes used throughout Emerson Electric provide a common approach to business strategy and allow comparisons across business units, so divisions work autonomously and there is no need for a large central headquarters staff. In Procter & Gamble's most advanced factories, work teams can function largely without managers thanks to a set of operating disciplines; workers are paid on the basis of their knowledge of these different disciplines. To build professionalism in frontline retail workers, the BhS chain is encouraging store sales personnel to take the British national retail exams, increasing their pay for each level of competence they attain.

Disciplines can also help solve the problem of delegation. To gain speed as well as efficiency, organizations have to delegate operational decisions and the pursuit of innovation. Top management cannot tell those below what decision to make in every circumstance. But while leaders cannot specify exactly what should be done in every circumstance, they can provide a *methodology* for analyzing and approaching tasks—the teaching function of leaders.

Process disciplines establish control that does not constrain. Total quality management (TQM) programs, for example, provide a common set of analytic and problem-solving techniques to be used in every part of the organization, regardless of the subdisciplines involved in particular functions like engineering or marketing. The "inspiration" part of quality programs (leaders encouraging quality values) is often less important than the "perspiration" component (people using analytic tools to manage difficult trade-offs on their own). Process disciplines such as planning routines or problem-solving techniques guide action without constraining the form that action takes. And it is easier for people to work together when they share such disciplines.

Xerox's decade-long quality effort replaced inefficient bureaucracy (costly layers of supervision and narrowly defined job charters) with empowerment-through-discipline. People learned how to analyze problems, display data, and hold meetings to find solutions. Now Xerox managers can trust people to do the right thing, because they know the mental habits and behavioral routines people will use.

For many employees, quality programs represent the first time that they have been treated as professionals and given analytic tools with which to assess problems and make decisions. In Fort Lauderdale, Florida, for example, quality improvement techniques involved all 2,300 city employees in the budgeting process.

Shared disciplines facilitate teamwork and allow organizational flexibility. People can get to work faster—and more easily work together in new groupings—when they share a methodology, or planning and problem-solving framework. While different approaches might work equally well, the important thing in a disciplined organization is that everyone uses the *same* approach. People can stop wondering about how to get started, or arguing about whose way is better, and just get on with it.

Teamwork goes up and costs go down in disciplined organizations. In a highly rated cost-efficient medical clinic, nurses and physicians operate as a team, seeing patients interchangeably. Because they have all learned to go through exactly the same steps, each can pick up on the process at any point, ensuring that patients do not have to wait for any particular professional to be available. Similarly, Legal Sea Foods, a small chain of crowded popular restaurants in the Boston area offering high quality at low prices, gains efficiency because waiters and waitresses act as a team—performing any task for any customer whenever they are nearby, then pooling and sharing tips.

Process disciplines, used in a consistent fashion throughout an organization, permit people to take more responsibility, even people who are viewed as "poorly skilled" or "not yet ready to work without supervision." At a recent gathering in Jakarta, for example, Indonesian managers wondered whether new management philosophies stressing flatter organizations and a minimum of hierarchy were applicable to their less sophisticated work force. The answer lies in giving people a set of specific process tools. The Institute of Cultural Affairs, a worldwide not-for-profit network of facilitators, devised a nuts-and-bolts technology of participation (called ToP) for community development in third-world countries. In a kind of reverse technology transfer, ToP has now spread from mountaintop retreats in Jamaica to the boardrooms of Brussels.

Common disciplines also help organizations manage cultural and racial diversity. Whenever people can be taught a common methodology, they can communicate more easily with fewer misunderstandings or conflicts. Engineers from Asia, North America, and Europe who work together in a London-based high technology venture find that the power of their shared discipline transcends their cultural differences.

Whenever there are clear standards and certifiable training in known methodologies, equal opportunity is more likely to prevail. By putting promising minority youth through a rigorous, highly disciplined program, Reginald Dickson's Inroads lays the foundation for its graduates to learn other disciplines in the corporations that hire them.

When people share a methodology, they can check each other's work and count on each other's results. To do this effectively, however, they need performance data. Professional discipline is aided by measures that enable professionals to monitor and correct their own work. Robert Kaplan and David Norton's "balanced scorecard" adds three important measures to the more traditional financial ones: customer satisfaction, internal operational processes, and innovation and improvement activities. Just as these measures are too strategically important to be designed by the control function, they are too tactically important to be reported only to top management. Banc One Corporation's success at balancing local autonomy with systemwide coherence rested on an elaborate set of identical process measures reported to every unit every month.

Of course, even discipline is subject to excess. Disciplines can become mindless rituals, empty exercises that substitute for thinking. Methodologies can become outmoded. Planning can become a fetish, with plans detached from reality. Measures can substitute for goals, as when people try to get high scores rather than results. One chemical company's effort to establish planning disciplines degenerated into silly jargon, such as the need to speak "comvoc" (its "common vocabulary").

Disciplines are not necessarily antithetical to creativity, however. They can be the grounding that permits creativity. After all, intuition often stems from deep knowledge gained through constant practice, which then permits imaginative leaps.

The key to discipline is always consistent practice. Diets, whether to lose weight or shed corporate costs, work because a regimen is practiced day after day after day, year after year after year.

And not just in January.

15

A Walk on the Soft Side

A man drove up to a gasoline pump to get his gas tank filled. The gas station attendant noticed three penguins in the back seat of the car and, curious, asked about them.

"I don't know how they got there," the driver said. "They were in the car when I took it out of the garage this morning."

The attendant thought for a moment. "Why don't you take them to the zoo?"

"Good idea," the driver replied and drove away.

The next day, the same man returned to the same gas station. In the back seat were the same three penguins, but now they wore sunglasses.

The attendant looked at the car in surprise. "I thought you took them to the zoo!" she exclaimed.

"I did," the driver said. "And they had such a good time that today I decided to take them to the beach."

People talk past one another all too frequently in organizations. But most of the time it's not as funny as three penguins at the beach.

Now, more than ever, businesses must rely on good communication across organizational boundaries. Brainpower in search of partners is an apt description of the situation facing many companies, and many departments inside companies. The sharing and use of ideas is as important as their development.

To promote innovation, businesses need to tap and share "soft knowledge"—insights, intuitions, and hunches. To raise productivity, they must unravel and explain the mysteries of knowledge and service workers' craft, which involves skills and insights not captured in job manuals. To increase quality, they should promote understanding across functions and learning across companies. To drive expansion, businesses need flexible relationships with allies in other countries. And to build teams, managers must be sensitive to difficult dilemmas faced by employees with diverse lifestyles.

When communication takes place across differences of background, training, professional expertise, or national culture, the opportunities for missed messages multiply.

In theory, there can be as many ways to interpret a situation as there are people in it. The classic film *Rashomon* turned on the striking differences in how the same event was described by four participants—each convinced his or her version was the right one.

People easily become fixated on their own interpretations of reality, unable to see or hear different views. Try asking people to make a human figure from the pieces of a square like the one on this page *(Figure 15-1)*. Some will give up in frustration; others find the "only" solution. In fact, dozens of human silhouettes and a thousand other shapes are possible *(Figure 15-2)*. When people listen to each other, more creative solutions happen.

Leaders have always faced communication challenges. But the same lessons need to be learned again and again. Consider how relevant classic lessons about listening skills preached by psychologists for decades are to high performance teams in companies that try to learn subtle skills from experts, or how applicable traditional systems such as open employee meetings or suggestion systems are to fast growth companies seeking innovation. Leaders

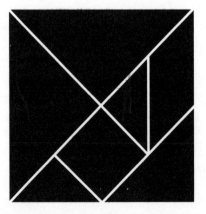

Figure 15-1. Can you make human figures from this square? Use all seven pieces without overlapping them.

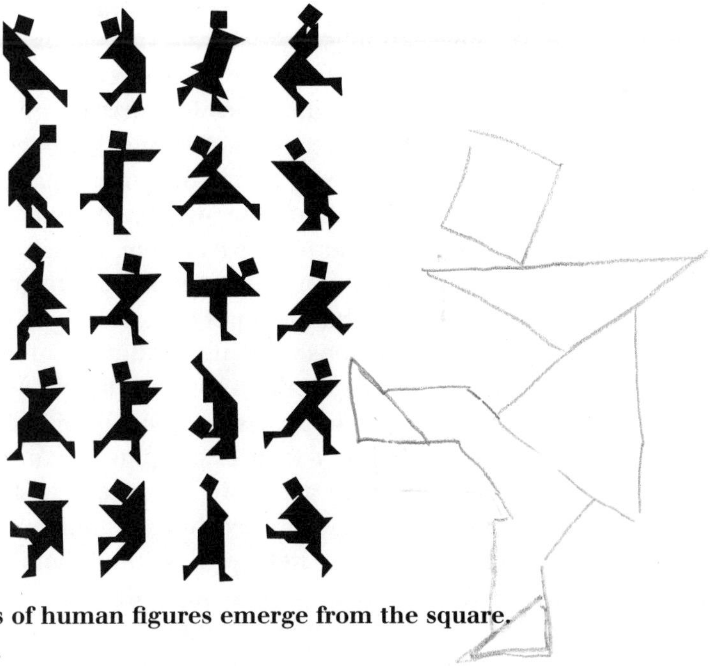

Figure 15-2. Dozens of human figures emerge from the square. Here are just a few.

still need to listen, carefully, and they need to open the channels for others to talk, listen, contribute, and reflect. They need to encourage people to tell each other stories—that's the essence of the sharing of best practices—and to understand them the same way to build a culture of organizational learning.

Open communication that leads to shared knowledge is easier when organizations are relatively homogeneous, as in Japan—or when everyone in them shares the same aspirations. But when people take pride in emphasizing their differences and seek sovereignty for their own cultural group (as in current movements throughout splintering Eastern Europe), the ability to take another's perspective which is fundamental to good listening becomes both more difficult and more essential. Indeed, many managers consider cultural differences the number one barrier to successful alliances and partnerships.

Sometimes relationships improve when participants listen to feedback about how others perceive the same situation. One executive from the United States who now heads a British company learned by trial and error that behavior lauded in his previous American jobs as "decisive" was considered "pushy" by his new European organization. But often it is important to go further. Irene Rodgers, director of a Paris-based consulting firm, analyzed breakdowns in negotiations between Anglo-Saxon and French managers. She found that participants often lacked concrete knowledge about the organizational context from which their adversaries came. For example, British interviewees felt the French took too much time in negotiations and attributed this to their cultural emphasis on personal relationships. In fact, in many French organizations, the negotiator is often not the decision maker; he chats to fill the time until he can get to the boss.

Understanding context is one part of effective communication. The other is making tacit assumptions explicit—that is, making personal knowledge accessible to others, as Japanese expert Ikujiro Nonaka puts it. "The learning organization must be a teaching organization" to help professionals analyze their work and spread their craft to others. According to Nonaka, the ability to translate subjective understandings into objective information is exactly what makes Japanese organizations learning-rich innovators. Similarly, judges for the U.S. Malcolm Baldrige National Quality Award have reported that they want to see the subtle harmony that occurs when functions are tuned to the same wavelength translated into hard indicators of performance. People must be willing to articulate what they know, share what they feel, and make others aware of their assumptions and ways of working.

Even so, no amount of sharing and communicating may be enough to overcome barriers between organizations or people. Sometimes people want to see things differently because of what they stand to gain or lose. In cross-border alliances, disagreements often reflect divergent strategies, not national misunderstandings. Tensions increase when both partners are strong, presumably because both have interests they can legitimately push. Thus the effectiveness of soft management depends on a number of hard realities. Unbalanced incentives can interfere with any relationship regardless of how well those involved understand each other.

Some conflicts that supposedly reflect cultural differences are really power struggles. In one European airline consortium, the Italian representative succeeded in having a major project named after an Italian hero. One British observer thought this was because Italians are especially conscious of symbols; however, others suggested it was an example of a smaller partner seizing any opportunity to assert its will over larger, more important partners. Understanding Italian culture would not have helped in this situation as much as a grasp of power dynamics. Even the best listening skills cannot paper over power games.

Furthermore, the soft side of management is inevitably imperfect. The more managers acknowledge their vulnerabilities, the more chances there are to slip. When information is widely shared, mistakes or setbacks are more likely to be exposed. Increased communication simply whets the appetite for more, which explains why some of the corporations known for good communication still get low ratings on employee surveys. As high-participation organizations have discovered, employee expectations about how much say they have in a business often cannot be fulfilled by management.

Willingness to be exposed has a cultural component. Americans are noted for self-disclosure as well as their interest in the inner workings of others. International participants in Harvard's Advanced Management Program marvel at the willingness of Americans to discuss organizational matters Europeans and Japanese consider private company secrets. (One Japanese executive confessed that his company sends people to U.S. business schools for just that reason.) Perhaps Japanese organizations appear so perfect to Westerners because so little is known about them from inside. When a glimpse of the private side is permitted, cracks appear in the facade of harmony and consensus.

There is nothing cushy about the soft side of management. It involves hard work. But a sense of humor can help smooth the rougher spots. *Now where should we take those penguins today . . . ?*

16

The Attack on Pay

Status, not contribution, was traditionally the basis for the numbers on employees' paychecks. Pay reflected where jobs rank in the corporate hierarchy—not what comes out of them.

Today this system is under attack. More and more senior executives are trying to turn their employees into entrepreneurs—people who earn a direct return on the value they help create, often in exchange for putting their pay at risk. In the process, changes are coming into play that will have revolutionary consequences for companies and their employees. For example:

- To control costs and stimulate improvements, a leading financial services company converts its information systems department into a venture that sells its services both inside and outside the corporation. In its first year, the department runs at a big profit and employees begin to wonder why they can't get a chunk of the profits they have generated instead of just a fixed salary defined by rank.

- In exchange for wage concessions, a manufacturer offers employees an ownership stake. Employee representatives begin to think about total company profitability and start asking why so many managers are on the payroll and why they are paid so much.

- To encourage initiative in reaching performance targets, a city government offers large salary increases to managers who can show major departmental improvements. After a few years, the amount in managers' paychecks bears little relationship to their levels in the organization.

In traditional compensation plans, each job comes with a pay level that stays about the same regardless of how well the job is performed or what the real organizational value of that performance is. Pay scales reflect such estimated characteristics as deci-sion-making responsibility, importance to the organization, and number of subordinates. If there is a merit component, it is usually very small. The surest way—often the only way—to increase one's pay is to change employers or get promoted. A mountain of tradi-tion and industrial relations practice has built up to support this way of calculating pay.

Proponents of this system customarily assert that the market ultimately determines pay, just as it determines the price of every-thing else that buyers wish to acquire. Compensation systems cannot be unfair or inappropriate, therefore, because they are incapable of causing anything. Actually, however, because it is so difficult to link people's compensation directly to their contribu-tions, all the market really does is allow us to assume that people occupying equal positions tend to be paid equally and that people with similar experience and education tend to be worth about the same. So while the market works in macroeconomic terms, the process at a microeconomic level is circular: we know what people are worth because that's what they cost in the job market; but we also know that what people cost in the market is just what they're worth.

Given logic like this, it's not hard to see why such strange bed-fellows as feminist activists and entrepreneurially minded manag-ers both attack this traditional system as a manifestation of the paternalistic benefits offered across the board by Father Corpora-tion. "We've got corporate socialism, not corporate capitalism," charged the manager of new ventures for a large industrial com-pany. "We're so focused on consistent treatment internally that we destroy enterprise in the process."

These old arrangements are no longer supportable. For eco-nomic, social, and organizational reasons, the fundamental bases for determining pay are under attack. And while popular attention has focused on comparable worth—equalizing pay for those doing comparable work—the most important trend has been the loosen-ing relationship between job assignment and pay level.

Four separate but closely related concerns are driving employ-ers to rethink the meaning of worth and look beyond job assign-ments in determining pay—equity, cost, productivity, and the re-wards of entrepreneurship.

It's Not Fair!

Numerous surveys in large corporations have shown a decline in the number of employees willing to say that traditional pay practices are fair. Moreover, top management compensation has been assailed by the public, the media, and some politicians as unjustifiably high, especially when executives get large bonuses while their companies suffer financial losses or are just recovering from them.

Despite economic data showing an association between executive compensation and company performance, many professionals still argue that absolute amounts are excessive and reflect high status rather than good performance. Likewise, the existence of layers on layers of highly paid managers no longer seems entirely fair. Employees question why executives should be able to capture returns others actually produce. And they are beginning to resent compensation plans like the one in a leading well-run bank that gives managers bonuses of up to 30% of their pay for excellent branch performance, while branch employees get annual increases of only 6% to 8%.

If executives get bonuses for raising profits, many urge, so should the workers who contribute to those profits. Indeed, this is the theory behind profit sharing in general. Although there are many specific variations, such programs have in common the very appealing and well-accepted notion that all employees—not just management—should share in the gains from enhanced performance.

Profit sharing is ordinarily a straightforward arrangement in which a fraction of the net profits from some period of operation are distributed to employees. The distribution may be either immediate or deferred, and the plan may not include all employees.

The long-standing plan at Lincoln Electric, the world's largest manufacturer of arc-welding products, is particularly generous. Every year, Lincoln pays out 6% of net income in common stock dividends—the "wages of capital." The board determines another sum to be set aside as seed money for investment in the future. The balance, paid to all employees, ranges from 20% of wages and salary, already competitive, to more than 120%. The company remained profitable even in the face of sales declines during recessions, to the benefit of employees as well as stockholders.

Overall, probably about a half million companies have some form of profit sharing, if both deferred and cash payouts are included. In private enterprises other than those categorized as small businesses, government statistics show that by 1983 19% of all production employees, 27% of all technical and clerical employees, and 23% of all professional and administrative employees were covered by profit-sharing agreements.

The variant known as gain-sharing takes profit-sharing one giant step further by attempting, usually with some elaborate formula, to calculate the contributions of specific groups of employees whose contingent pay depends on those varying results. Although the basis for calculation varies from one gain-sharing plan to another, the plans have two principles in common: first, the payout reflects the contribution of groups rather than individuals (on the theory that teams and collective effort are what count), and second, the rewards to be shared and the plan for their distribution are based on objective, measurable characteristics (so that everyone can see what is owed and when).

In the United States, estimates vary about the use of gain-sharing; one study estimated that it was in use in several thousand companies by 1987. These programs already involve millions of workers and seem to be growing in popularity. The Scanlon Plan, probably the oldest, best-known, and most elaborate gain-sharing system, usually distributes 75% of gains to employees and 25% to the company. In addition, this plan is organized around complex mechanisms and procedures that spell out how employees at various levels are to participate, not only in control of the process but also in opportunities to help improve performance and thereby their own shares. At Herman Miller, Inc., gain-sharing is described not simply as a compensation system but rather as a way of life for the company.

Group or all-employee bonuses, especially when linked to specific performance indicators, provide another way to share some of the benefits of good performance more equitably. But evidence shows that their potential far exceeds their use. Although group performance bonuses are continuing to grow, top executives are much more likely to capture a portion of the benefits of increased profitability than employees are. In a Conference Board study of 491 companies, 58% had top executive bonus plans but only 11% had profit-sharing plans, 8% all-employee bonuses, 3% group productivity incentives, and fewer than 1% group cost-control incentives.

Performance-related compensation plans generally ignore employees other than top management and, to a lesser extent, some middle managers. And even in incentive-conscious high-technology companies, gain sharing is rare. While more than half the high-tech companies included in a Hay Associates compensation survey had cash or stock awards for individuals, only 6% had gain-sharing or group profit-sharing programs. Concerns about equity—including those framed in terms of comparable worth—are not altogether misplaced.

Companies have long been concerned with one fundamental fairness issue—the relative compensation of employees in general. Now, however, they face two new issues that are complex, hard to resolve, and rapidly getting worse. The first, evident in the debate over gain-sharing and profit-sharing, considers what employees get against what the organization gets from their efforts. The second, evident in the debate over comparable worth, is how groups in an organization fare in relation to each other. At the very least, these issues call for better measurement systems or new principles on which various constituencies can agree.

Let Them Eat Dividends

Facing greater challenges from competition for cost-and-value-conscious customers, companies in every field are seeking ways to reduce fixed labor costs. One sure way is to peg pay to performance—the company's as well as the individual's. Merit awards, bonuses, and profit-sharing plans hold out the promise of extra earnings for those who truly contribute. But it is their cost-reduction potential that really makes executives' eyes sparkle with dollar signs.

Making pay float to reflect company performance is the cornerstone of MIT economist Martin L. Weitzman's proposal for a "share economy." If many companies can be induced to share profits or revenues with their employees, Weitzman argued, then the cure for stagflation would be at hand. Among other things, companies would have an incentive to create jobs because more workers would be paid only in proportion to what they have brought in.

For companies themselves, these macroeconomic implications are a lot less tantalizing than the more immediate benefits to be gained by asking workers to take their lumps from business cycles—or, employees would add, poor management decisions—along with their companies. Moreover, a similar logic clearly accounts for some of the appeal of employee ownership, especially to companies in industries where deregulation has created enormous cost competitiveness. According to one recent book about employee ownership, *Taking Stock: Employee Ownership at Work,* the wave of deregulation in the 1980s encouraged at least 6 major airlines and 15 trucking companies to adopt employee ownership plans. Overall, the authors estimated that some 11 million employees in 8,000-plus businesses now own at least 15% of the companies employing them.

While many companies have found employee ownership attractive primarily as a financing scheme, there is little doubt that, properly designed and managed, it can positively affect corporate success. Take Western Air Lines as an illustration. After losing $200 million over four years, this company created the Western Partnership by trading a 32.4% ownership stake, a meaningful profit-sharing plan, and four seats on the board of directors for wage cuts and productivity improvements of 22.5% to 30%. In 1985 Western distributed more than $10 million to its 10,000 employees—$100 each in cash and the rest in employees' accounts. When Western was sold to Delta as part of continuing industry consolidation, employees netted about $75 million on the sale.

Such schemes have obvious advantages over another highly visible alternative for fixed-labor-cost reduction—two-tier wage systems, which bring in new hires at a lower scale than current employees. Most of us can see the obvious inequity in paying two groups differently for doing exactly the same job. But pay pegged to actual performance? Earnings tied to company profits? What could be more fair? The clear problems—that lower paid employees cannot afford income swings as readily as the more highly paid and that employee efforts are not always directly related to company profitability—do not seem to deter the advocates.

In general, the fixed part of the paycheck is already shrinking in many American companies. Even the bonus is being used to supplement these efforts, especially among manufacturing companies, continuing a trend starting in the 1980s. The Bureau of National Affairs found that one-shot bonus payments, replacing general pay increases, were called for in almost 20% of all 1985 union contract settlements outside the construction industry, up from a mere 6% in 1984. Similarly, 20% of the 564 companies in Hewitt Associates' 1986 compensation survey gave one-time bonuses to white-collar workers, up from 7% in 1985. These one-time payments do not raise base pay, nor do they affect overtime calculations. In fact, just the opposite occurs: they reduce the cost of labor. More than two-thirds of the bonus provisions the BNA studied were accompanied by wage freezes or decreases.

Bucks for Behavior

The cost attack is one straightforward way for companies to become more competitive, at least in the short run. In the long run, however, pay variations or rewards, contingent on specific and measurable achievements of individuals at every level, are likely to be even more effective in stimulating employee enterprise and channeling behavior. What better way could there be, proponents argue, to help employees recognize what is most useful and to guide their efforts appropriately?

Merrill Lynch's compensation system for over 10,000 brokers, first introduced in 1986, is a good example. To encourage brokers to spend more time with larger, more active customers, the firm has cut commissions for most small trades and discounts and rewards the accumulation of assets under its management. The pay system was developed in direct response to new products like the firm's Cash Management Account because the old system wasn't adequate to reward performance in new and growing areas management wanted to stress.

Commissions and bonuses for sales personnel are standard practice in most industries, of course. What seem to be changing are the amounts people can earn (for example, more than double one's salary at General Electric Medical Systems' Sales and Service Division), the number of people who can earn them, and the variety of productivity bonuses, especially in highly competitive new industries.

Take PSICOR, a small Michigan company supplying equipment and professionals (called perfusionists) for open-heart surgery. Perfusionists are in great demand and frequently change employers, so founder Michael Dunaway searched for a way to give them immediate rewards because the standard 10% increase at the end of the year was too remote.

First he tried random bonuses of $100 to $500 for superior performance, but tracking proved difficult. Then he hit on the idea of continuous raises—increases in every paycheck—calculated to add up to at least a 5% annual raise over base salary, with up to 8% more in a lump sum at year-end based on overall performance. Employee response was positive, but the accounting department was soon drowning in paperwork.

PSICOR's third system combined quarterly raises of up to 5% a year, based solely on performance, with a series of additional bonuses to reward specific activities: higher caseloads, out-of-town assignments, professional certification, and the like. In response to this system, turnover declined to less than 2%, dropping to less than 1/2% for those employed two years or more.

Of course, some companies are going in exactly the opposite direction—for seemingly good reason. As an ex-director of sales compensation for IBM confessed, "We used to give bonuses and awards for every imaginable action by the sales force. But the more complex it got, the more difficult it was to administer, and the results were not convincing. When we began to ask ourselves why Digital Equipment had salespeople, who are tough competitors, on straight salary, we decided perhaps we'd gone overboard a bit." Even in commercial real estate leasing, long a highly performance-oriented business, one major and very effective Boston company—Leggat, McCall & Werner, Inc.—for years had its brokers on salary.

Nevertheless, the tide is moving in the other direction—toward more varied individual compensation based on people's own efforts. This trend reaches its fullest expression, however, not in pay-for-performance systems like those just described but in the scramble to devise ways to reward people in organizations for acting as if they were running their own businesses.

A Piece of the Action

The prospect of running a part of a large corporation as though it were an independent business is one of the hottest old-ideas-refurbished for the twenty-first century information age of virtual organizations. Many companies are encouraging potential entrepreneurs to remain within the corporate fold by paying them like owners when they develop new businesses. And even very traditional organizations are looking carefully at the possibility of setting up new ventures with a piece of the action for the entrepreneurs. "If one of our employees came along with a proposition, I'm not sure how anxious we'd be to do it," one bank executive said. "But ten years ago, we wouldn't have listened at all. We'd have said, 'You've got rocks in your head.'"

Most of the new entrepreneurial schemes pay people base salaries, generally equivalent to those of their former job levels, and ask them to put part of their compensation at risk, with their ownership percentage determined by their willingness to invest. This investment then substitutes for any other bonuses, perks, profit sharing, or special incentives they might have been able to earn in their former jobs. Sometimes the returns are based solely on percentages of the profits from their ventures; sometimes the returns come in the form of phantom stock pegged to the companies' public stock prices. Potential entrepreneurs cannot get as rich under this system as they could if they were full owners of independent businesses who shared ownership with other venture capitalists. But they are also taking much less risk.

AT&T was one of the large companies experimenting with ways to stimulate entrepreneurship by giving innovators a piece of the action when "intrapreneurship" was the flavor of the month. Its new venture development process spawned seven venture units over a three-year period, each sponsored by one of AT&T's lines of business, with the earliest growing to 90 employees by the time the seventh venture started. Venture participants were offered three compensation alternatives corresponding to three levels of risk.

Option one allowed venture participants to stick with the standard corporate compensation and benefits plan and to keep the salaries associated with their previous jobs. Not surprisingly, none of the seven chose this option.

Under option two, participants agreed to freeze their salaries at the levels of their last jobs and to forgo other contingent compensation until the venture generated a positive cash flow and the AT&T investment was paid back (or, with the concurrence of the venture board, until the business passed certain milestones). At that point, venture participants could get one-time bonuses equal to a maximum of 150% of their salaries. Five of the seven venture teams selected this option.

The third option, chosen by two self-confident bands of risk takers, came closest to simulating the independent entrepreneur's situation. Participants contributed to the venture's capitalization through paycheck deductions until the venture began to make money and generate a positive cash flow. Investments were limited only by the requirement that salaries remain above the minimum wage—to avoid legal problems and prevent people from using personal funds. In exchange, participants could gain up to eight times their total investment. Five years into the program, participants had put in from 12% to 25% of their salaries, and one of the two ventures had paid several bonuses at a rate just below the maximum. The other, a computer-graphics-board venture housed outside Indianapolis, was expected to return $890,000 to its 11 employee-investors by the program's seventh year.

The numbers show just how attractive AT&T employees found this program: ideas for new ventures began coming in before the program was announced, and in the planning year alone, 300 potential entrepreneurs developed proposals. About 2,000 ideas were submitted in the next five years, netting a venture formation rate of about 1 from every 250 ideas. People from every management level were funded, including a first-line supervisor and a senior officer.

Entrepreneurial incentives are especially prevalent at high-technology companies—not surprising given the importance and mobility of innovators. For example, a random sample of 105 Boston-area companies employing scientists and engineers compared the high-tech enterprises, dependent on R&D for product development, with their more traditional, established counterparts. The high-tech companies paid lower base salaries on average but offered more financial incentives, such as cash bonuses, stock options, and profit-sharing plans.

The entrepreneurial paycheck is on the rise wherever management thinks that people could do as well or better if they were in business for themselves—in high tech and no-tech alike. Au Bon Pain, a Boston-based international chain of bakeries and restaurants, created a partnership program to turn over a big piece of the action to store managers. Under the plan, annual revenues exceeding $170,000 per store were to be shared fifty-fifty with the partners.

If business developers and revenue growers are getting a chance to share in the returns, will inventors in the same companies be far behind? Probably not. The inventors' rights challenge is another nudge in the direction of entrepreneurial rewards.

Traditional practice has rewarded salaried inventors with small bonuses (often $500 to $1,000) for each patent received and some nonmonetary incentives to encourage their next inventions. Recognition ranges from special awards and promotion to master status entailing the use of special laboratories, freedom of project choice, sabbaticals, and the like. Cash awards are often given, but they are generally not tied to product returns. For outstanding innovation, it was standard practice in larger companies such as IBM to offer cash awards of $10,000 or more.

By the early 1990s, there were strong competitive and legal pressures to reward employed inventors as if they were entrepreneurs by tying their compensation to the market value of their output. Inventors, like business developers, want a piece of the action and a direct return on their contributions. They would rather work for start-ups where they can be treated like owners, particularly in hot new technology fields involving information technology and the Internet, than hand over their ideas to a big company for a pat on the back and a small check.

The Challenge to Hierarchy

If pay practices continue to move toward contribution as the basis for earnings, as I believe they will, the change will unleash a set of forces that could transform work relationships as we know them now. To illustrate, let's look at what happens when organizations take modest steps to make pay more entrepreneurial.

A surprising example comes from government—even more surprising because it began in the 1980s, before public attention turned to the need to reinvent government. The city of Long Beach, California, established a pay-for-performance system for its management as part of a new budgeting process designed to upgrade the city government's performance against quantifiable fiscal and service delivery targets. Under the new system, managers could gain or lose up to 20% of their base salaries, so the pay of two managers at the same level could vary by up to $40,000. Job category and position in the hierarchy were far weaker determinants of earnings. Soon there were people in lower ranks paid more than the city manager.

While the impact of a system like this on productivity and entrepreneurship is noticeable, its effect on work relationships is more subtle. People don't wear their paychecks over their name badges in the office, after all. But word does get around, and some organizations face the problem of envy head-on. In two different companies with new-venture units that offer equity participation, the units are being attacked as unfair and poorly conceived. The attackers are aggrieved that venture participants can earn so much money for seemingly modest or even trivial contributions to the corporation overall, while those who keep the mainstream businesses going must accept salary ceilings and insignificant bonuses.

In companies that establish new-venture units, this clash between two different systems is self-inflicted. But sometimes the conflict comes as an unwelcome by-product of a company's efforts to expand into new businesses via acquisition. On buying a brokerage firm, a leading bank found that it had also acquired a very different compensation system: a generous commission arrangement means that employees often earn twice their salary in bonuses and, once in a while, five times. Six people made as much in salary and commissions as the chairman did in his base salary, or roughly $500,000 each. These people all made much more than their managers and their managers' managers and virtually everyone else in the corporation except the top three or four officers, a situation that would have been impossible a few years ago.

Now such discrepancies cannot be prevented or kept quiet. "People in the trade know perfectly well what's happening," the bank's senior administration executive told me. "They know the formula, they see the proxy statements, and they are busy checking out the systems by which we and everybody else compensate these people."

To avoid the equivalent of an employee run on the bank—with everyone trying to transfer to the brokerage operation—the corporation has felt forced to establish performance bonuses for branch managers and some piece-rate systems for clerical workers, though these are not nearly as generous as the managers' extra earning opportunities.

This system, though it solves some problems, creates others. The executive responsible recognized that although these new income-earning opportunities were pegged to individual performance, people do not work in isolation. Branch managers' results really depended on how well their employees perform, and so did the results of nearly everyone else except those in sales (and even there a team effort can make a difference). Yet instead of teamwork, the bank's practices encouraged competition, the hoarding of good leads, and the withholding of good ideas until one person could claim the credit. "We talk about teamwork at training sessions," this executive said, "and then we destroy it in the compensation system."

Team-based pay raises its own questions, however, and generates its own set of prickly issues. There is the "free rider" problem, in which a few nonperforming members of the group benefit from the actions of the productive members. And problems can arise when people resent being dependent on team members, especially those with very different organizational status.

There are also pressure problems. Gain-sharing plans, in particular, can create very high peer pressure to do well, since the pay of all depends on everyone's efforts. Theodore Cohn, a compensation expert, liked to talk about the Dutch company, Philips, in which twice-yearly bonuses could run up to 40% of base pay. "Managers say that a paper clip never hits the floor—a hand will be there to catch it," Cohn recounted. "If a husband dies, the wake is at night so that no one misses work. If someone goes on vacation, somebody else is shown how to do the job. There is practically no turnover."

Similarly, Cohn claimed that at Lincoln Electric, where performance-related pay is twice the average factory wage, peer pressure can be so high that the first two years of employment are called purgatory.

Another kind of pressure also emerges from equity-ownership and profit-sharing systems—the pressure to open the books, to disclose managerial salaries, and to justify pay differentials. Concerns like these bubble up when employees who may never have thought much about other people's pay suddenly realize that "their" money is at stake.

These concerns and questions of distributional equity are all part of making the system more fair as well as more effective. Perhaps the biggest issue, and the one most disturbing to traditionalists, is what happens to the chain of command when it does not match the progression of pay. If subordinates can outearn their bosses, hierarchy begins to crumble.

Social psychologists have shown that authority relationships depend on a degree of inequality. If the distance between boss and subordinate declines, so does automatic deference and respect. The key word here is *automatic.* Superiors can still gain respect through their competence and fair treatment of subordinates. But power shifts as relationships become more equal.

Once the measures of good performance are both clearly established and clearly achieved, a subordinate no longer needs the goodwill of the boss quite so much. Proven achievement reflected in earnings higher than the boss's produces security, which produces risk taking, which produces speaking up and pushing back. As a result, the relationship between boss and subordinate changes from one based on authority to one based on mutual respect.

This change has positive implications for superiors as well as subordinates. For example, if a subordinate can earn more than the boss and still stay in place, then one of the incentives to compete for the boss's job is removed. Gone, too, is the tension that can build when an ambitious subordinate covets the boss's job and will do anything to get it. In short, if some of the *authority* of hierarchy is eliminated, so is some of the *hostility.*

In most traditional organizations, however, the idea of earning more than the boss seems insupportable and, to some people, clearly inequitable. There are, of course, organizational precedents for situations in which people in lower ranked jobs are paid more than those above. Field sales personnel paid on commission can often earn more than their managers; star scientists in R&D laboratories may earn more than the administrators nominally placed over them; and hourly workers can make more than their supervisors through overtime pay or union-negotiated wage settlements. But these situations are usually uncommon, or they're accepted because they're part of a dual-career ladder or the price of moving up in rank into management.

To get a feeling for the kinds of difficulties pay imbalances can create in hierarchical organizations, let's look at a less extreme case in which the gap between adjacent pay levels diminishes but does not disappear. This is called pay compression, and it bothers executives who believe in maintaining hierarchy.

In response to an American Management Association survey of 613 organizations, of which 134 were corporations with more than $1 billion in sales, 76% reported problems with compression. Yet only a few percentage points divided the organizations expressing concern from those that do not. For example, the average earnings difference between first-line production supervisors and the highest paid production workers was 15.5% for organizations reporting compression problems, and only a little higher, 20%, for those not reporting such problems. In the maintenance area, the difference was even less—a 15.1% average earnings difference for those who said they had a problem versus 18.2% for those who said they did not. Furthermore, for a large number of companies claiming a compression problem, the difference between levels was actually greater than their official guidelines stipulate.

What was most striking to me, however, was how great the gap between adjacent levels still is—at least 15% difference in pay. Indeed, it is hard to avoid the conclusion that the executives concerned about compression are responding not to actual problems but to a perceived threat and the fear that hierarchy would crumble because of new pay practices.

What organizations say they will and won't do to solve compression problems supports this interpretation. While 67.4% of those concerned agree that an instant-bonus program would help, 70.1% say their companies would never institute one. And while 47.9% say that profit sharing for all salaried supervisors would help, 64.7% say that their companies would never do that either. In fact, the solutions least likely to be acceptable were precisely those that would change the hierarchy most—for example, reducing the number of job classifications, establishing fewer wage levels, and granting overtime compensation for supervisors (in effect, equalizing their status with that of hourly workers). On the other hand, the most favored solutions involved aids to upward mobility like training and rapid advancement that would keep the structure of the hierarchy intact while helping individuals move within it.

The Future of Pay: Beyond Status to Contribution

The attacks on pay I've identified all push in the same direction. Indeed, they overlap and reinforce each other. For example, a decision to reward individual contributors makes otherwise latent concerns about equity much more visible and live. Without options, private concerns can look like utopian dreams. Once those dreams begin to appear plausible, however, what was "the way things have to be" becomes instead a deliberate withholding of fair treatment.

By creating new forms for identifying, recognizing, and ultimately permitting contributions, the attack on pay goes beyond pay to color relationships throughout an organization. In the process, the iron cage of bureaucracy is being rattled in ways that will eventually change the nature, and the meaning, of hierarchy in ways we cannot yet imagine.

Wise executives, however, prepare themselves and their companies for these revolutionary changes and are experimenting with new forms of compensation and reward. The shift toward contribution-based pay makes sense on grounds of equity, cost, productivity, and enterprise. And there are ways to manage that shift effectively. Here are some options to consider:

- Think strategically and systematically about the organizational implications of every change in compensation practices. If a venture unit offers an equity stake to participants, should a performance-based bonus with similar earning potential be offered to managers of mainstream businesses? If gain sharing is implemented on the shop floor, should it be extended to white-collar groups?

- Move toward reducing the fixed portion of pay and increasing the variable portion. Give business unit managers more discretion in distributing the variable pool, and make it a larger, more meaningful amount. Or allow more people to invest a portion of their salary in return for a greater share of the proceeds attributed to their own efforts later on.

- Manage the jealousy and conflict inherent in the more widely variable pay of nominal peers by making standards clear, giving everyone similar opportunities for growth in earnings, and reserving a portion of the earnings of stars or star sectors for distribution to others who have played a role in the success. Balance individual and group incentives in ways appropriate to the work unit and its tasks.

- Analyze—and, if necessary, rethink—the relationship between pay and value to the organization. Keep in mind that organizational levels defined for purposes of coordination do not necessarily reflect contributions to performance goals, and decouple pay from status or rank.

- And finally, be prepared to justify pay decisions in terms of clear contributions—and to offer these justifications more often, to more stakeholder groups.

17

Service Quality: You Get What You Pay For

It takes hubris to name a baseball championship the "World Series" when the only teams that can participate are from North America. Americans do tend to assume that their own issues and techniques have universal applicability and appeal.

But at times, American experiences, problems, and solutions can usefully be examined by the rest of the world. Consider the shift to a service economy. The United States is in the forefront of this important change. Therefore, U.S. companies face service-industry challenges before other countries do—challenges that require rethinking aspects of society as well as business.

The richest and deepest service market in the world is found in the United States, economist Stephen Roache observed. By the early 1990s the United States accounted for 85% of the service transactions in the Group of Seven nations (the United States, Canada, France, Germany, Italy, Japan, and Great Britain), with an annual expenditure on services of $2.4 trillion, double that of Japan, the number two services consumer. In recent decades, white collar jobs have shown explosive growth, and knowledge-based industries benefiting from widespread higher education have sprung up.

The number of service jobs is, of course, far greater than the employment in service-providing organizations; more people work in service jobs in some manufacturing firms than in direct production. With government, education, and health care in the equation, the vast majority of Americans work in services.

Growth in service jobs has kept unemployment in check while manufacturing jobs were being lost, but the quality of those new jobs has been controversial. Some politicians warned that America was losing higher value-added work, turning into a "nation of hamburger-flippers."

Now international competition, deregulation, and cost pressures force once-invulnerable service industries to shed rather than create jobs. The time is ripe for scrutinizing productivity and quality in the service sector—which includes the quality of service jobs.

Services are inherently local: frontline people shape the customer's experience. Understanding this truth about service quality is the first step to restoring service excellence because it makes concern for people the cornerstone of service strategy. People at lower rather than higher organizational ranks make or break service strategies. No matter what strategy leaders inside the organization devise, what customers see is at the front line. It's not politicians and managers in corner offices who set operative policy in city government, MIT's Michael Lipsky proposed in his book *Street-Level Bureaucracy,* but the legions of teachers, firefighters, police, and trash collectors whose day-to-day activities tell customers what the strategy really is.

Thus while the *cost* of service delivery may benefit from economies of scale in large global enterprises, the *act* of service delivery is still intensely local. As an Italian apparel company manager observed, "The company may be global, but the consumer is not." And this means that large (and even not-so-large) organizations may need a physical presence in many locations to be where the customers are.

Service quality can stand or fall on the relationship between providers and recipients, especially when no tangible products are involved. For customers, the specific provider *is* the organization. For example, strong bonds between sales representatives and their customers are common, especially in Europe; loyalty dictates that customers transfer their business if their sales rep moves on. Consultants and attorneys can also usually count on favored clients to follow when they move to a new firm. And restaurant customers may not return, regardless of the quality of the food, if they dislike the treatment they received from their waiter.

Which brings us once more to the people in services and the jobs they fill. Bankers, consultants, physicians, and other highly paid, prestigious knowledge workers constitute only a small portion of the service front line. The largest portion of service workers includes receptionists, waiters, telephone operators, insurance company claims processors, flight attendants, salesclerks, and others with low pay and little voice in their organizations. Services also employ large numbers of the "working poor," who constitute 90% of those below the poverty line in the United States, according to former U.S. Health and Human Services officials Mary Jo Bane and David Ellwood.

It is hard to deny the marginal appeal of many service jobs. Critics of such jobs abound. In *The Electronic Sweatshop,* Barbara Garson showed how the McDonald's system of beeps and buzzers that turns inexperienced teenagers into short-order cooks controlled by computers was adapted to stockbrokers and financial planners, turning them into clerks and machine operators. In *The Managed Heart,* based on extensive research on flight attendants and people in similar roles, Arlie Hochschild questioned the manipulative, demoralizing aspects of service jobs that encourage workers to feign emotions they do not feel. And many service jobs are female pink-collar ghettos, poorly paid and bereft of opportunities for advancement. No wonder they become revolving-door jobs; one large retailer turns over 80% of its grocery stores' non-managerial personnel every 11 months.

Try to motivate people in repetitive, dead-end jobs to care about the quality of service they provide. Try to keep the attention on customers when working parents are worried about their children because child care is scarce, undependable, and unaffordable. Try to get people to expedite the service for one more rude, demanding customer when they are earning wages barely above the poverty level.

Contradictions like these set destructive cycles in motion. There's no point investing in training for people who will leave, the company says, so it takes even more skill out of the job. Replace some people with computers and use computers to monitor the rest, the company says, because people cannot be entrusted to work hard or well. Reduce costs, the company decides—and pushes wage rates down still more. These are the traps that service companies must avoid. Service companies should not emulate the manufacturing sector's single-mindedness and simple-mindedness about cost-cutting as the solution to financial woes.

Effective restructuring of the service sector to meet competitive challenges will require massive reskilling. This lesson was learned by the United Services Automobile Association's CEO Robert F. McDemmott—and it is the secret of his company's success.

Reskilling Service Jobs

Raise pay. Create the incentives to encourage professionalism.

New incentives were an important part of a British retailer's turnaround. Everyone at the store level can earn an extra week's salary for meeting performance targets, and workers receive raises as their skills are certified on a national retail exam. According to the CEO, better pay substitutes for the "mental compensation" people took by goofing off "because we didn't pay enough." Now the company has fewer people, working harder, earning more, and feeling recognized.

Equity ownership and performance measures that support motivation—and better pay—are other ways to foster professionalism. Establishing and communicating precise goals are important to help ensure high-quality outputs, especially with respect to new tasks.

Subordinate technology to people. Use technology to empower.

Companies should use technology to remove walls, not to wire them, so it is easier for people in every job to make decisions and connections. Consider the information flows at a prosperous Dutch retailer with U.S. operations: any in-store clerk can see scanner data instantly; a video with best-practice cases arrives at every store weekly; data from supermarket scanners in Connecticut goes right to the president's home computer screen in the Netherlands.

Learn from the field. Let the front line teach the top floor.

Taco Bell has attempted to turn managers into coaches and supporters of the customer-contact employees. At the Dutch grocery chain, the best performer in a unit becomes the coach. At the Royal Bank of Canada, field managers are becoming agents of change through their task networks.

Manufacturing can use these lessons as well, of course. Italian apparel company Gruppo GFT is decentralized into small units with a great deal of autonomy to mold themselves to the particu-

---

larities of local markets, which results in innovations influencing the direction of the whole company.

To enable and pay for these changes, cut "corporate." Harvard Business School Professor Jay Jaikumar argues that most technological progress occurs at smaller, flatter companies staffed with generalists. So does most people progress: eliminating levels of bureaucracy accelerates decision making in the field, empowers talented people formerly hidden in the hierarchy, and saves enough money to pay for major information systems improvements. The successful Dutch retailer has only 128 corporate headquarters personnel for a business with 103,000 employees.

It is dangerous to give lip service without real service—lots of rhetoric but no change in customer relationships. The warning applies with equal force inside a company. To ensure service excellence, companies need to ensure the excellence of the service worker's job.

18

A New Human Resources Agenda

New management models, derived from large Japanese companies, often urge lifetime employment as a central component of high-commitment, high-productivity work systems. But the job-tenure ideal is colliding with the job-insecurity reality.

Labor mobility is now a fact of life. "Migrant managers" soon may become as common as migrant workers—moving from company to company as frequently as they move from country to country.

As business globalizes, local loyalties decline. Global managers feel comfortable moving operations—and themselves—anywhere. The decisions made by migrant managers often dislocate stay-put workers. Simultaneously, recessionary pressures and sweeping industrial transformations are forcing large companies to down-size—a euphemism that masks the human turmoil involved.

Flexibility can hurt people, but stability can hurt even more by depressing economies. According to French economist Robert Boyer, job security was associated with higher productivity (though not with product innovations) in industrialized countries through the 1970s, but in the 1980s, this connection disappeared. France and other nations loosened regulations to permit greater flexibility in hiring and firing.

A decade ago, IBM—the major U.S. role model for lifetime employment—worried that its very low turnover created too much deadwood. Besides blocking opportunities to bring in new talent with fresh ideas, insiders reported, career security enabled some of the long-tenured to refuse to do things, knowing that they could always transfer to another job. Meanwhile, many fast-growing startups that now compete with giants like IBM base their human resource policies on offering great jobs, not guaranteed ones. Entrepreneurial dynamism often involves wandering talent; Silicon Valley was built by roving engineers.

Mobility is both a cause and an effect of a mismatch between people and jobs. In many parts of the world, labor shortages and labor surpluses coexist. The work force has one skills profile, but jobs have another. Education and skills are increasing in developing countries, but the jobs are in industrialized countries.

In OECD surveys, Europeans worry about a scarcity of skilled workers. Many countries worry about future adaptability. For Japan, the problem is work force aging; for Germany, the absorption of East German workers, a relatively small percentage of working women, and rote education favoring precision over breadth.

In the United States, according to a University of Michigan study, there are too few electrical engineers, dentists, biological scientists, and legal assistants but too many telephone operators, butchers, barbers, and plumbers. (Vocational counselors also are in short supply—part of the problem?)

There are disturbing indications that the mismatch is the result of a failure to upgrade and retrain. The United States has too many data processors and statistical clerks but too few computer scientists; too many typists, stenographers, and machine operators but too few computer systems analysts. Surely some of those handling the data could learn to handle the systems?

The fact of mobility and the problem of mismatch are intertwined. Both require new human resource policies with lifelong learning as their centerpiece.

A skill-poor labor pool makes it easier for global companies to search for more productive people elsewhere. Communities and nations best protect their economies by investing in their people. But unless businesses provide jobs that reinforce the value of learning, mismatches will continue, and mobility will be defined not by voluntary migrations but by wrenching dislocations that hurt people.

A better match between work force abilities and business needs means ensuring that people can grow into higher skill jobs without such trauma. New policies must reflect new forms of security while embracing the emerging realities of flexibility, mobility, and change.

From Employment Security to Employability Security

If security no longer comes automatically with being employed, then it must come from being *employable*. Employability security rests on the knowledge that competence is growing to meet tomorrow's challenges, that today's work includes the learning and experience to enhance future opportunities—whether with a current employer, with another company, or as an entrepreneur.

Some prominent companies have always been able to attract top talent despite their stringent up-or-out systems that offer no security at all. They are seen as a training ground, a good place to learn, and a valuable addition to the résumé.

Even companies that want to keep the same employees long term can afford to only if they keep people growing and learning through challenging jobs, continuing education, and complete retraining when circumstances require a major shift in tasks. Continuous upgrading of skills in order to help people and companies pursue new opportunities is no longer a luxury but a necessity. Encouraging learning builds innovation and entrepreneurship; it is an essential motivational tool when traditional carrots like promotions and raises are less common.

Some companies worry about the consequences of lavish training: What if we invest in people and then they leave? Singapore solves this problem by bonding; employees sign notes agreeing to pay back the cost of their training if they leave the organization before a specified time. But such legal handcuffs may not be necessary. What data there is suggests that most employees stay with companies that provide training. While the people become more valuable to the company, the company also becomes more valuable to the people.

"Education" in the abstract is not enough. There must be a strong link between the workplace and learning. An elaborate adult education system in the United States is largely underutilized because people want their education on company time. More classrooms in the formal sense is not the solution; businesses should emulate the best schools, becoming laboratories for learning, not mechanistic factories. The best French management de-

---

velopment is informal and work-related and occurs through mentoring and special assignments. Formal training classes, not taken very seriously, are for the lower tiers.

Yet when many human resource directors imagine the "learning organization," they see a building with high-tech, video-equipped classrooms and a lockstep curriculum resembling grade school. Rarely considered are less expensive and often more effective learning opportunities: field studies of other companies, projects to explore a new issue, or a lunchtime seminar series.

Education also comes from the job itself, which can either stretch or numb the mind. If people are tested for their IQ (intelligence quotient), why don't we rate jobs according to their LQ (learning quotient)? Flexibility and innovation require people who easily learn, not people who are easily taught.

From Stability Policies to Portability Policies

Employability-security principles fit the coming world labor market: global managers who easily pick up stakes, expatriate professionals on temporary assignments, Turkish "guest workers" in Germany, "south of the border" illegal aliens in the United States, emigrant Irish nurses, or engineers from India. All are part of a freer flow of human capital.

As the work force grows more diverse, some human resource policies must become more standardized. It is difficult for people to move across boundaries marked by different vacation, workweek, safety, rights, fringe-benefit, bonus, and licensing policies. It is difficult for companies to compete in attracting talent if they adhere to noticeably lower standards. Strategic alliances and joint ventures also face problems of joining two work forces subject to different policies. For example, a manufacturer of copiers launched a joint development team with a manufacturer of workstations that had better bonuses; the first company had to put its team members on the second company's system.

Just as industry standards are emerging to make computers portable and plug-comparable, standards should be developed to help people become learners who can adapt to many circumstances, carrying their skills and pensions with them to plug into new companies. Instead of relying on GATT (General Agreement on Trade and Tariffs) talks to manage economies, perhaps the major trading nations should start GAPP talks—toward a General Agreement on People Policies.

Promising Employability Security: A Sample "Contract"

"Our company faces competitive world markets and rapidly changing technology. We need the flexibility to add or delete products, open or close facilities, and redeploy the work force. Although we cannot guarantee tenure in any particular job or even future employment, we will work to ensure that all our people are fully employable—sought out for new jobs here and elsewhere. We promise to:

■ Recruit for the potential to increase in competence, not simply for narrow skills to fill today's slots.
■ Offer ample learning opportunities, from formal training to lunchtime seminars—the equivalent of a month a year.
■ Provide challenging jobs and rotating assignments that allow growth in skills even without promotion to "higher" jobs.
■ Measure performance beyond accounting numbers and share the data to allow learning by doing and continuous improvement.
■ Retrain employees as soon as jobs become obsolete.
■ Recognize individual and team achievements, thereby building external reputations and offering tangible indicators of value.
■ Provide three-month educational sabbaticals or external internships every five years.
■ Find job opportunities in our network of suppliers, customers, and venture partners.
■ Tap our people's ideas to develop innovations that lower costs, serve customers, and create markets—the best foundation for business growth and continuing employment."

V

Crossing Boundaries:
Business and Its Partners

Overview

As industries deregulate, markets open, governments rethink their roles, and communications technology links the world, businesses are learning to open their own boundaries to closer collaboration with a range of partners—their key connections globally and locally.

How widespread is the crossing of traditional boundaries? To find out, I led a global survey of nearly 12,000 managers from 25 countries, who responded to the questions in their own languages (see "Transcending Business Boundaries"). The survey confirmed that change is part of corporate life everywhere, especially in large companies. Manufacturing companies are ahead of service companies in thinking globally. Awareness is growing that business should play a greater role in solving social problems. But some walls inside and outside of business are coming down more slowly than others. Hierarchy still rules in most places. Despite greater interest in closer relationships with suppliers and customers, businesses are proceeding cautiously in bringing partners inside their own operations. Yet the trend is clear. Not just the corporate giants and not just U.S. companies are getting rid of walls and thinking about the value of connections: Companies throughout the world are beginning to embrace the value of partnering.

"Collaborative Advantage: The Art of Alliances" offers a framework for forming and managing productive partnerships. Relationships between organizations proceed a little like marriages, from courtship to meeting one another's families to learning to live together. But there are many pitfalls along the path, and partnerships are unstable, sometimes fragile. Some are on a trajectory toward full merger; others dissolve or change shape, such as the FCB-Publicis venture described in "Collaborative Advantage," which began with romantic promise and splintered when the companies began to cohabit. The numbers of partners can change—for example, three-way formal coalitions like the European Retail Alliance can become informal two-partner affiliations. But supplier-customer relationships tend to endure. And the companies that know how to leverage their connections and to learn from them are more likely to derive lasting value from even fleeting relationships. "Collaborative Advantage" outlines eight factors that can make the crucial difference.

Government connections have always been important to businesses, but can collaborative advantage also extend to business-government relationships? Countries vary in the extent to which their businesses know how to approach government and citizens as allies and partners. Those that do can derive advantages from diplomatic or philanthropic moves that foster cooperation (see "Competing on Politics").

There are many issues to examine in the political realm, fraught as it is with legal and ethical perils. These include the role of lobbyists and campaign contributions to the need to preserve government's role as protector of wider public interests. A strong legal framework, a skeptical press, and an alert public can help guard against abuses, such as unwarranted intrusions of foreign companies into domestic policies. Nonetheless, public-private partnerships are increasing in number and importance. Political tasks and public outreach will play a greater part in the work of every business leader in the future.

Public-private partnerships certainly play a role in helping local and regional economies to thrive. Communities can be a source of the 3Cs introduced in chapter one—concepts, competence, and connections—that help companies succeed (see "Thriving Locally in the Global Economy"). Such partnerships are more likely to develop when the interests of business and of government align.

Those regions destined to flourish as prosperous centers of the global information economy have many partnerships among businesses and civic organizations through which business as well as community tasks are performed. "Thriving Locally" offers a case study demonstrating the benefits to business of working across boundaries with its newest partner: the community.

19

Transcending Business Boundaries: How 12,000 World Managers View Change

For much of the twentieth century, business managers around the world confronted a series of walls. Walls between nations that establish the boundaries of national markets, national practices, or national social, economic, and political systems. Walls between the company and the society in which it exists, drawing sharp distinctions between corporate interests and social interests. Walls between work and home, separating those activities that involve earning a living from those that constitute just plain living. Walls within the workplace itself, dividing managers from workers, function from function, line from staff. And walls between the company and its stakeholders, including suppliers, customers, and venture partners.

Now, we are told, the walls are crumbling.

Globalizing markets, instantaneous communications, travel at the speed of sound, political realignments, changing demographics, technological transformations in both products and production, corporate alliances, flattening organizations—all these and more are changing the structure of the corporation. The once very rigid and unbreachable boundaries of business are fading in the face of change.

Or so many experts say. But what is the experience of real managers around the world?

To find out, colleagues and I conducted a World Leadership Survey exploring the boundaries of business. After constructing and testing the survey questionnaire, we distributed it through *Harvard Business Review* and 25 publications in 25 countries on 6 continents, with each publication reproducing the survey in its own language. In 1991, 11,678 responses to the 91 survey questions were received for analysis at Harvard University.[1] Details of each nation's findings were returned to the appropriate magazine editor for further analysis and comment.

The Global Reach of the World Leadership Survey

Country	Magazine	Number of Responses
Argentina	Mercado	59
Australia	Business Review Weekly	265
Austria	Austrian Management Club	114
Belgium	Trends	217
Brazil	Exame	605
Canada	Harvard Business Review	180
Estonia	Teataja	4
Finland	Talouselama	495
France	Harvard L'Expansion	446
Germany	HARVARDmanager	134
Great Britain	Business	560
Hungary	Figyelö	117
India	Business India	224
Italy	Harvard Espansione	483
Japan	Diamond Harvard Business	639
Mexico	Expansion	1,322
The Netherlands	Financieel Economisch	583
New Zealand	National Business Review	251
Nigeria	Management in Nigeria	24
Singapore	Singapore Business	340
South Korea	Harvard Sogang Business	569
Spain	Harvard Deusto Business	871
Sweden	Ledarskap	363
United States	Harvard Business Review	2,737
Venezuela	Asociacion Venezolana de Ejecutivos	76

If there was a single message from the survey results, it was this: change is indeed everywhere—regardless of country, culture, or corporation. But the idea of a corporate global village where a common culture of management unifies the practice of business around the world is more dream than reality.

The survey themes fall into five major areas:

- Internationalists vs. economic patriots; how corporate and country interests conflict and coincide in the face of global markets.

- Businesses as citizens; which social responsibilities are embraced—or rejected—by business leaders.

- Productivity and parenting; the ways in which work and family interests can support each other, and the emerging sources of conflict.

- Fissures inside the workplace; issues of loyalty and hierarchy that create a still-divided organization.

- Anxious alliances, cautious coalitions; what companies say about the importance of their ever-closer relationships with customers and suppliers, and how this compares with what they are actually doing.

Since the respondents were not selected at random, it is impossible to know how representative their views are. In addition, language barriers, cultural assumptions, and other national differences can lead to distortions or limitations on comparability. Nevertheless, the survey is a worldwide dialogue with managers whose voices are not always heard beyond their own country's borders. Because the survey appeared in the language of each country, in a domestically published magazine, participants did not have to belong to a select set of managers who speak English, read international publications, work in global corporations, or travel internationally. In that respect, despite the survey's limitations, it also overcame many of the hurdles that inhibit open communication about the heart of business practice inside many countries.

This business mainstream was reflected in the profile of the average respondent. Across countries, the typical survey respondent turned out to be:

- A male senior manager in his early 40s, married and bilingual.

- Employed in an established, privately held, midsize organization with several thousand employees and a two- to four-year planning horizon; the company has a small number of foreign facilities but derives the largest proportion of its revenues domestically, faces mainly domestic competition, and is competitive in its industry but not dominant, having increased profits and market share last year.

- Cautiously optimistic about the future and assuming that the next generation will live a more comfortable, secure life.

- More concerned about customer service, product quality, work force skills, and technology than about macroeconomic and political issues, and sure that trade rules, government policies, currency risks, and even capital availability are neither significant success factors for his business nor significant worries.

- Strongly in favor of work-site child care and very concerned about the quality of education, believing that business should play a major role in improving it.

In addition to profiling the views of this average manager, the survey detected the deep and powerful national differences that overwhelm age, sex, or industry distinctions among respondents. For example, Germans appeared the most cosmopolitan. South Koreans most clearly favored country over company. Japanese reported the strongest work ethic among top managers and the greatest worries about the work ethic of the rest of their work force.

Interestingly, managers' views tended to correspond more to their country's cultural heritage and less to its geographic location or its regional economic affiliations. Cultural alliances appeared to unite the views of Italians and Spaniards with those of Mexicans, Brazilians, and Venezuelans, superseding the bonds of the new Europe. English-speaking countries tended to have deep similarities, regardless of continent. Japan and South Korea each stood alone.

Cultural Affinity More Than Geographic Proximity Is a Major Determinant of Managers' Views

Cultural Allies

Group 1: Australia, Canada, Great Britain, New Zealand, Singapore, United States.
Common traits: A preference for family over work, and the least "cosmopolitan." (Cosmopolitan is defined as being multilingual and having international experience.)

Group 2: Argentina, Brazil, Italy, Mexico, Spain, Venezuela.
Common traits: More privately held companies, fewer joint ventures, and a higher reliance on trade policy for industry protection.

Group 3: Austria, Belgium, Finland, France, Germany, the Netherlands, Sweden.
Common traits: Most cosmopolitan, more close partnerships, and more pessimistic about the future.

Cultural Islands

Japan: The strongest work ethic, the greatest concern about the work ethic of the rest of the work force, and strongly in favor of "free trade."

South Korea: Strongly favors protectionism, puts country ahead of company, a strong sense of corporate responsibility toward employees, and more optimistic about the future.

India: More optimistic about the future and strongly favors protectionism.

Hungary: Organizationally different from companies in other countries and very focused on economic regeneration.

The above allies and islands were determined by statistical analysis. This clustering technique compares the responses by country for each survey question and evaluates the degree of overall country difference.

While the survey results indicated that the emergence of a global culture of management is more dream than reality, they also uncovered the leaders of the dream. For the most part, traditional industrial enterprises—larger, older, publicly held manufacturing companies with long planning horizons—were leading the drive toward globalization. These organizations were more "cosmopolitan" in their outlook and were reshaping their boundaries faster. They were the most international in scope, least protectionist, and most closely involved in cross-boundary relationships with suppliers, customers, and venture partners. They also had undergone the most pervasive changes in recent years: more downsizings, reorganizations, CEO changes, mergers or divestitures *(Figure 19-1)*. Respondents from this sector reported less satisfaction with their own jobs and a decline in loyalty and commitment to their companies.

Such companies and such managers are in the vanguard of changes that could confront business with new political and social struggles.

Internationalists vs. Economic Patriots

Economics has not yet triumphed over politics. While most survey respondents presented themselves as "internationalists"—free trade advocates who reject government favoritism or assistance for domestic companies—country differences and contradictions in response patterns suggested continuing local political battles over the rights and responsibilities of businesses *(Figure 19-2)*. Those in more domestically focused companies and those in countries whose national competitiveness was eroding joined newly industrialized countries in sounding notes of ambivalence about internationalism.

Most of the survey respondents naturally wanted businesses to have the freedom to make decisions in their own interests, without having to take "patriotic" considerations into account. As expected, the most internationalist views on the survey were expressed by German, Swedish, Finnish, Dutch, and Belgian respondents. It was no surprise to find the capital of the European community (Belgium) and the European community's unofficial leader (Germany)

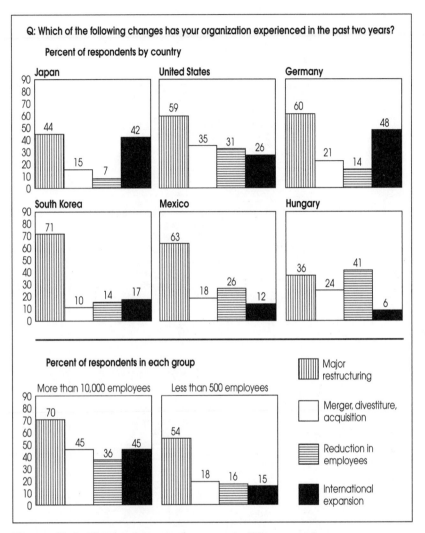

Figure 19-1. Change is part of corporate life everywhere . . .
Especially in large companies

among a group of nations whose size or situation made trade a
necessary component of a healthy economy.

This internationalist tendency on the part of northern European
countries was mildly associated with the greater cosmopolitanism
of their managerial populations, especially in Germany. "Cosmopolitan" respondents (those who speak more than one language

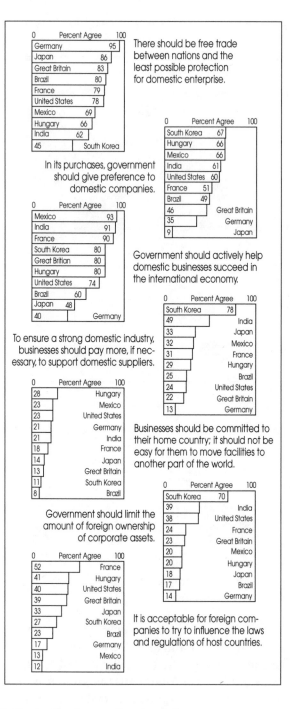

There should be free trade between nations and the least possible protection for domestic enterprise.

0 Percent Agree 100	
Germany	95
Japan	86
Great Britain	83
Brazil	80
France	79
United States	78
Mexico	69
Hungary	66
India	62
45	South Korea

In its purchases, government should give preference to domestic companies.

0 Percent Agree 100	
South Korea	67
Hungary	66
Mexico	66
India	61
United States	60
France	51
Brazil	49
46	Great Britain
35	Germany
9	Japan

Government should actively help domestic businesses succeed in the international economy.

0 Percent Agree 100	
Mexico	93
India	91
France	90
South Korea	80
Great Britian	80
Hungary	80
United States	74
Brazil	60
Japan	48
40	Germany

0 Percent Agree 100	
South Korea	78
49	India
33	Japan
32	Mexico
31	France
29	Hungary
25	Brazil
24	United States
22	Great Britain
13	Germany

To ensure a strong domestic industry, businesses should pay more, if necessary, to support domestic suppliers.

Businesses should be committed to their home country; it should not be easy for them to move facilities to another part of the world.

0 Percent Agree 100	
28	Hungary
23	Mexico
23	United States
21	Germany
21	India
18	France
14	Japan
13	Great Britain
11	South Korea
8	Brazil

0 Percent Agree 100	
South Korea	70
39	India
38	United States
24	France
23	Great Britain
20	Mexico
20	Hungary
18	Japan
17	Brazil
14	Germany

Government should limit the amount of foreign ownership of corporate assets.

It is acceptable for foreign companies to try to influence the laws and regulations of host countries.

0 Percent Agree 100	
52	France
41	Hungary
40	United States
39	Great Britain
33	Japan
27	South Korea
23	Brazil
17	Germany
13	Mexico
12	India

Figure 19-2. Protectionism or free trade?

and were born or hold citizenship in countries other than the ones in which they currently work) were somewhat more likely to hold internationalist views—the only area in which their attitudes toward business practices differed significantly from those of their "local" counterparts. These cosmopolitan respondents often worked for cosmopolitan companies—those doing business in many countries—and therefore reflected the interests of their companies in eliminating barriers to operating anywhere in the world.

Japanese antiprotectionist responses were most surprising in light of Western "conventional wisdom" that says Japanese companies benefit from government protection and assistance. Assuming the honesty and accuracy of the responses, three interpretations seem most plausible. First, this group of Japanese managers, drawn primarily from older companies competing domestically, having heard recent exhortations in the Japanese media about the inevitability of internationalism, was now playing that message back. Or, second, the responses could simply reflect a growing confidence within Japan over the quality and performance of Japanese products. Or, third, it is possible that Western conventional wisdom is simply wrong.

Underneath the world majority's endorsement of globalism are some potentially difficult contradictions. Look at the third of the survey respondents who said that businesses should be willing to pay a premium to support domestic suppliers, or the quarter who wanted business owners to care more about their country's success than their company's. These managers were indicating their willingness to put patriotism before profits. They represented a sizable business group available for political mobilization in the name of protectionism.

Even in the unlikely event that trade barriers disappear, other contentious issues remain around the rights and responsibilities of global companies. Respondents appeared to draw a clear line between economic freedom and political rights. While foreign ownership of local assets is acceptable around the world, foreign voice in local affairs is not.

Will local politicians simultaneously court foreign investors and exploit xenophobia in trying to keep their country free of foreign influence? If a freer flow of capital across country borders is not accompanied by the ability to protect that capital through the political system, will global companies exit, or will they enter into the political fray?

If the internationalists do challenge the economic patriots over political rights and economic freedom, they will be up against groups likely to have a great deal of local clout. Economic patriots could have a larger voice in domestic politics than even their numbers suggest. The survey showed a correlation between patriotic responses, a more local business orientation, and a slightly greater willingness for business to help solve social problems.

Thus, if managers act on their espoused values, domestically oriented companies with a protectionist agenda could play a disproportionate role in shaping political policy because of the credibility they gain from local philanthropy. This pattern is already apparent in many regions of the United States.

Even if the scope of economic activity is increasingly global, many social problems remain firmly local. More internationally oriented companies could find their local political voice reduced by their managers' greater reluctance to get involved in the social arena. It is understandable that cosmopolitan managers might not identify with a community's problem if they can easily pull up stakes and move elsewhere. But if cosmopolitan managers in global companies show reduced commitment to the places in which they operate, then political voice could be ceded to more protectionist and patriotic localists.

Businesses as Citizens: Which Social Responsibilities?

Respondents everywhere singled out the quality of education as the most significant social issue affecting their organizations, and they felt business should take the lead in improving it (*Figures 19-3* and *19-4*). A scant 5% felt business should not be involved at all. While 18% said that businesses should limit their contribution to financial support, another 77% approved of a very active role. And a great many respondents felt business can make a very useful contribution to basic literacy skills.

Environmental issues such as waste disposal and pollution were

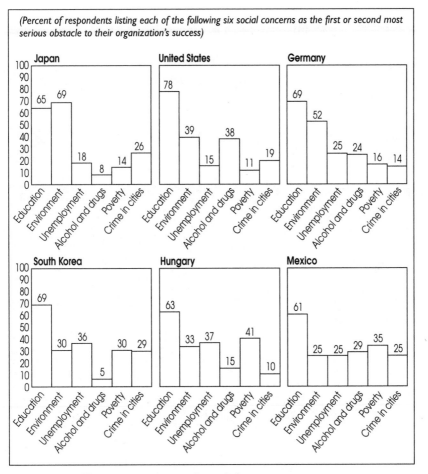

Figure 19-3. How managers rank social concerns

the second highest social priority, though falling well behind education in degree of importance to the respondent's own business. But solving environmental problems is the responsibility of those that create them. Most respondents were willing to shoulder *all* the burdens; only 3%—one of the lowest responses on any item on the survey—thought business should not be involved at all.

Consensus broke down, however, around somewhat messier human problems that are country-specific: alcoholism and drug addiction, crime-ridden cities, and poverty. Argentinians, for ex-

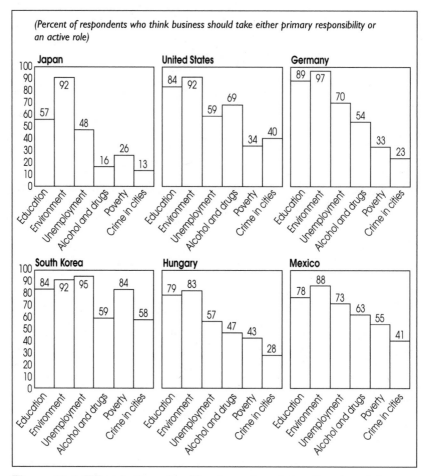

(Percent of respondents who think business should take either primary responsibility or an active role)

Figure 19-4. What is the role of business in solving these social problems?

ample, worried more about the impact of poverty and unemployment on business, while Americans saw unsafe cities and substance abuse as more pressing problems.

Regardless of the strength of concerns, there tended to be little interest in business involvement in solving the problems of urban life. In some countries, of course, business leaders can count on a strong welfare-oriented government to prevent problems or address them if they arise. There are low crime rates, stiff antidrug laws, and social safety nets. Singaporeans, for example, were much less likely than the average respondent to feel that unsafe cities are a critical problem for their businesses or that business has to improve literacy. Government simply ensures that such problems do not occur.

But consider the situation in countries like the United States whose respondents identified urban problems as urgent. Responses hint that business leaders are turning their backs on decaying cities, either because they can move facilities internationally or because they do not know what to do. This may cause downward spirals: as businesses abandon deteriorating cities, poverty and crime grow, literacy drops, and such places become even less attractive to business. If businesses do not accept citizenship responsibilities in areas they say affect them, will there be a backlash against business? Or will social activists push businesses to take more responsibility in exchange for economic concessions?

Managers often appear more politically conservative than the general population, and their responses to the survey are no exception. They are willing to shoulder those welfare burdens involving wealth creation that have already been established as part of the standard benefit package in industrialized nations. But they draw the line at taking on new responsibilities, such as helping employees care for elderly dependents.

Productivity and Parenting

Respondents voiced strong support for practices that help working parents. While world averages were skewed slightly because Americans take the lead in this area, Japanese, Brazilian, Mexican, and Canadian respondents were also strong supporters. Only South Korean managers were dissenters.

Finding world consensus in a direction some consider "women's" issues—and from a survey response that is 90% male—is noteworthy. Attitudes toward work and family are fraught with cultural overlays, colored by deeply held personal values. Yet respondents agreed on three win-win practices that are good for both families and organizations.

First, child care at the work site was overwhelmingly supported by respondents. Indeed, there was more agreement in this area than in any other on the survey *(Figure 19-5)*.

A second practice considered good for both families and organizations is for both husbands and wives to hold important paid jobs *(Figure 19-6)*. There was strong support for dual-career families even among those who believe that it is good for the family to have one parent at home to take care of children. Still, the line between work and family should not be erased too much, respondents said; a sizable group felt a husband and wife should not work for the same organization. Clearly, respondents' views reflected a deep ambiguity and continuing conflicts for women, who are expected to work at demanding paid jobs while "someone" stays home with the children.

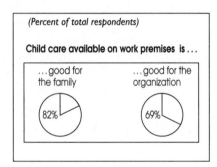

Figure 19-5. Most respondents are strong supporters of child care

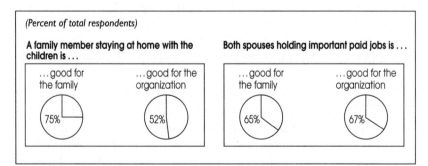

Figure 19-6. Wanting it both ways: Tension between work and family

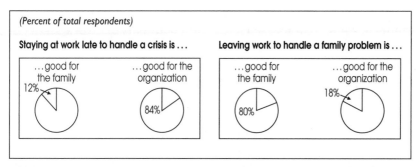

Figure 19-7. Juggling time: The source of most work-family conflict

Flexible work hours is the third practice considered good for both families and organizations. Support for flextime appeared connected to a desire for family members to be able to provide care for one another, instead of relying on child care centers—though fewer supported stay-at-home family members than supported work-site child care. But flexible work hours were seen as good for the family just as often as a family member at home *(Figure 19-7)*.

The strongest endorsement of a working parent's agenda came from Japanese and U.S. respondents. The reasoning, however, appeared to be quite different in these two groups. Japanese respondents seemed to support any practice that makes it easier for people to dedicate themselves single-mindedly to work. Japanese scores on a "precedence for work over family" scale were off the charts—higher and statistically more distant from the scores of other countries than any other measure. Japanese respondents were nearly alone in finding it *good* for the family to have vacations, weekends, or evenings interrupted for work. What parents do "for the family" seems viewed in financial terms—to keep working and earning. Support for working parents could be seen by the Japanese as tilting the work-family balance in favor of work; by U.S. respondents, as tilting it toward family.

Organizations want productivity; families want time. The greatest work-family tensions center around conflicting time demands—the trade-offs involved in working weekends, interrupting vacations, or staying late at the office. Child care facilities make it easier for people to work and not spend time with their families. The tensions are clear when both parents work and both parents value their families—the combination is true for many survey respondents.

By supporting child care and flextime, managers were endorsing the work side of the work-family equation; the family side remains unaddressed. This area is ripe for new solutions that go beyond parenting leaves and sabbaticals. Will we see flex-year—the opportunity to work intensively for periods of time, then ease up, perhaps around school vacations? Or will solutions lie in technology—making work flexible and portable, or adding labor-saving innovations to increase productivity while freeing up time? A new work force, composed of more working parents, requires a new look at the workplace itself.

Fissures Inside the Workplace

Today's work force was generally viewed everywhere as more skilled and motivated than it was ten years ago *(Figure 19-8)*. This positive aura was even stronger for successful, growing companies. Managers from growing companies reported more positive views of their own jobs, their employers, and their people than did those from stagnant companies—one of the few differences between the groups on the survey.

Many respondents counted work force skills among the most important business success factors, but successful companies had a higher percentage of managers who believe their people actually have better skills. Are the people in such companies really better, or does a "halo effect" surround anyone who works in a successful organization? Research suggests that positive views of people's abilities can cause high performance as well as result from it. A "culture of pride," based on success, increases confidence and motivation. It's a virtuous cycle: performance stimulating pride stimulating performance.

But the widely noted decline in employee loyalty and commitment was also confirmed by survey respondents from many countries *(Figure 19-9)*. And the respondents expressed a higher level of satisfaction with their jobs than with their employers—a pattern

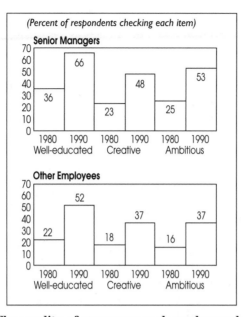

Figure 19-8. The quality of managers and employees has improved . . .

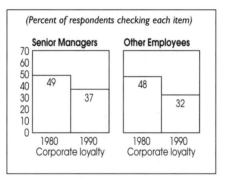

Figure 19-9. . . . But they are more willing to leave their employer than before

indicative of the shift in managerial loyalty from company to profession.

That gaps remain between managers and nonmanagers is not surprising, but the nature of the gaps is suggestive. Workers were seen as having a widening edge over managers in their ability to

Table 19-1. Hierarchy still rules corporate life

Q: How do your organization's "top" and "bottom" groups compare in each category?
(percent of total respondents who say each category is "somewhat different" or "very different")

	Japan	United States	Germany	South Korea	Mexico	Hungary
Access to information about the company	86	81	86	90	76	83
Level of pay	92	96	97	93	81	87
Ability to initiate new projects	87	81	84	82	76	81
Contact with customers	83	73	69	86	74	74

work well in teams; managers were seen as increasing their cross-functional knowledge more than nonmanagers. Managers also tended to reserve strategic information and project initiation for themselves *(Table 19-1).*

Such gaps could limit the ability of either group to contribute fully to the organization's success. If employees' teamwork is not associated with better knowledge about the whole business and where its work fits in, how can the team help solve problems or improve performance, especially with limited power to initiate projects? And if managers' strategic knowledge is not associated with cooperation, then how well can the organization develop cross-functional integration or other forms of synergy? This suggests a dual corporate education agenda for the future, one in which companies both upgrade the team skills of managers and increase the strategic knowledge of employees.

Respondents from Japanese companies reported some of the greatest differences between the organizational "top" and "bottom" and were least optimistic about work force improvement. They saw a widening gap between the better discipline and motivation of managers today and the declining work ethic of other employees. But these respondents were also unusual in counting on product development and the quality of management more than work force skills to make their companies successful *(Table 19-2).* Perhaps Japanese society is beginning to move away from its traditional work ethic, as some Japan-watchers suggest; but a continued emphasis on innovation still provides productivity ad-

Table 19-2. Key success factors differ among the three industrial leaders

Q: What are the three most important factors for your organization's success? *(percent of respondents checking each item)*

Japan		Germany		United States	
① Product development	54	① Work force skills	63	① Customer service	52
② Management	41	② Problem solving	47	② Product quality	40
③ Product quality	36	③ Management	44	③ Technology	36

vantages. This is a reminder that great products, well-designed processes, and effective strategic planning can sometimes play a bigger role in business outcomes than worker attitudes.

Is hierarchy still inevitable in all but the smallest companies? Maybe so, but respondents in Finland, Austria, and New Zealand reported much more egalitarianism in their companies. Clearly some countries are beginning to blur the distinction between managers and others. Social distance—differences of appearance and lifestyle—fades fastest; organizational power distinctions linger longer.

Anxious Alliances, Cautious Coalitions

While boundaries within the organization are shifting slowly, the blurring of external boundaries is apparently happening faster. Larger, older manufacturing companies are in the vanguard, but they are proceeding cautiously.

Customer service was saluted as the top success factor in nearly every country. Product quality, often involving close relationships with suppliers, was also highly ranked. Many companies represented in the survey claim to have long-term relationships both with their customers and suppliers *(Table 19-3)*. But according to survey results, "long-term" does not necessarily translate into "close." In practice, customers are kept at arm's length and suppliers only a little closer. Only a small minority of companies claiming long-term supplier relationships said that they train suppliers or work closely on product development with those suppliers *(Table 19-4)*.

Is ambivalence about breaching company boundaries a function of the difficulties involved in making this change? Most respondents' companies were engaged in at least a few joint ventures or alliances, though more often in countries like Sweden or Belgium than in Argentina or Brazil. The more joint venture experience respondents had, the more they identified *managerial* issues as worrisome *(Table 19-5)*. For instance, Belgians were more concerned about loss of control and information in collaborative ventures. In contrast, Austrians, who reported less joint

Table 19-3. While companies claim they are getting closer to their customers and suppliers . . .

	Always	Often	Sometimes	Never

Q: Does your organization have long-term relationships with suppliers? *(percent of total respondents)*

	Always	Often	Sometimes	Never
Total	24	52	20	4
Greater than 10,000	20	57	20	3
Less than 500	27	49	19	5

Q: Does your organization share strategic information with customers?

	Always	Often	Sometimes	Never
Total	7	26	44	23
Greater than 10,000	6	26	47	21
Less than 500	8	28	42	22

venture activity, considered the biggest risks to involve political and macroeconomic factors such as exchange rates.

It is one thing for less experienced managers to be unaware of the corporate culture clashes and ongoing managerial dilemmas of cross-company coalitions. But if so many experienced managers recognize that ongoing management issues are the biggest risks in alliances and partnerships, why do companies devote considerably more resources and top management time to negotiating the deal than they do to managing the subsequent relationship?

According to respondents' reports, companies in some countries do more than give lip service to the importance of their external allies. Germans, for example, were higher than the average on scales measuring closeness to *both* customers and suppliers—perhaps reflecting the industrial goods sectors in which many small-to-midsized German companies operate (they tend to be weak in consumer products and consumer marketing).

Other country differences are provocative. Americans scored

Table 19-4.   . . . Most of these relationships, especially with suppliers, are still infrequent

	Always	Often	Sometimes	Never
Q: Does your organization work with suppliers to design a product? *(percent of total respondents)*				
Total	8	29	46	17
Greater than 10,000	8	36	45	11
Less than 500	9	27	44	20
Q: Does your organization offer seminars or training programs for suppliers?				
Total	4	14	33	49
Greater than 10,000	5	22	44	29
Less than 500	3	10	26	61
Q: Does your organization include customers on a product-planning team?				
Total	9	23	41	27
Greater than 10,000	9	24	44	23
Less than 500	11	24	38	27
Q: Does your organization offer seminars or training programs for customers?				
Total	13	27	35	25
Greater than 10,000	17	35	33	15
Less than 500	12	24	33	31

somewhat higher than average on *customer* closeness and lower than average on *supplier* closeness. The Japanese pattern on the survey was the opposite. Though appearing cautious and protective in all relationships, the Japanese were more likely to open their boundaries to suppliers than to customers. This is consistent with other findings. Japanese respondents placed a much higher

Table 19-5. What companies worry about the most in their supplier-customer relationships

(percent of total checking each item)

Different corporate cultures	59
Coordinating plans	43
Quality standards	32
Other company's personnel	27
Stealing secrets	24
Personality clashes	24
Different size companies	18
Customer confusion	17
Incompatible accounting	17
Political risk	9
Currency risk	8

emphasis on product innovation than did U.S. respondents, who preferred to count on customer service for their success.

Does this tell us anything about systematic managerial biases that can subtly influence strategies, resource allocation, and patterns of attention? Imagine that the survey findings are an early indicator of where companies are placing their bets for the future, and consider the plausibility of this possible division of global labor between the triad powers: will the U.S. role be to distribute and service products developed in Japan—while Germany tries to compete effectively with both?

Agenda for the Next Conversation

Comparing and contrasting opinions from managers in many countries provide an opportunity for leaders to hold a mirror to themselves, their companies, and the countries in which they do business. Like an image in a mirror, the images they see could be distorted by any number of cultural factors, or the self-selection of respondents. Still, taken as a whole, the survey results suggest some topics for the next conversation:

- *Look to Germany for small and mid-sized industrial goods companies "fit" for global competition.* German cosmopolitanism is associated with less reliance on government and more cooperation with suppliers and customers. Working effectively across boundaries could come more easily to smaller German companies, giving them an edge in the global economy. In contrast, smaller companies in English-speaking countries, including the United States, are still comparatively inward-focused.

- *Worry about the Japanese emphasis on product innovation and the Japanese work ethic.* In fact, worry about Japanese worries. A tendency to be dissatisfied, for example, with the work force, coupled with a productivity emphasis could spur Japanese companies on to more achievements, especially in labor-saving technology.

- *Expect less from one's country and give more.* Conflicts and contradictions around political rules for the economic game still have to be sorted out. International companies are not expecting much direct government economic assistance. At the same time, companies that are excellent local citizens contributing to the improvement of society can have a stronger voice in political affairs.

- *Get on the child care and education bandwagons.* The overwhelming worldwide consensus about the importance of these issues suggests that companies that do not contribute could lag behind their competitors. While cleaning up the environment is also an important arena for action, business leaders already see this as their responsibility. A greater challenge for business is to develop a social agenda that identifies ways to contribute to today's families and tomorrow's work force.

- *Close the gap between values and practices.* Do too many managers lack faith in the capabilities of nonmanagers? General agreement about the importance of people to a company's success should be translated into opportunities for those at the bottom to get more information, initiate projects, and mingle with management. Similarly, endorsement of the importance of customer service and product quality should be reflected in new ways of including customer and supplier perspectives in decision making.

A smaller world creates a bigger agenda for business. There are more cultures to understand, more social responsibilities to master, more time pressures to juggle, and more relationships to rethink.

Note

1. Data were examined item by item (raw frequencies, means, and standard deviations) as well as organized into 40 scales based on statistical tests, such as cluster analysis and factor analysis. Translations were double-checked for accuracy and for universality of meaning, and questionable items were excluded from certain analyses. Patterns were analyzed by the country in which respondents currently work, respondent sex and age, and company type (by industry, size, ownership, degree of recent growth and profitability, and international orientation). Tests of statistical significance, effect size (measuring the degree of difference in a particular group's responses from the mean), and intercorrelations between scales were also conducted.

20

Collaborative Advantage: The Art of Alliances

Alliances between companies, whether they are from different parts of the world or different ends of the supply chain, are a fact of life in business today. Some alliances are no more than fleeting encounters, lasting only as long as it takes one partner to establish a beachhead in a new market. Others are the prelude to a full merger of two or more companies' technologies and capabilities. Whatever the duration and objectives of business alliances, being a good partner has become a key corporate asset. I call it a company's collaborative advantage. In the global economy, a well-developed ability to create and sustain fruitful collaborations gives companies a significant competitive leg up.

Yet, too often, top executives devote more time to screening potential partners in financial terms than to managing the partnership in human terms. They tout the future benefits of the alliance to their shareholders but don't help their managers create those benefits. They worry more about controlling the relationship than about nurturing it. In short, they fail to develop their company's collaborative advantage and thereby neglect a key resource.

To develop lessons about productive partnerships, especially but not exclusively those intercompany relationships that spanned two or more countries and cultures, my research group and I observed more than 37 companies and their partners from 11 parts of the world (the United States, Canada, France, Germany, the United Kingdom, the Netherlands, Turkey, China, Hong Kong, Indonesia, and Japan). We included large and small companies in both manufacturing and service industries that were involved in many kinds of alliances. To ensure that the lessons were widely applicable, we sought companies less prominent in the business press than giants like IBM, Corning, Motorola, or Ford. Several of the relationships that we studied were more than 20 years old; others had formed only recently in response to industry and geopolitical changes. In multiple visits, we conducted more than 500 interviews with leaders and staffs of both partners. Over time, we saw relationships blossom after good or rocky starts; change goals or structures; and wither or dissolve—amicably or contentiously. Our research uncovered three fundamental aspects of business alliances:

- They must yield benefits for the partners, but they are more than just the deal. They are living systems that evolve progressively in their possibilities. Beyond the immediate reasons they have for entering into a relationship, the connection offers the parties an option on the future, opening new doors and unforeseen opportunities.

- Alliances that both partners ultimately deem successful involve collaboration (creating new value together) rather than mere exchange (getting something back for what you put in). Partners value the skills each brings to the alliance.

- They cannot be "controlled" by formal systems but require a dense web of interpersonal connections and internal infrastructures that enhance learning.

Moreover, we observed that North American companies, more than others in the world, take a narrow, opportunistic view of relationships, evaluating them strictly in financial terms or seeing them as barely tolerable alternatives to outright acquisition. Preoccupied with the economics of the deal, North American companies frequently neglect the political, cultural, organizational, and human aspects of the partnership. Asian companies are the most comfortable with relationships, and therefore they are the most adept at using and exploiting them. European companies fall somewhere in the middle.

Exploring the different outcomes of the business relationships of other companies can help companies manage their own. Successful alliances build and improve a collaborative advantage by first acknowledging and then effectively managing the human aspects of their alliances.

Varieties of Relationships

Cooperative arrangements between companies range along a continuum from weak and distant to strong and close. At one extreme, in *mutual service consortia,* similar companies in similar industries pool their resources to gain a benefit too expensive to acquire alone—access to an advanced technology, for example. At midrange, in *joint ventures,* companies pursue an opportunity that needs a capability from each of them—the technology of one and the market access of the other, for example. The joint venture might operate independently, or it might link the partners' operations. The strongest and closest collaborations are *value-chain partnerships,* such as supplier-customer relationships. Companies in different industries with different but complementary skills link their capabilities to create value for ultimate users. Commitments in those relationships tend to be high, the partners tend to develop joint activities in many functions, operations often overlap, and the relationship thus creates substantial change within each partner's organization.

Companies can participate simultaneously in many kinds of relationships, and partners in any relationship may play a variety of roles. The 65 partners in Inmarsat, a consortium that operates a telecommunications satellite, are simultaneously *owners* investing capital, *customers* routing calls through the satellites, *suppliers* of technology to the venture, *regulators* setting policy, and *competitors* offering services similar to Inmarsat's. Netas, Northern Telecom's joint venture with local investors in Turkey, is simultaneously an *investment* asset for Northern, a *customer* for Northern equipment, a *supplier* of new software and systems, and a *gatekeeper* to other relationships.

In every case, a business relationship is more than just the deal. It is a connection between otherwise independent organizations that can take many forms and contains the potential for additional collaboration. It is a mutual agreement to continue to get together; thus its value includes the potential for a stream of opportunities.

Selection and Courtship

Relationships between companies begin, grow, and develop—or fail—in ways similar to relationships between people. No two relationships travel the same path, but successful alliances generally unfold in five overlapping phases.

In the first—courtship—two companies meet, are attracted, and discover their compatibility. During the second—engagement—they draw up plans and close the deal. In phase three, the newly partnered companies, like couples setting up housekeeping, discover they have different ideas about how the business should operate. In phase four, the partners devise mechanisms for bridging those differences and develop techniques for getting along. And in phase five, as old-marrieds, each company discovers that it has changed internally as a result of its accommodation to the ongoing collaboration.

"Love at first sight?" "The company of our dreams?" In fact, many executives use romantic analogies to describe the enthusiasm that accompanies their discovery of a new corporate partner. "One of the reasons our alliance was consummated so quickly," reports a Foote, Cone & Belding executive about the Chicago ad agency's partnership with Paris-based Publicis SA, "was that it was . . . love at first sight."

Such analogies are appropriate because business pairings aren't entirely cold-blooded. Indeed, successful company relationships nearly always depend on the creation and maintenance of a comfortable personal relationship between the senior executives.

Alliances and partnerships are initially romantic in another sense: their formation rests largely on hopes and dreams—what might be possible if certain opportunities are pursued. Strategic and financial analyses contribute a level of confidence, but, like all new business ventures, collaborative relationships draw energy largely from the optimistic ambition of their creators. COMCO, a Swiss diversified services company, seeing a big demand for environmental cleanup in Eastern Europe, touted enthusiastically the benefits of its joint venture with the U.S. expert, Martech. COMCO

---

optimistically made the Martech joint venture a linchpin of its future growth strategy and assumed Martech felt the same way. Only later, when a cash infusion was needed and Martech backed off, did COMCO realize that its infatuation had been one-sided. Eastern Europe was less important to Martech than it was to COMCO, and more remote; also, Martech had wanted quick returns.

The risk of missing a rare opportunity also motivates company leaders to enter into relationships with open-ended possibilities beyond just clear financial payoffs. For example, newly privatized telecommunications businesses in Europe, Latin America, and Asia often find many foreign companies bidding for their affections, even when financial payoffs are uncertain and venture strategies confusing. Those companies offer a rare chance for outsiders to acquire inside positions in country markets.

Furthermore, distance lends enchantment. Company leaders often don't know each other well enough to be aware of, never mind bothered by, a potential partner's subtle differences. Selective perceptions reinforce the dreams, not the dangers. Leaders see in the other what they want to see and believe what they want to believe, often realizing only later that infatuation blinded them to early warning signs. One leader on the European side of an alliance with a U.S. company blamed himself for believing that his country unit would become the lead center for both companies' products worldwide. "I was ignoring the fact that we were two separate companies," he says, "and that our partner would never accept part of its business being run by an outsider."

The selection process may go better if companies look for three key criteria:

1. *Self-analysis.* Relationships get off to a good start when partners know themselves and their industry, when they have assessed changing industry conditions and decided to seek an alliance. It also helps if executives have experience in evaluating potential partners. They won't be easily dazzled by the first good-looking prospect that comes along.

2. *Chemistry.* To highlight the personal side of business relationships is not to deny the importance of sound financial and strategic analyses. But deals often turn on rapport between chief executives. And the feelings between them that clinch or negate a relationship

transcend business to include personal and social interests. Also, a good personal rapport between executives creates a well of goodwill to draw on later if tensions develop.

Northern Telecom was not even on the list when Matra Hachette of France began to seek partners for its Matra Communication subsidiary. In late 1991, negotiations with Philips, Siemens, and AT&T were well under way when Northern chairman Paul Stern asked Matra chairman Jean-Luc Lagardère to consider his company. Eventually Matra executives flew to North America to meet Stern and other senior staff. Two weeks later, Stern flew to France to dine with Lagardère. Skeptical at first, Lagardère was won over. "Our views on business," Stern says, "were similar: speed, disdain for bureaucracy, a willingness to make decisions. We hit it off socially; we share an interest in the arts and fast cars." Northern also impressed Lagardère and other Matra managers because Stern got personally involved; CEOs from other companies had left all contact to lower functionaries. In July 1992, Northern and Matra closed the deal.

Signs of the leader's interest, commitment, and respect are especially important in certain countries. In China, as well as in Chinese-dominated businesses throughout Asia, company suitors should give "face" (honor and respect) to a potential partner's decision makers by investing the personal time of their own leaders.

3. *Compatibility.* The courtship period tests compatibility on broad historical, philosophical, and strategic grounds: common experiences, values and principles, and hopes for the future. While analysts examine financial viability, leaders can assess the less tangible aspects of compatibility. When British retailer BhS decided to form partnerships with a small number of key suppliers instead of continuing its "promiscuity" with many suppliers, to use one executive's term, then CEO David Dworkin met with the head of each prospective partner to explore business philosophies—not products and finances.

The initial relationship building between ad agencies Foote, Cone & Belding and Publicis involved the discovery of many commonalities. Publicis, operating in 39 major European cities by 1987, was twentieth in the world in billings. FCB, also with an extensive international presence, ranked fifteenth. Both agencies shared the same industry imperative—to improve their international reach—and the same important catalyst, the announcement by Nestlé, a leading client of both, that it would reduce its ad agencies from 100 to 5.

FCB and Publicis both brought humility to their growth plans, which made them open to sharing control; each believed that it could not grow alone and that industry globalization was blunting its competitive edge. Both had searched for several years without finding the right partner, so they had sufficient experience with other potential partners to be satisfied with what they found in each other. Each company was strong in territories that the other was not, but there was reasonable equivalence in the strengths each brought to the relationship. The companies had similar creative principles and operating philosophies, similar experiences with common clients, and few areas of direct business conflict.

In 1987, "Nestlé told us it wanted five global agencies and that, unless we did something, we would not be one of them," Publicis managing director Gerard Pedraglio recalls. Meanwhile, he had tried to hire Antonio Beja to manage the company's Spanish operations. Though Beja did not take the offer, the two men stayed in touch. Beja eventually became head of Asian and Latin American operations for FCB. In December 1987, Beja and Pedraglio met for dinner, and in the course of their conversation, Beja described his chairman's strategy for FCB. Pedraglio interrupted. "Now, Antonio," he said, "You stop, and I will finish." He did, and Beja was astounded. "How did you know?" he asked. "That's our plan too," Pedraglio replied.

Beja told FCB chairman Norman Brown about his dinner discussion with Pedraglio, and soon after that, Publicis representatives were on a plane to Chicago. Six months and five meetings later, having seen in each other a fulfillment of their needs, Publicis and FCB announced their alliance. "We found early on a remarkable degree of similarity in our creative and operating philosophies," an FCB executive explains.

The results of their collaboration initially confirmed those findings. Publicis and FCB operated an innovative global alliance and built a network of 173 agencies in 43 countries. Together the partners constituted the second largest agency in Europe and North America, and the eighth largest in the world. But initial compatibility proved superficial, and later the alliance dissolved.

The FCB-Publicis alliance is evidence that, especially in fast-moving industries, potential partners must find compatibility in legacy, philosophy, and desires, because specific opportunities are often short-lived and won't sustain a long-term relationship. A relationship that falters or fails as soon as the first project is concluded precludes other opportunities from developing. Moreover, side deals can quickly become significant in a sustained relationship. The potential to tap Matra Communication's cellular radio technologies was a side benefit of Northern Telecom's alliance with Matra Hachette. Within a year, the side benefit had become the most important and productive piece of the alliance.

Powersoft entered into an alliance with Lotus to share manufacturing space and soon discovered that sharing Lotus's new packaging technology was even more valuable. Inmarsat's original maritime communications venture, which joined partners such as Comsat, British Telecom, Teleglobe, and Japan's KDD, has been dwarfed in growth potential by newer activities in aeronautical and land mobile communications. For TechRidge, a small manufacturer of specialized cameras for identification card photos, a long-standing relationship with Polaroid took a new turn when a Polaroid ally included Polaroid in a large contract in Mexico, and Polaroid brought along TechRidge. This unanticipated opportunity gave TechRidge a platform for further globalization.

Sometimes, particularly in Asia, partners are selected more for their potential to open future doors than for immediate benefits. Lippo Group, a rapidly growing financial conglomerate, has tapped a network of Japanese, European, and U.S. partners to expand from its Indonesian home base to Hong Kong and China. Founder and chairman Mochtar Riady believes that promising relationships should be nurtured for their future value, even when initial joint ventures are not very profitable.

Many relationships die an early death when they are scrutinized for quick returns. COMCO's alliance with Martech for environmental cleanup services in Eastern Europe dissolved in less than two years because of disputes over slower-than-expected returns

and the need for new investment, even though the market potential was still great.

Getting Engaged

What starts out as personal rapport, philosophical and strategic
compatibility, and shared vision between two companies' top executives eventually must be institutionalized and made public.
Other stakeholders get involved, and the relationship begins to
become depersonalized. But success in the engagement phase of
a new alliance still depends on maintaining a careful balance
between the personal and the institutional.

Meeting the family

The rapport between chief executives and a handful of company
leaders must be supplemented by the approval, formal or informal,
of other people in the companies and of other stakeholders. Also,
each partner has other outside relationships that need to approve
of the new tie: government ministries, major customers and suppliers, other partners, and investors. Sometimes those meetings
don't go well.

In the early stages of an alliance in Europe, a French company
representative took his U.S. counterpart to meet with a French
government official in a ministry that had partial oversight of the
deal. The U.S. manager proceeded to lecture the French official,
a socialist, about the virtues of free-market capitalism. French
leaders pride themselves on their intellect, so both the form and
the substance of the meeting created significant problems. Later,
the French managers had to smooth things over at the ministry
and educate the American on appropriate behavior.

The vows

Third-party professionals—lawyers, investment bankers, and their
staffs—play their most important roles at this point in the process.

But if they dominate, the relationship can become too depersonalized and lose the leaders' vision. It is important to remember
that outside professionals don't have to live with the results of their
work. Also, because of their professional bias, they are less likely
to be interested in the symbolic substance of relationship building:
the gestures of respect or the mutual give-and-take that cement a
relationship.

One alliance between a U.S. company and a French company in
the North Sea oil fields involved a few perfunctory meetings between the chief executives. Then the legal, financial, and strategy
staffs took over under the guidance of external law firms. The alliance collapsed in just three years. The professionals were savvy
about finance and contracts but not about what it would take to
operate the joint venture or whether the two companies were
operationally compatible. When the U.S. company later formed a
productive alliance with a Dutch company, executives and key
managers spent a great deal of time together discussing principles
as well as specific agreements; lawyers' and analysts' roles were
minimized.

The best agreements between companies contain three important components. First, they incorporate a specific joint activity, a
first-step venture or project. This project makes the relationship
real in practice, helps the partners learn to work together, and
provides a basis for measuring performance. Having real work to
do makes it possible to get the relationship started; the longer a
courtship drags on without consummation, the more likely conditions or minds or both can change and jeopardize it.

Second, the vows should include a commitment to expand the
relationship through side bets such as equity swaps or personnel
exchanges. Such a commitment reflects a willingness to connect
the fates of the companies, as in the European Retail Alliance,
formed in 1989 by three large food retailers: Ahold in the Netherlands, Argyll in the United Kingdom, and Groupe Casino in France.
The ERA collaboration gave partners low-cost opportunities for
scale efficiencies and innovation. To cement the relationship, the
partners bought modest amounts of one another's stock. The three
ERA partners sold products to one another and collaborated in
joint projects in insurance, data processing, hardware purchasing,
quality assurance, and personnel development. They have also

developed an 11-company marketing association based in Switzerland that works closely with manufacturers on product development.

ERA enlarged each member's international supplier base by sharing relationships already tested by another ERA company. These new alliances, in turn, provided new product offerings that enhanced the companies' reputations as taste leaders in their home markets. For example, Argyll's Safeway stores bought 320,000 cases of wine from Casino for their 1992 Christmas promotion; Casino used Safeway suppliers in the United Kingdom to introduce Scottish smoked salmon products and other high-quality U.K. fresh foods to French consumers. Safeway's store-of-the-future, which opened in Edinburgh in November 1993, featured ERA-derived concepts new to the U.K. market—French-style delis, for example. ERA helped its partners test future opportunities that might emerge as Europe integrates further. Argyll's chairman, Sir Alistair Grant, stressed ERA's long-term benefits: "Perhaps above all, the Retail Alliance has helped our team to become serious about Europe. I believe that our successors will be grateful for this." Externally, ERA opened borders. Inside member companies, it opened minds.

Third, the vows should incorporate clear signs of continuing independence for all partners. The FCB-Publicis alliance appointed an American as chairman of the European joint venture, so FCB's European staff and clients wouldn't think FCB was ceding its European operations to its French partner. When Matra allied with Northern Telecom, it preserved continuity in its product lines, even at the price of duplication with Northern products, to show customers that it would continue to upgrade and service installed machines.

Setting Up Housekeeping

The romance of courtship quickly gives way to day-to-day reality as partners begin to live together. Joint ventures are also new ventures and are thus fraught with uncertainty and unanticipated roadblocks. Now more than just the upper echelons of management must work together to make the partnership succeed.

Problems of broader involvement

As actual projects get under way, many more people filling many more roles must work with members of the other organization. This broader involvement threatens to undermine the commitment forged at the top, for four reasons.

1. People in other positions may not experience the same attraction and rapport as the chief executives did. For example, during their alliance's early years, Publicis and FCB top executives maintained close contact, traveling often to each other's headquarters. They spent a lot of time together both informally and formally. Other employees had not been in touch with one another, however, and in some cases had to be pushed to work with their overseas counterparts.

2. Employees at other levels in the organization may be less visionary and cosmopolitan than top managers and less experienced in working with people from different cultures. They may lack knowledge of the strategic context in which the relationship makes sense and see only the operational ways in which it does not. For example, a member of the team developing a new financial product to be launched with a foreign partner complained repeatedly to his boss about the risks inherent in the product and the difficulties in introducing it, even recommending termination of the venture. He didn't realize that the foreign partner was a key gatekeeper for a lucrative development deal in another country. Senior managers were tolerating this risky venture in the hope of a larger payoff elsewhere.

3. Usually only a few staff people are dedicated full-time to the relationship. Others are evaluated on the performance of their primary responsibilities and therefore often neglect duties relating to the new alliance. Venture managers, more concerned about their future in the parent company that appointed them, often give priority to their own company's events or executives and subordinate those of the partner.

4. People just one or two tiers from the top might oppose the relationship and fight to undermine it. This is especially true in organizations that have strong independent business units or among professional groups whose incentives aren't aligned with the interests of the organization as a whole. For example, a health care

services company formed an alliance with a group of hospitals to create a single new facility to replace duplicate capacity in the hospitals. All the hospitals invested in the alliance, and the services company assumed they would bring enough business to make the venture profitable quickly. But that assumption proved wrong. While the hospital heads had committed to the relationship, they had ignored the views and needs—and the power—of the staff at the units to be closed. The staffs fought back. They cited issues about quality for not sending business to the new venture, and because it was having start-up problems, their claims were plausible. They also cut the transfer prices to internal customers to win their backing in keeping their units alive. And they neglected to send their people to work with the venture, which began to hemorrhage money badly. Eventually the alliance folded.

Discovery of difference

Operational and cultural differences emerge after collaboration is under way. They often come as a surprise to those who created the alliance. That failure could reflect blind spots on the part of the legal and financial analysts who dominate the engagement period, but even operating people see the similarities more often than the dissimilarities in potential partners. Experience has a way of opening their eyes.

Differences in authority, reporting, and decision-making styles become noticeable at this stage in the new alliance: which people get involved in decisions; how quickly decisions are made; how much reporting and documentation are expected; what authority comes with a position; and which functions work together.

Before the alliance, for example, Publicis was a 75% privately held company whose chief executive dominated strategic decisions. FCB was a public company with a large number of senior managers trying to operate by consensus and generating a lot of paperwork: reports, financial statements, and lengthy meeting minutes. One key U.S. manager, who worked slowly through others according to a philosophy of empowerment, was regarded as weak by the French, who were used to a more directive style. Early in the relationship, some U.S. managers found Publicis too hierarchical, but some French managers found FCB's frequent meetings and paperwork too bureaucratic. And the French managers' abstractions and penchant for theory contrasted with the Americans' desire for concrete empirical facts.

Differences in structuring authority can have immediate practical consequences. In China, a chief engineer reports typically to the chief executive, whereas in Canada, at Northern Telecom, he or she reports to the manufacturing director. Numerous other logistical and operational differences are soon discovered to be hiding behind the assumed compatibility: different product development schedules, views of the sales process, or technical standards, for example. Also, when the partners extend their areas of collaboration, the relationship becomes more difficult to govern and to evaluate on a purely financial basis.

The most common conflicts in relationships occur over money: capital infusions, transfer pricing, licensing fees, compensation levels, and management fees. Also, the complexity of roles each partner has with respect to the other can make economic decisions difficult. Remember, the relationship is larger than any one venture.

All operational dissimilarities require working out. More communication than anyone anticipated is necessary, and different languages make things even harder. In a Franco-American joint venture, meetings were conducted in both languages and thus took twice as long. Differences between companies do not disappear because of an alliance, but they can be handled so they don't jeopardize it. Companies that are good at partnering take the time to learn about the differences early and take them into account as events unfold.

Respect versus resentment

People will take the time to understand and work through partnership differences to the extent that they feel valued and respected for what they bring to the relationship. Using stereotypes to explain people's behavior—the French always do this, or the Germans always do that, for example—denigrates individuals and therefore diminishes their incentive to bridge troubling differences.

Stereotyping polarizes the partners, setting up us-versus-them dynamics that undermine the desire to collaborate. One North American manager observed soon after forming an alliance with a European company, "You're an ugly American to them, backwater folks from across the pond, here to purchase, steal, whatever." A cynical countryman wondered whether the European partner's motive was to push the North American company out of the market.

Mistrust, once introduced, sets off a vicious cycle. It makes success harder to attain, which means someone has to be blamed for the lack of success. Because of their differences, outsiders are the most suspect—a fact that only increases mistrust. Respect that builds trust begins with an assumption of equality: all parties bring something valuable to the relationship and deserve to be heard. In one alliance, tension began to build after the local partner felt shut out of decisions, even though local knowledge was vital to the venture's success. A Chinese manager commented on the resentment that Western companies create when they assume that their superior technology gives them the right to make all the decisions. "The focus here," the manager said, "is on face, reputation. Even if people are poor, you need to give them face. North Americans feel that because they gave us jobs, we can't argue. But the Chinese people don't need their jobs. We can replace them with another foreign company; we can import from another place."

Learning to Collaborate

Active collaboration takes place when companies develop mechanisms—structures, processes, and skills—for bridging organizational and interpersonal differences and achieving real value from the partnership. Multiple ties at multiple levels ensure communication, coordination, and control. Deploying more rather than fewer people to relationship activities helps ensure that both partners' resources are tapped and that both companies' own needs and goals are represented.

The most productive relationships achieve five levels of integration.

1. *Strategic integration,* which involves continuing contact among top leaders to discuss broad goals or changes in each

company. Leaders should not form an alliance and then abandon its nurturing to others. The more contact top executives have, the more changes they will hear about, the more chances they will have to work things out, the more information they will be able to turn into benefits, and the greater the possibility that the companies will evolve in complementary rather than conflicting directions.

Often, new governance forums evolve after the relationship is under way. The chief executives in the European Retail Alliance devoted a day a month to their meetings, rotating among the three countries. Investment bankers Wertheim of the United States and Schroders of the United Kingdom began their alliance in 1986 with infrequent board meetings but soon saw the need for broader and more frequent contact. FCB and Publicis built their Alliance Operating Committee after realizing that having the CEOs sit on each other's boards didn't produce enough communication.

2. *Tactical integration,* which brings middle managers or professionals together to develop plans for specific projects or joint activities, to identify organizational or system changes that will link the companies better, or to transfer knowledge.

The ERA developed projects in insurance, information technology, and transportation that involved staff from member companies. Leadership for each project came from the company with the most experience or the best practices in that area. Northern Telecom and Matra Communication pinpointed four product domains in which potential synergies existed. Then they created four working groups of eight to ten people that met monthly to define specific ways of cooperating in each area. Members of all four groups convened in a general assembly every three months to report progress and problems to management. The small British apparel supplier Cohen & Wilks and its large retail partner, BhS, developed joint planning projects, including team efforts to improve computer linkups and financing mechanisms, such as a proposed retrospective discount scheme. BhS buying director Liz Broughan meets frequently with Cohen & Wilks staff members to plan product designs.

Establishing formal integrator roles is another way to ensure tactical integration. Lotus, Powersoft, and other partner-rich software companies have senior executives dedicated to alliance management, equivalent in status to the heads of finance or human resources. Worldwide account directors (WWADs) at FCB and Publicis work to make the best use of all resources of both partners on behalf of major clients. That task is complicated by another dynamic, the fact that each client relationship is very different. Some have highly centralized global marketing efforts; others give companies or regions autonomy to develop their own. Salomon Salto, WWAD for the FCB-Publicis relationship with Nestlé, communicated ideas to all parties but also intervened in local conflicts. He was viewed as an impartial observer with experience in many countries and brands. "My job is more diplomacy and negotiation than power," he observed. His ability to speak French, Spanish, English, and German helped a lot.

3. *Operational integration,* which provides ways for people carrying out the day-to-day work to have timely access to the information, resources, or people they need to accomplish their tasks. Participation in each other's training programs helped two companies in a technology-based relationship develop a common vocabulary and product development standards. Computer connections between Cohen & Wilks and BhS provided direct data interchange, which speeds product development and delivery cycles. Inmarsat engineers in London shared a technical vocabulary and systems with counterparts at the earth stations where partners receive satellite signals.

4. *Interpersonal integration,* which builds a necessary foundation for creating future value. As relationships mature beyond the early days of scrambling to create initial projects and erect structural scaffolding to manage them, the network of interpersonal ties between members of the separate companies grows in extent and density. Leaders soon feel the need to bring people together to share information. FCB and Publicis first expanded their initial Alliance Operating Committee to include more people. They then initiated worldwide conferences for executives and country managers. Next, they brought creative directors and account managers from both companies and many countries together to make recommendations for business development, creative excellence, and international client management.

Broad synergies born on paper do not develop in practice until many people in both organizations know one another personally and become willing to make the effort to exchange technology, refer clients, or participate on joint teams. Lippo Group, which has many partners involved in its network of banks and property development ventures, uses senior management conferences to sell the concept of synergy, identify cross-unit business opportunities, and build personal ties among managers.

Many strong interpersonal relationships help resolve small conflicts before they escalate. "There really is no good system for working out problems except through personal relationships," observes a European manager experienced in transatlantic relationships. "If you don't establish good rapport with your counterparts, you haven't got a prayer of making it work. Formal structures of decision making don't do anything for you unless you've got the relationship to start with."

5. *Cultural integration,* which requires people involved in the relationship to have the communication skills and cultural awareness to bridge their differences. Northern Telecom and Matra picked executives for their Matra Northern Cellular joint venture who had shared a similar foreign assignment. Chief executive Émile Gratton, a bilingual Canadian, had worked in the United States, South America, and Saudi Arabia. Chief operating officer Olivier de Pazzis, deployed by Matra in France, had run a joint venture with a U.S. company in Saudi Arabia.

Managers from both partners or affiliated companies must become teachers as well as learners. Managers at Tong Guang Nortel, the successful venture in China between Tong Guang Electronics and Northern Telecom, have committed themselves to teaching and learning. TGNT managing director Gerry Jones, deployed from the Northern side, arranged for Chinese deputy managing director Frank Yong to participate in a three-month training program in Canada to become familiar with Western business practices. That experience enabled Yong to raise questions with Northern managers in China and educate them about how situations appeared from the Chinese side of the venture. In turn, Yong arranged for his Western partners to visit important Chinese historic sites, such as the Great Wall and the Summer Palace, and invited them to Chinese weddings and to employees' homes.

When managers accept teaching and learning roles, they demonstrate interest and respect, which helps build the goodwill that's so useful in smoothing over cultural and organizational differences. TGNT's Canadian manufacturing director learned to speak Mandarin. Although he could hold only a simple conversation in Chinese, the enthusiastic applause he received at quarterly meetings in Shekou attested to his popularity. An American expatriate heading part of Lippo Group's insurance joint ventures knew that his primary job was to teach local managers analytic skills, but he also took the time to set up classes for himself and other expatriates to learn the local language and customs.

Integration in all five of these dimensions—strategic, tactical, operational, interpersonal, and cultural—requires that each party be willing to let the other parties inside, which entails a risk: the risk of change.

Changing Within

Productive relationships usually require and often stimulate changes within the partners, changes that they may not anticipate at the outset of the collaboration. When two companies place themselves in intimate contact with each other through an alliance, it is almost inevitable that each will compare itself with the other: How do we measure up to our partner in systems sophistication or operational efficiency? What lessons can we learn from our partner? In fact, learning and borrowing ideas from partners is part of realizing the full value of the relationship. FCB and Publicis used the formation of their alliance as the occasion to rethink the nature of an advertising agency and to create new roles for regional and country managers as well as for worldwide account directors.

Empowerment of relationship managers

Because collaborative ventures often make new demands, managers involved in the relationship must be able to vary their own companies' procedures to make venture-specific decisions. Staff involved in alliance activities often need more knowledge and skills. When British retailer BhS established partnerships with suppliers like Cohen & Wilks, buyers on both sides needed new strategic and financial information and negotiating skills to work effectively with one another. One success factor in Northern Telecom's joint ventures in Turkey and China was the autonomy of each venture's board of directors and expatriate managers, an autonomy that allowed them to depart from the practices the company follows in North American markets. In China, the ability to adapt to local markets—for example, in accounts receivable policies or incentive schemes for sales personnel—helped TGNT succeed. Developing flexibility—"letting go," as one manager describes it—may be difficult for tightly managed companies with detail-oriented managers.

Infrastructure for learning

Companies with strong communications across functions and widely shared information tend to have more productive external relationships. Thus other desirable internal changes include greater cross-functional teamwork and exchange of ideas. At BhS, cross-functional teamwork is crucial for achieving the speed, innovation, and quality the company seeks from supplier partnerships. Liz Broughan had to build bridges to marketing director Helena Packshaw and trading manager Sandee Springer.

Many businesses fail to realize the full potential from their relationships because internal barriers to communication limit learning to the small set of people directly involved in the relationship. One large U.S. company's highest award for quality went to a joint venture operating in a developing country, yet managers in that venture had a hard time convincing their colleagues in other countries that they had anything to teach them.

The company's systems are usually the culprit in such situations, not its people. In the early stages of its relationship with Northern Telecom, Matra learned that Northern put designs into production earlier than Matra did. Despite a common stereotype that speed is less important in France, the French engineers rose quickly to the challenge and proudly demonstrated a new capability several months ahead of schedule.

Specific forums to exchange ideas can help companies import lessons from their partners. In addition to top management's participation in the ERA, Argyll's Safeway stores have created a regional managers' forum and a senior executive development program. Cross-functional projects, such as offering discounts to customers who buy combinations of products, link marketing, information technology, and stores.

Managing the Trade-offs

There are limits to how much a company should change to accommodate the demands of an alliance. The potential value of the relationship must be weighed against the value of all the other company activities, which also make demands on its resources—including the time and energy of executives. Even when relationships have high value, an organization can handle only so many before demands begin to conflict and investment requirements (management time, partner-specific learning, capital, and the like) outweigh perceived benefits.

Sometimes companies must face the challenge of terminating an alliance. Relationships can end for a number of reasons. A partner may be suitable for one purpose and not another. Managers or other venture participants may be needed for more urgent tasks. Shifts in business conditions or strategy can mean that a particular relationship no longer fits as well as it once did. For whatever reason, ending a partnership properly is difficult to do and requires much skill and diplomacy. Partners should be fully informed and treated with integrity. If they are not, future relationships will be jeopardized—especially in Asian countries, where business and government leaders have long memories.

Like all living systems, relationships are complex. While they are simpler to manage when they are narrow in scope and the partners remain at arm's length, relationships like these yield fewer long-term benefits. Tighter control by one partner or development of a single command center might reduce conflicts and increase the manageability of a relationship. Many benefits, however, derive from flexibility and being open to new possibilities. Alliances benefit from establishing multiple, independent centers of competence and innovation. Each center can pursue different paths, creating in turn new networks that go off in new directions. Flexibility and openness bring particular advantages at business frontiers—in rapidly changing or new markets or in new technology fields.

The effective management of relationships to build collaborative advantage requires managers to be sensitive to political, cultural, organizational, and human issues. In the global economy today, companies are known by the company they keep. As the saying goes, success comes not just from what you know but from who you know. Intercompany relationships are a key business asset, and knowing how to nurture them is an essential managerial skill.

Eight I's That Create Successful We's

The characteristics of effective intercompany relationships challenge many decades of Western economic and managerial assumptions. For example, most Westerners assume that modern industrial companies are run best by professional managers operating within limited, contractual Western obligations. And most Westerners assume that any person with the requisite knowledge, skills, and talents can be a manager in the modern corporation. Although smaller companies, family businesses, and companies that are operating in developing countries have retained "premodern" characteristics, the "rational" model has been considered the ideal to which all organizations would eventually conform.

Intercompany relationships are different. They seem to work best when they are more familylike and less rational. Obligations are more diffuse, the scope for collaboration is more open, understanding grows between specific individuals, communication is frequent and intensive, and the interpersonal context is rich. The best intercompany relationships are frequently messy and emotional, involving feelings like chemistry or trust. And they should not be entered into lightly. Only relationships with full commitment on all sides endure long enough to create value for the partners.

Indeed, the best organizational relationships, like the best marriages, are true partnerships that tend to meet certain criteria:

Individual Excellence. Both partners are strong and have something of value to contribute to the relationship. Their motives for entering into the relationship are positive (to pursue future opportunities), not negative (to mask weaknesses or escape a difficult situation).

Importance. The relationship fits major strategic objectives of the partners, so they want to make it work. Partners have long-term goals in which the relationship plays a key role.

Interdependence. The partners need each other. They have complementary assets and skills. Neither can accomplish alone what both can together.

Investment. The partners invest in each other (for example, through equity swaps, cross-ownership, or mutual board service) to demonstrate their respective stakes in the relationship and each other. They show tangible signs of long-term commitment by devoting financial and other resources to the relationship.

Information. Communication is reasonably open. Partners share information required to make the relationship work, including their objectives and goals, technical data, and knowledge of conflicts, trouble spots, or changing situations.

Integration. The partners develop linkages and shared ways of operating so they can work together smoothly. They build broad connections between many people at many organizational levels. Partners become both teachers and learners.

Institutionalization. The relationship is given a formal status, with clear responsibilities and decision processes. It extends beyond the particular people who formed it, and it cannot be broken on a whim.

Integrity. The partners behave toward each other in honorable ways that justify and enhance mutual trust. They do not abuse the information they gain, nor do they undermine each other.

21

Competing on Politics

Productivity. Cost-effectiveness. Quality. Innovation. Customer service. Just when we thought that all the bases for business success had been identified, labeled, and dissected, along comes another one: *Politics.*

"Political advantage" derives from a stable and constructive relationship that makes government and the public allies in the battle for competitiveness. The Japanese case is instructive. Japanese businesses have been notably successful at advancing Japanese interests with governments around the world, especially in the United States. And they have done this as commercial entities working through civilian channels. The U.S. equivalent to the Japanese business-government alliance was once called the military-industrial complex—for good reason. Since World War II, there have been numerous cases of U.S. military or CIA intervention in behalf of American commercial interests: for example, in the Middle East (oil) and in Latin America (sugar and fruit). But today's wars are largely economic. The exceptions—terrorist provocation or invasions by power-hungry dictators—do not justify extending military approaches to commercial realms, where they are unsuitable.

Has American business caught up with the change? Alan Wolff, a former U.S. trade negotiator, observed that the U.S. State Department historically favored military over business interests on trade issues. The adversarial relationship between American business and its government created a vacuum. By embracing simplistic free-market rhetoric and wanting to operate "without government interference," U.S. businesses ensured that only military interests could speak with a united voice. But now the global economy has pulled the United States into competitive contests not of Boeing versus McDonnell Douglas but of Boeing versus Airbus *and* helpful European governments, as political strategist Kevin Phillips reminded the Republican party in a recent book.

In some countries, seeking political advantage for a company or an industry is routine. Because commercial success is difficult without political support, a tradition of cooperative alliances exists at all levels of industry and between business and government. The political dimension of the work of a general manager is much greater in France and Italy, for example, than it is in the United States. The European Community is thus more likely to understand Japanese political strategies and defend against them.

But American business is showing signs of growing political sophistication, as these examples illustrate:

Industries are learning. The semiconductor industry succeeded in welding apolitical entrepreneurs from smaller companies into a political force. In 1983, the industry established an ambitious agenda for government action. Four years later, industry members received more favorable tax treatment, relaxed antitrust regulation of joint R&D, greater protection of chip designs, and tougher fair-trade policies.

CEOs are learning. For example, Bob Malott, head of FMC Corporation, committed enormous time and energy to product-liability law reform over a period of more than a decade.

Once-protected corporate giants are learning. AT&T revamped its approach to political management after losing the opportunity to break into the French digital-switch market to L.M. Ericsson, the Swedish telecommunications company. In 1989, AT&T scored a big victory over both Ericsson and Siemens by winning a contract to modernize the Italian telecommunications system.

Is this learning too little, too late?

Consider the French success in commercializing remote satellite-sensing systems. In his book *Perestroika for America,* Harvard Business School Professor George Lodge showed how political advantage in the form of cooperative business-government relationships helped the French and cost the Americans. In 1981, the French space agency established the world's first commercial satellite venture, SPOT (Satellite pour l'Observations de la Terre), with help from the French, Swedish, and Belgian governments and from private companies like Matra, the French defense giant.

SPOT's first satellite was launched in 1986 with a government investment about one-third the amount the U.S. government invested in EOSAT (Earth Observation Satellite), a joint venture of Hughes (now General Motors) and RCA (now General Electric). By 1989, SPOT had more than 30% of world market share and was growing fast, while EOSAT was languishing.

There was more at stake in this French-American competition than a private company's loss of market share. Whoever controls the system can adjust the timing of data delivery, affecting a country's as well as a company's access to intelligence. You would think the United States would have marshaled its technological and financial resources to win in this realm, where there are enormous military implications.

Lodge argued that EOSAT's failure stems from fundamental flaws in U.S. business-government relationships. The EOSAT venture was not connected to a coherent long-term national strategy, and it lacked a following in Congress. Neither the venture's prominent parent companies nor their customers—a hundred companies dependent on the satellite data—bothered to get involved in the political sector.

When companies need government support to win a contract or change the rules, the need to put a political strategy into play seems obvious. But the European and Japanese cases demonstrate that a successful political strategy involves long-term investment in relationships, education, and diplomacy. Action must be taken at every point in the political value-creation chain. Shaping the agenda, framing the debate, or simply creating a positive image in the minds of the public can be as important as weighing in on a specific issue.

Japanese successes in the United States should be examined carefully, with respect as well as concern, for their lessons about competing on politics. Many of the management traits that earned Japanese companies success in the product marketplace also operate in the political realm: Consistency. A larger sense of purpose. Coherent activities involving the coordinated efforts of many organizations. Attention to detail. Willingness to spend large sums. Commitment to be in the game for the long haul. Patience. Perseverance.

Furthermore, the entire political spectrum is covered: Lobbying for favorable rules. Hiring the best-connected experts. Working the rules to advantage. Gathering abundant intelligence and analyzing it carefully. Practicing diplomacy. Winning friends for later contests. Making generous philanthropic donations. Spreading ideas and images through the educational system.

In short, an effective strategy for competing on politics means learning how the system operates and then working through it. It also means preventing reciprocity—not letting the competition do the same thing back in the home country.

Of course, political success cannot be detached from other aspects of business. An effective political strategy has to involve educating, mobilizing, and, especially, pleasing the public. In many countries, consumers are more active and more demanding. They vote—and not only with their pocketbooks. Many Japanese companies have been able to mount effective political strategies in the United States because the public perceived better value in some Japanese products. As Japanese companies expanded their U.S. operations in some regions, the public equated Japanese financial success with job creation and job security for Americans. Politicians actively courted Japanese companies for the benefits Japanese investment could bring their constituencies.

Without direct benefits to consumers and voters, no strategy of political intelligence gathering or of "buying" influence could last very long. Indeed, the U.S. cable TV industry is threatened with re-regulation because numerous consumer complaints about shabby service have reached congressional mailboxes. In contrast, a Swiss pharmaceutical company that distributes its products through physicians has recognized the public's role in influencing health care regulation; the company has added consumer and government outreach to its marketing agenda even though it doesn't sell products directly to consumers.

Undeniably, competing on politics is a touchy subject. There are many difficult ethical and moral questions, issues that reach to the heart of a country's values and interests. If political advantage comes principally from putting politicians and former government officials on the payroll, as Ross Perot's 1996 running mate Pat Choate argued, then the public has a right to be profoundly troubled about the outcomes. In some African and Arab countries where officials may expect a monetary token of "appreciation" for helping businesses operate, American multinationals are learning how to substitute *public* benefits (such as funding a community amenity) for bribery. Yet some of the same companies are silent on whether U.S. officials should be permitted to sign on as lobbyists after they leave office. Serving as a representative for a foreign organization is perfectly legal, of course; but "foreign agent" sounds sinister—and may indeed have troubling implications.

The subject of political advantage is also controversial because companies often keep political operations behind the scenes. Indeed, a company's political strategy is likely to be less transparent than its product strategy. Businesses don't offer tours of the inner workings of the political factory. Even those analysts who manage to get inside have to piece together a story. George Lodge, a welcome observer of IBM's Office of Governmental Programs, can only speculate about how IBM influenced changes in Brazil's restrictive computer-import policies.

These complexities should not deter businesses from thinking harder and more often about their relationships with government and the public. Indeed, as globalism grows in markets, localism in politics becomes more important. Officials whose mandate derives from local opinion determine the rules of the game. As trade boundaries between nations blur, governments become more relevant because they can make it easier or harder for businesses to operate. Understanding and influencing public opinion becomes as critical as understanding and influencing consumer preferences.

Competing on politics is not simple. Nor will it alone guarantee success today. Clearly, there is no substitute for the basics of providing high-quality products to customers. But there is also no excuse for naiveté and inaction on the political front.

22

Thriving Locally in the Global Economy

In the future, success will come to those companies, large and small, that can meet global standards and tap into global networks. And it will come to those cities, states, and regions that do the best job of linking the businesses that operate within them to the global economy.

Sweeping changes in the competitive landscape, including the presence of foreign competitors in domestic markets, are driving businesses to rethink their strategies and structures to reach beyond traditional boundaries. Increasing numbers of small and midsize companies are joining corporate giants in striving to exploit international growth markets or in trying to become world-class even if only to retain local customers.

At the same time, communities are under considerable pressure to understand what they need to do to enhance—and in some cases even preserve—their local vitality. Local residents and civic leaders are expressing concern about their communities' economic future, particularly in light of the impact of global forces on where businesses locate and how they operate. Some see a basic conflict between social and community interests that are largely domestic or even local, and business competitiveness issues that often are international in scope. If the class division of the industrial economy was between capital and labor, or between managers and workers, the class division of the emerging information economy could well be between cosmopolitans with global connections and locals who are stuck in one place.

To avoid a clash between global economic interests and local political interests, businesses must know how to be responsive to the needs of the communities in which they operate even as they globalize. And communities must determine how best to connect cosmopolitans and locals and how to create a civic culture that will attract and retain footloose companies. The greatest danger to the viability of communities is not globalization but a retreat into isolationism and protectionism. In the global economy, those people and organizations that are isolated and cut off are at a disadvantage. They are targets for nativists who feed on discontent by blaming outsiders, scapegoating foreigners, and urging that barriers be erected to stem the global tide. But if communities retreat into isolationism, they are unlikely to solve the very problems that led to their discontent in the first place. Ironically, the best way for communities to preserve their local control is to become more competitive globally.

This lesson began to come into sharp focus for me when I started to explore over 37 emerging business alliances and partnerships around the world. I saw that those companies often were surpassing their peers by linking forces in international networks. But I also saw how controversial their actions were in their own countries and cities, and how irrevocably they were altering life back home. What I saw made me wonder how the rise of a global economy changes the meaning of community, which is largely rooted in place. And I started thinking about how global forces could be marshaled to support and develop communities rather than cause their demise.

Beginning in 1993, I undertook a civic-action research project in five regions of the United States that connect with the global economy in different ways: the areas surrounding Boston, Cleveland, Miami, Seattle, and Greenville and Spartanburg in South Carolina. By looking at those cities and regions through the lens of business, I was able to view local economies not as abstractions or aggregate statistics but from the point of view of those inside the organizations that struggle every day to make and sell goods or services. I could listen to what real people had to say about how they were faring. I was able to sound out business and civic leaders about their strategies for improving their constituents' economy and quality of life in light of the global changes. And I identified some ways in which the global economy can work locally by capitalizing on the availability of those resources that distinguish one place from another.

The New Criteria for Success

In the industrial economy, place mattered to companies because it gave them control over the means of production—capital, labor, and materials—and access to transportation centers that minimized the cost of moving products from one location to another. In the global information economy, however, power comes not from location per se but rather from the ability to command one of the intangible assets that make customers loyal. These assets are concepts, competence, and connections. Today a place has value if it can provide companies with at least one of these resources.

Concepts are leading-edge ideas, designs, or formulations for products or services that create value for customers. *Competence* is the ability to translate ideas into applications for customers, to execute to the highest standards. *Connections* are alliances among businesses to leverage core capabilities, create more value for customers, or simply open doors and widen horizons. Unlike tangible assets, these intangible resources are portable and fluid, and they decline rapidly in value if not constantly updated. World-class companies keep their supplies of these assets current by being more entrepreneurial, more learning oriented, and more collaborative. They continuously seek better concepts and invest in innovation. They search for ideas and experience and nurture their people's knowledge and skills. And they seek partnerships with others to extend their competencies and achieve common objectives.

Companies have several ways of deriving concepts, competence, and connections from the communities in which they are located. Regions can be superior development sites for concepts because innovators can flourish there, come into contact with new ways of thinking, and find support for turning their ideas into viable businesses. Regions also can distinguish themselves by enhancing production competence through maintaining consistently high quality standards and a highly trained workforce. And they can provide connections to global networks in which businesses find resources and partners to link them with other markets. Cities can thrive as international centers if the businesses and the people in them can learn more and develop better by being there rather than somewhere else. Places can—and do—establish linkages to world-class companies by investing and specializing in capabilities that connect their local populations to the global economy in one of three ways: as thinkers, makers, or traders.

Thinkers specialize in concepts. Such places are magnets for brainpower, which is channeled into knowledge industries. Their competitive edge comes from continuous innovations and they set world standards in the export of both knowledge and knowledge-based products. Thinkers count on their absolute dominance in technological creativity and intellectual superiority to ensure their position on the world stage. The Boston area, for example, specializes in concepts—in creating new ideas and technologies that command a premium in world markets.

Makers are especially competent in execution. They have superior production skills and an infrastructure that supports high-value, cost-effective production. As a result, maker places are magnets for world-class manufacturing. Spartanburg and Greenville, South Carolina, are good examples of world-class makers: They have an exceptional blue-collar work force that has attracted more than 200 companies from many countries.

Traders specialize in connections. They sit at the crossroads of cultures, managing the intersections. They help make deals or transport goods and services across borders of all types. Miami, with its Latin American and increasingly global connections, is a quintessential trader city. Organizations such as AT&T selected Miami for their Latin American headquarters because of the city's Pan-American characteristics. Miami bridges Anglo and Latino cultures in the same way that Singapore and Hong Kong tradition-ally have linked British and Chinese cultures.

Boston, Miami, and Spartanburg and Greenville are distinctive as models of emerging international cities because of their em-phasis on one core capability. Each must develop a broader range of capabilities for its success to continue, but their stories offer lessons for businesses and cities everywhere about how to harness global forces for local advantage. For example, through a combi-nation of local and foreign leadership and influence, the Spartan-burg-Greenville area systematically upgraded its ability to meet the needs of world-class manufacturers. The history of the region's economic development is a lesson for business and community leaders seeking to understand what is required to achieve world-class status and bring local residents into the world economy.

An Unlikely Success Story

Spartanburg and Greenville, in the hill country of South Carolina, make an unlikely center for international industry. Yet these neighboring cities are the site of the highest diversified foreign investment per capita in the United States. Their success rests on the second intangible asset: competence. By achieving superiority in their ability to produce goods, these cities have derived benefits from the global economy as makers.

As in other U.S. cities, the center of activity has shifted from downtown to the shopping malls and industrial belts on the periphery. But what is found on the outskirts of Spartanburg and Greenville, and throughout the seven-county area called the Upstate, is unusual: a concentration of foreign manufacturing companies on I-85, the interstate highway that stretches from Atlanta, Georgia, to Charlotte, North Carolina. The local section of this highway is known as "the autobahn" because of the many German companies located there.

For decades, business leaders have worked with civic leaders to shape an economic development strategy that is almost a foreign policy. For the Spartanburg-Greenville region, foreign investment has been a positive force, bringing benefits to local businesses, workers, and the community beyond the infusion of capital and job creation. The presence of foreign companies has unleashed and renewed entrepreneurship and innovation, stimulated learning, heightened awareness of world standards, and connected local companies to global networks.

The cities of Spartanburg (population 46,000) and Greenville (population 58,000) and the seven surrounding counties contain almost a million people and share an airport. The region has a diversified economic base that includes textiles, high technology, metalworking, and automobiles. Unemployment stays well below the national average, and the I-85 business belt boasts the largest number of engineers per capita in the United States and the country's lowest work-stoppage rate. South Carolina's nationally recognized worker training program has upgraded the workforce and raised the average wage rate across the region.

The Upstate is now home to more than 215 companies from 18 countries, 74 of which have their U.S. headquarters there. The largest manufacturing employer is Michelin North America, a subsidiary of France's Michelin Groupe. It has three facilities in the region, a total investment of $1.5 billion, more than 9,000 employees in the state, and comparatively high factory wage rates of $15 to $16 per hour. R&D for Michelin North America also is in Greenville, and a test track and distribution center are located nearby. In 1985, the company moved its headquarters to Greenville.

The area entered the international limelight in 1992, when BMW announced it would locate its first-ever manufacturing facility outside Germany in Spartanburg County. Newspapers and magazines took note of the "boom belt" in the Southeast along I-85. The BMW facility promised to provide 2,000 jobs directly and create perhaps 10,000 more at a time when the U.S. auto industry was only beginning to emerge from recession and U.S. cities were desperate for sources of new jobs. Ecstatic locals donned T-shirts proclaiming the arrival of "Bubba Motor Works."

BMW's announcement made international headlines and created a local stir because BMW is a well-known upscale consumer product and a household name. But behind this highly visible investment stood several decades of investment by companies that were not household names but that had contributed to the worldwide reputation for competence in industrial skills that would attract BMW to the area.

The history of economic development in the Upstate represents one model for success in the global economy: a solid base of midsize entrepreneurial companies that innovate continually in basic manufacturing and employ a work force whose skills are regularly upgraded against world standards. Four factors are critical for success:

- visionary leaders with a clear economic development strategy who work actively to recruit international companies;

- a hospitable business climate and a positive work ethic that attract innovative manufacturing companies seeking to make long-term investments;

- customized training and gradual upgrading of workers' skills; and

- collaboration within the business community and between business and government to improve quality and business performance.

Leadership with a Global Strategy

The first major businesses in a region often provide the leadership and platform for the community's growth and development. Their industrial base and character shape the prospects for those who come later and provide connections between the community and the wider economy.

In the Upstate, foreign investment began in Spartanburg, and the foundation was large textile companies. When Roger Milliken, CEO of Milliken & Company, moved the company's headquarters and his family from New York to Spartanburg in 1954, he set in motion a number of forces that eventually brought economic strength to the region as a global center. Milliken saw the need to compete with inexpensive imports by modernizing equipment and raising skill levels to improve quality and bring labor costs under control. In the late 1950s, he started urging German and Swiss manufacturers that supplied the textile industry to set up shop in Spartanburg close to their customers. For many local residents, the arrival of Milliken and other northern executives was the first "foreign" influence in the area. It highlighted the need for improvements in education and brought cosmopolitan attitudes even before the foreign companies arrived.

Richard E. Tukey, executive director of the Spartanburg Area Chamber of Commerce from 1951 until his death in 1979, was the driving force behind efforts to attract foreign investment to the Upstate. Tukey was a visionary who realized that opportunities had to be cultivated for a declining textile industry that was the area's principal economic base. People in Spartanburg were open to for-

---

eign investment because the alternatives were poor jobs in textile or poultry plants or no jobs at all. Tukey went overseas to textile machinery shows to find investors and developed a wide network of business contacts in Europe. In 1965, he helped establish the U.S. base for Menzel of Germany in just four days, including locating housing for the plant manager and finding someone to write articles of incorporation for the company. When Kurt Zimmerli, CEO of Zima, first explored moving to the area, Tukey escorted him to banks and introduced him to community leaders. Tukey sometimes was criticized for paying more attention to outside investors than to local companies, but his persistence paid off in job growth that ultimately benefited local suppliers from construction crews to retailers.

Tukey was highly regarded by many civic leaders, and his allies included South Carolina's governors and lieutenant governors. He urged them to make the Upstate more attractive to Europeans by, for example, amending alcohol laws to make it easier to import wine. Tukey helped establish a variety of institutions that gave Spartanburg an international look, and he improved its cultural and educational offerings by initiating community events such as a German-style Oktoberfest and by working with local officials to create a state educational TV capability that was top-notch.

Reinforcing the Cycle of Development

The Upstate's business climate was hospitable to long-term outside investment, and the local work ethic was attractive to innovative companies. Spartanburg was the first of the two cities to catch the foreign wave, which started in the 1960s with a set of midsize companies that established their own greenfield sites rather than acquiring U.S. companies. Those companies stayed and expanded, often because their entrepreneurs were committed to growth in Spartanburg; some expatriates eventually became U.S. citizens and community leaders.

Several aspects of foreign investment in the area are noteworthy:

Industry Diversification Based on Core Skills. The textile industry provided a customer base, but the technical capabilities of the companies that moved into the area were not confined to one industry; they could be extended to many others.

Expansion and Upgrading. The foreign companies gradually expanded the region's functions, markets, and skills. Functions tended to expand from sales and service to manufacturing. Markets tended to expand from regional to North American to overseas. A regional office often became the North American headquarters. Initially, the companies transferred technology, standards, and skills from the foreign parent; eventually, many of the U.S. units outperformed the parents and educated them. According to a 1993 Greenville Chamber of Commerce survey of 87 foreign-owned companies, 80% had expanded since their arrival in the Upstate, and about 55% were planning a capital investment project in the next three years.

Entrepreneurship and Innovation. The first foreign companies were generally midsize. They had sent over individuals who could build new ventures from scratch and had granted them considerable autonomy to do so. U.S. operations were thus highly independent rather than subordinate branches of multinational giants; and foreign managers in the United States were entrepreneurs committed to growing the local business, not expatriates on short career rotations. Survival depended on a high degree of technological innovation.

Assimilation into the Local Culture. Companies generally sent over only a few foreigners, some of whom became U.S. citizens; the large number of U.S. hires gave the companies an American flavor. The first foreign company representatives were well-educated, English-speaking, cosmopolitan Europeans who could blend easily into the local population. Switzerland, Austria, and Germany—countries not intent on maintaining language purity or separatist traditions—were most often represented. Moreover, the original companies were not household names, not particularly visible, and not of particular interest to average citizens. But the new companies had a cultural style that complemented the local culture; they tended to sink roots and assimilate. According to local leaders, it took a long time for most people to realize just how many foreign companies there were in Spartanburg.

Among the first foreign companies to locate in the region was

Rieter Machine Works of Winterthur, Switzerland. Rieter, whose first U.S. chief was a friend of Roger Milliken's, located its sales and service office in Spartanburg in 1959 because the U.S. textile industry was at the time 30% to 35% of its market. (It is now 20%.) Rieter gradually expanded into manufacturing, increasing its investment in South Carolina. Although the company found numerous differences between operating in Switzerland and in the United States—from measurement to quality standards—it found that it could blend American entrepreneurial flair with Swiss technical precision to achieve outstanding results. Ueli Schmid, the current CEO of Rieter in the United States, joined Rieter in Switzerland in 1970, moved to the States in 1980, and became a U.S. citizen.

As the Upstate proved hospitable to foreign investors, expansion from sales and service offices to manufacturing began. Menzel, from Bielefeld, Germany, established its sales office in Spartanburg in 1965 but soon realized it was more practical to build machinery there. It was the first European company to do so, and its presence paved the way for others. Menzel created an innovative material-handling system for large-roll batching used in plastics, fiberglass, rubber, and other applications besides textiles. Now three times its original size, it produces machinery in the United States that it does not build in Germany and derives less than 40% of its revenue from the textile industry.

Cosmopolitan entrepreneurs such as Hans Balmer came with the initial German and Swiss wave. In 1972 at the age of 25, Balmer was sent on a two-year assignment from Switzerland as Loepfe Brothers' U.S. representative. Instead of staying just two years, he married an American and, in 1985, founded his own business, Symtech. Now, with nearly $50 million in sales, Symtech uses the best models of supply-chain partnering to integrate manufacturing equipment from multiple suppliers for its customers. Balmer also has brought other foreign companies to Spartanburg, and he succeeded Kurt Zimmerli as international committee chair for the Spartanburg Area Chamber of Commerce.

An exception to the predominance of small and midsize companies in the initial foreign surge was the German chemical giant Hoechst. Hoechst traces its local origins to its 1967 joint venture with Hercules, a U.S. chemical company. (In 1987, Hoechst merged with Celanese to form Hoechst Celanese.) The company has both raw materials and fiber plants in the area; in the chemical plant alone, equity investment totals close to half a billion dollars. A truly global organization, Hoechst is a cosmopolitan force in Spartanburg. It gives its U.S. business relative autonomy but creates cross-cultural linkages through employee exchanges and technology transfers between Spartanburg and other worldwide facilities.

Besides bringing jobs to Spartanburg, Hoechst brought another important local leader: Paul Foerster. In 1967, Foerster moved to Spartanburg from Germany on a four-year contract to run the fibers facility. The contract was extended until his retirement in 1990. A cultural cross-fertilizer, Foerster turned Hoechst Celanese into an important charitable contributor to the region despite the absence of a charitable tradition in Germany. Today Foerster is honorary consul for Germany, liaison to Europe for South Carolina, past chairman of the Spartanburg Area Chamber of Commerce, and the person responsible for much of the international traffic through Spartanburg.

In the 1980s, attracting foreign investment became an explicit strategy for Greenville as well as for Spartanburg. Greenville has had a successful Headquarters Recruitment Program since 1985, and in 1993, 14 foreign companies announced that they would open new regional headquarters or expand existing offices in the city. By 1994, German companies still dominated in the Upstate with 65 of the region's 215 foreign companies; British companies were second with 43, and Japanese third with 29. Although there were only 16 French companies, employment in them was almost as great as in the German companies because of Michelin's size. Foreign-owned service companies located in the region, as well. Supermarket conglomerate Ahold of the Netherlands, a member of the European Retail Alliance, employs 4,000 people in the Upstate through its Bi-Lo chain, headquartered in Greenville.

Improving Training and Education

Good attitudes are not enough; workers' skills must meet international standards. For more than 30 years, the state has led a collaborative effort to provide outstanding technical training—a crucial factor in expanding high-wage manufacturing jobs in the Greenville-Spartanburg area.

Contrary to popular belief, low wages or tax incentives were not the primary reason the first foreign companies were attracted to South Carolina's Upstate region. Indeed, recent studies by James Hines of Harvard University's John F. Kennedy School of Government have shown that state and other local tax incentives play little or no role in where foreign companies locate their businesses in the United States. Foreign investors sometimes do decide to locate in a particular place in the United States if they will get tax credits at home for state tax payments, but generally, business factors play a larger role. South Carolina's principal attraction is the competence of its workforce.

The South Carolina State Board for Technical and Comprehensive Education offers free, customized technical training of prospective workers and supervisors to companies that bring new investment to the state. The board assigns staff to prepare manuals, interview workers, and teach classes based on technical requirements established by the company. The company is not obligated to hire any worker who completes the training, nor do workers have to accept any job offer. In some cases, the state will pay to send first-time line supervisors for training elsewhere, even in a foreign country. Training benefits apply to major facility expansions as well as to new sites. A related initiative is the Buy South Carolina program, which supports just-in-time inventory systems by finding local suppliers.

A network of 16 technical colleges runs the State Tech Special Schools, including Greenville Technical College, rated by *U.S. News & World Report* as one of the best technical schools in the country. Devised as a crash program to deal with economic desperation in 1961, the State Tech Special Schools are now a national model. Since the network's inception, it has trained more than 145,000 workers for about 1,200 facilities, including more than 30,000 for the textile industry, 34,000 for metalworking, and nearly 18,000 for electrical and electronic machinery trades. In fiscal year 1992–1993, more than 6,400 people were trained for 121 companies, including U.S. companies such as Tupperware and Perdue, at a cost to the state of about $6.4 million. Companies also can draw on training from the Quality Institute of Enterprise Development, a private nonprofit venture spun off from the state's economic development board, which partners with the Upstate's technical colleges, the University of South Carolina at Spartanburg, and local chambers of commerce.

For German and Japanese companies with high technical and quality standards, such training is a major incentive. Mita South Carolina, a Japanese toner producer, used the State Tech Special Schools to build its U.S. workforce after arriving in Greenville in 1991 to manufacture for the North American market. Of its 150 current employees, only the top dozen managers are Japanese (the heads of engineering and human resources are Americans), and Japanese technicians were present only to install machinery and troubleshoot when the company started up. Some foreign managers want the workforce to meet even higher standards, and German-style apprenticeships are on the agenda.

The quality of public education also has improved because of new business investment. Foreign companies contributed by providing a sound tax base and a strong vision of what education should be by setting high standards for workers' knowledge. But, according to educators, the presence of foreign companies was an excuse for change, not a cause of it. Local interest and investment in educational reform have been consistent since the 1950s, and in the 1980s the public and private sectors collaborated on an increase in the sales tax to provide for a 30% increase in school budgets. The state saw a rise of 128 points in average SAT scores, and Richard Riley, South Carolina's governor during this decade, went on to join the Clinton cabinet as the secretary of education. Although there were widespread improvements in the entire public education system, particular innovations came in the areas of language training, world geography, and world cultures. Spartanburg's District 7 high school was one of the first in the United States to offer advanced placement courses, and it continues to receive White House Achievement Awards—the only high school in the country said to have won three times. Greenville's Southside High School is the only high school in South Carolina, and one of a handful in the United States, that awards the International Baccalaureate Diploma. This program is modeled on the curricula of

European schools and enables interested students to prepare to attend European universities.

International awareness and world-class capabilities are a priority also in the Upstate's colleges and universities. Skills in mathematics, science, computers, and technology are especially important because of the region's industrial base. However, educators also are upgrading language training, exchange programs, and internships abroad. For the latter, in particular, foreign companies are a key resource connecting local residents to many parts of the world.

Raising Standards Through Collaboration

Companies new to the Upstate discover strong cross-business and cross-sector collaboration that not only enhances business performance for both domestic and foreign companies but also strengthens the area's economy. Company executives comment repeatedly about strong networking, exchange of learning among businesses, and cooperation between business and government.

Strong, active chambers of commerce are catalysts for much of the cooperation, making the connections and mounting the programs that serve as the infrastructure for collaboration. The Spartanburg Area Chamber of Commerce has 1,800 members from 13 municipalities forming seven area councils. In 1989, it joined with the Spartanburg County Foundation—a charitable organization that supports community activities—and other groups to launch the Consensus Project, a community priority-setting activity based on a set of critical indicators of Spartanburg's community "health." The project began with about 75 leaders and eventually got feedback from many citizens. It has led to adult education, programs to prevent teenage pregnancy, and Leadership Spartanburg, a program that trains community leaders.

The Spartanburg Chamber offers programs that have directly improved business performance. It has a "vice president for quality"—an unusual office signifying the Chamber's activist role in industry and one that encourages innovative companies to learn from one another. In 1981, Milliken instituted a pioneering internal quality program, leading to a string of awards: the American Malcolm Baldrige National Quality Award, the British Quality Award, Canada Awards for Business Excellence, and the European Quality Award. Milliken was the first, and in some cases the only, fabric supplier to receive quality awards from General Motors, Ford, and Chrysler. With inspiration from Milliken, the Chamber's committee on quality launched the Quality in the Workplace program in 1984, very early in the U.S. total quality movement. In addition to educating numerous local companies, including those without their own quality or training staffs, the program extended the principles of quality to nonprofits such as the United Way.

The Greenville Chamber of Commerce—the state's largest, with 3,000 members—also facilitates collaboration. Companies exchange best-practice ideas, screen employees for jobs, encourage new companies to come to the area, solve one another's problems, and sometimes even lend one another staff. A monthly Chamber-sponsored manufacturers' discussion group helps with employee relations problems—something particularly beneficial to foreign companies employing a U.S. workforce—and serves as a job-finding network by circulating resumes and lists of names. When Sara Lee opened a plant in Greenville, Fuji's plant manager helped the company implement worker teams. At a Chamber "prospect" dinner, the representative of a smaller company being enticed to the area mentioned that the company could not afford a human resources function right away. Other manufacturers present, including Mita, volunteered to build a team of their own people to serve in the interim, to screen resumes and do the hiring.

Collaboration increasingly extends beyond political jurisdictions. A joint airport helped break the barrier between the two cities, and the wooing of BMW involved still more cooperation. Encouraged by a call from the governor's office, Greenville's and Spartanburg's hospital systems wrote a joint proposal about medical services in the area for BMW. The two cities compete for business investment, and there are continuing turf battles, especially among local politicians. But there also is a great deal of cooperative and overlapping activity; Greenville relishes Spartanburg's successes and vice versa. Behind these attitudes is more than the simple desire to be friendly. Leaders of the region increasingly acknowledge their shared fate as the pressures of growth and the stress on the existing infrastructure increase the demands on local resources. Many Spartanburg businesspeople call for greater cooperation between Spartanburg and Greenville, and between business and government, and even for the merger of the cities and counties into one metropolitan area. The Upstate's record of success in addressing the challenges of becoming a world-class maker will continue to be tested as the opportunities that have resulted from achieving global competence give rise to the challenges of sustaining growth.

Localizing the Global Economy

Ask people in Spartanburg and Greenville about the influence of foreign companies on their area, and they immediately turn to culture and cuisine: the annual International Festival; the Japanese tea garden, said to be the only authentic one in the United States outside the Japanese embassy in Washington; a surprising number of international organizations per capita; and many sister-city relationships. But the real impact has to do more with opening minds than with changing eating habits. Local residents have become more cosmopolitan, with extended horizons and higher standards.

The presence of foreign companies raised the adrenaline level of the business community, providing a new perspective that increased dissatisfaction with traditional practices and motivated people to improve. It was impossible to sustain sleepy local companies in an environment in which world-class companies came looking for better technology and skills. Business leaders and the workforce are now more aware of global standards. Suppliers to foreign companies credit them with raising standards to world-class levels.

The main concern that residents have about foreign companies—a concern reluctantly but consistently voiced—is whether they will donate money or provide leadership to the community. Tensions often are framed in terms of community service, but the real problems come from local residents' suspicion that foreign companies that move capital into a community can all too easily move it out again and that locals will have no power to stop them.

It takes time to educate foreign companies, many of them from countries whose social network is supported by government alone, about the United States' self-help, volunteer, and charitable traditions. But there are notable exceptions and increasing community support from foreign companies. Kurt Zimmerli, Paul Foerster, and Hans Balmer are frequently mentioned as examples of immigrants who became community leaders. Ueli Schmid secured a pool of money from Rieter to spend on discretionary local contributions. BMW makes its new facility available for community events. The self-reinforcing cycle of welcome succeeds as the Upstate's hospitable business climate creates an environment in which cosmopolitan leaders are willing to make deep commitments to the community.

Moreover, the locals' view is generally positive because foreign and outside investment has helped retain—and expand—home-grown companies in the area. For example, one of Spartanburg's oldest companies, Hersey Measurement, was saved by a joint venture between a U.S. and a German company. Hersey was founded in 1859 to manufacture rotary pumps, bolts, and general machinery, and its new owners from Atlanta decided to keep the company in Spartanburg because of the excellent workforce. They expanded operations and built a new plant that doubled the size of its local facilities. Lockwood Greene Engineers, one of the oldest engineering-services companies in the United States, was reinvigorated by a German company after the failure of a management buyout. Metromont Materials, a leader in concrete, was rescued by a British company after large U.S. companies abandoned the industry. And locals report that even for residents not working at foreign-owned facilities, jobs are better paid and of better quality as a result of foreign investment in the region as a whole.

Becoming World-Class

The story of the Spartanburg-Greenville region illustrates what it takes to acquire the mind-set of the new world class. Cities and regions must become centers of globally relevant skills to enable local businesses and people to thrive. World-class businesses need concepts, competence, and connections, and world-class places can help grow these global assets by offering capabilities in innovation, production, or trade. Cities and regions will thrive to the extent that the businesses and people in them can develop better by being there rather than somewhere else.

To create this capability, communities need both magnets and glue. They must have magnets that attract a flow of external resources—new people or companies—to expand skills, broaden horizons, and hold up a comparative mirror against world standards. The flow might involve customers, outside investors, foreign companies, students, or business travelers. Communities also need social glue—a way to bring people together to define the common good, create joint plans, and identify strategies that benefit a wide range of people and organizations. In addition to the physical infrastructure that supports daily life and work—roads, subways, sewers, electricity, and communications systems—communities need an infrastructure for collaboration to solve problems and create the future. Community leaders must mount united efforts that enhance their connections to the global economy in order to attract and retain job-creating businesses whose ties reach many places.

And business leaders must understand how strong local communities can help them become more globally competitive. Businesses benefit from investing in a region's core skills. They derive advantages not only from creating company-specific resources but from establishing linkages outside the company as well. Local collaborations with international giants operating in their area can help smaller companies raise their standards and propel them into wider, more global markets. Leaders of large companies can strengthen their own competitiveness by developing a supportive environment in the primary places where they operate to ensure the availability of the highest-quality suppliers, workforce, living standards for their employees, and opportunities for partnership with local leaders.

VI

Values and Purpose:

The Meaning Behind Management

Overview

What are the responsibilities of business leaders, and to whom are they responsible? As the strategic connections of businesses continue to expand beyond links to customers, suppliers, and venture partners to encompass nonprofit organizations and community collaborations, questions of social values and social responsibilities inevitably arise. Evidence has mounted that the companies that endure, showing sustained profitability and growth over many decades, consider their purpose to involve more than money. Such businesses are not simply financial engines or production machines. They are human institutions filled with people who come to work as members of communities, bringing with them their social, religious, and ethical values. This is true of CEOs who ponder their legacies when the historical records are written. It holds for professionals who want to imbue their work with a sense of mission. It matters for the front-line associates who want to feel that the time spent at work is meaningful.

Writing statements of corporate values has become popular for companies. They try to articulate the higher purpose of the enterprise in order to unite employees in a common cause and to offer them codes of conduct to guide their everyday decisions. These statements can inspire pride and raise aspirations, or they can remain empty words on paper that reinforce cynicism (see "Values and Economics"). Stated values must be supported by policies and actions that make them real, and they must permeate the daily life of an organization. When Texaco preaches non-discrimination on paper while its executives make rude jokes about African-Americans in closed-door meetings, how much will employees believe in any of its stated values? Managing by values can be a powerful motivational tool, as earlier chapters in this book show, but it can also be a dangerous one if leaders are not prepared to hold themselves to the high standards they set for others. People can become more committed to companies with strong values, but before doing so they will scrutinize every aspect of the company to see whether its leaders live up to its declared values.

Whether companies should have values at all is at the heart of the shareholder versus stakeholder debate taking place in businesses around the world. Some would say that the only "value" worth mentioning is shareholder value, as capital markets seek high financial return. Clearly, capitalism is flourishing in nearly every nation, but the institutions of capitalism are social creations. The public will not long support uncaring capitalism; it demands demonstrated concern with societal well-being (see "Money Is the Root . . ."). Money is no longer considered the root of all evil; it is clearly a tool that can be used to increase quality of life. But by itself, without communal values, the search for wealth can be empty and devoid of meaning. Business leaders need to ask fundamental questions about the kind of life their enterprises make possible—or fail to make possible—for themselves and for others.

We must think long-term about the kind of world we're creating for the twenty-first century. We need businesses that consider the impact of their activities on future generations and invest for long-term success, not short-term quick hits (see "The Long View"). We need leaders who create shared visions that motivate and inspire because they are based on enduring values that will serve society well into the future.

23

Values and Economics

"The vision thing" is giving way to "the values thing" in the lexicon of business leaders. Established corporations are searching for values in their pasts; entrepreneurs are formulating philosophies they hope will last well into the future. One CEO wiles away the airplane miles adjusting the items on the company mission statement to fit the acronyms on his statement of values. Another, well known for his bias for action and impatience with philosophizing, slows down long enough to engage his top management in crafting guiding principles. Nonprofit organizations, long the stepchildren of the management world, are suddenly admired for their capacity to instill a sense of mission and purpose.

Some companies see their values as a source of competitive advantage. Jim Burke, former chairman of Johnson & Johnson, is a legendary advocate, arguing that J&J's credo was responsible for the company's rapid action in taking Tylenol off the market after a poisoning scare. To prove his point, he commissioned a study of the financial performance of U.S companies that have had a written value statement for at least a generation. The net income of those 20 companies increased by a factor of 23 during a period when the GNP grew by a factor of 2½.

For other companies, values are a kind of corporate glue. Global enterprises in volatile markets may use values to provide a common denominator, a source of structure and stability for people of many nationalities in far-flung units.

Chuck Exley, former CEO of NCR, looked for longer range principles that could guide business practice even in light of shrinking high-technology product life cycles; he chose an Italian executive based in Latin America to shape the communication of NCR's "recreating value for stakeholders" philosophy. Jack Welch sees

GE's management principles as a primary source of corporate value added for highly diverse business units.

Values also offer guidance and control for workers, who increasingly function as independent decision makers—for example, the team with the power to stop production if a core principle is violated. Internalization of values and standards can replace direct surveillance in ensuring conformity. And values are a powerful motivational tool for the new work force, especially when promotion prospects are dimmer and the do-good drive supplants monetary success in the popular imagination.

But there are reasons to be skeptical about the values push in business. The relationship between values and performance remains equivocal. Research nets mixed results, with uncertain causality. Critics argue that financial success gives companies the luxury of considering and proclaiming their values. Anyway, many corporate value statements ring hollow, invoking the same lofty generalizations that are tacked up on every company's bulletin boards: "Our customers come first." "Our people are our greatest assets." Important ideas, certainly. But meaningless when they become soundalike clichés.

Moreover, the company value statement can mask hypocrisy and sham. If a company that deifies "quality" sacrifices it for short-term profits, cynicism prevails. Worse yet, in some companies the attempt to spread corporate values is viewed as authoritarian, an excuse for intrusion into people's innermost thoughts or for the imposition of one group's beliefs on another. One prominent multinational found the equal opportunity principles in its code of conduct challenged on religious grounds by employees in a rural location. A company widely praised for its esprit de corps alienated a few managers who experienced its team-building exercises as "brainwashing."

So it is important to think carefully before jumping on the values bandwagon. Some key conditions must be met for values to matter.

Where credos make a difference, the values are appropriate to the business. They fit what the business is trying to achieve; they reflect a theory of the business, a model of its success factors, that clarifies the relationship between its values and economics. Banc One's "uncommon partnership" philosophy, valuing both local autonomy to serve the customer and shared operating standards to create a unified team, derived from a shrewd understanding of profit drivers and people motivators. Without a theory linking a company's values and economics, any statement of values contributes more to global warming than to competitive advantage; it is just hot air.

Clearly, it is also important for corporate values to be appropriate to the people comprising the organization, congruent with their skills and consistent with their goals. Values should be inclusive—general enough to embrace diverse parts of the organization and diverse people. One company's attempt to spread a new management philosophy relevant to its traditional operations wing failed in a publicly humiliating way because the marketing group—mostly young MBAs—rebelled.

To be meaningful, values must enter into the daily life of the organization, with violators punished and exemplars rewarded. That way, the organization will equate abstract statements of principle with concrete models and lessons. But the values must reflect enduring commitments, not ephemeral notions. Thus leaders who are tempted to manage through values had better be prepared to examine their own—and to put their actions where their hearts are.

24

Money Is the Root . . .

Money and its management are at the heart of much of the institutional restructuring taking place around the world. Political and economic reform in Brazil. German unification. The shift to convertible currencies and market economies in Eastern Europe. Proposals for rethinking the American banking system. Controversies over the role of debt in corporate performance. Calls for new corporate performance measures and new management accounting systems.

Money cannot be viewed only in terms of rational efficiency. Social values—and the politics associated with them—inevitably intrude on "rational" business plans. So to be effective, restructuring and revitalization must involve revisiting root principles.

Consider our future world economic system. "Capitalism has won," we are told. But capitalism of what kind? The "Three Capitalisms"—American, Japanese, and German—vary in their social values and cultural habits as well as in their financial institutions. In fact, capitalism, once assumed to be exemplified by American individualism, now finds some of its best practitioners flourishing in other value systems. German scholar Max Weber's 1904 classic, *The Protestant Ethic and the Spirit of Capitalism,* could be retitled *The Confucian-Buddhist Ethic and the Spirit of Capitalism.* Today asceticism, diligence, and thrift are associated with rapidly growing Asian nations. Singapore, South Korea, and Hong Kong enjoyed the world's highest mean economic growth over a 20-year period; Taiwan and Japan were not far behind.

Values are being debated wherever capitalist institutions are being created or recreated. Consider the call for changes in the financial services industry in the United States. Distaste for the savings and loan bailout came from more than its price tag. The

American public was concerned not just with monetary losses but also with how those losses occurred—speculation. Thus both economic and social purposes must influence banking reform.

At stake is not just the value of money itself but also the value we put on money. In the United States, Main Street has long been suspicious of Wall Street—and even more suspicious of Easy Street. Similarly, distrust of speculators and traders, whether merchants or bankers, has a long tradition in Western history. Even in Florence, which financed the Renaissance, secular authorities fined bankers for usury and tried to prohibit credit transactions altogether, according to British historian R. H. Tawney. The German word *Schuld* means both "guilt" and "debt."

Today debt has lost its moral sting, and money too easily becomes detached from purpose. But both business and society are endangered when people see themselves as making money rather than products, or growing rich from speculation rather than labor. Some Japanese worry that too many of their compatriots are obsessed with money technology—*zaitek*—instead of real technology. There are concerns about a declining Japanese work ethic.

It is time to ask root questions: Is wealth production really the goal of business, as some economists say, or is wealth a by-product, an incentive en route to other ends? When a corporate mission statement contains only one goal—to create shareholder value—has an essential ingredient been lost? Entrepreneurs, considered the quintessential wealth producers of our time, certainly do not grow businesses on that kind of empty mission. Many entrepreneuers and business heads today—from Ben Cohen of Ben & Jerry's to Jeffrey Swartz of Timberland—are successfully pursuing goals to which money is merely the means. In both cases, the idea came first, the money later.

By design, money is anonymous and purposeless—a universal, easily counted medium of exchange whose value is independent of its origin or destination. Legend has it that Parisian urinals are sometimes called *vespasiennes* after the Roman emperor Vespasian, who taxed public urinals and claimed that "money has no smell."

Money also has no loyalty. As it speeds instantaneously around the world and the last barriers to currency convertibility disappear, money earned in one locale can be spent anywhere. Communities can too easily be drained and not built. Even the savings of the poor flow out to more affluent communities. By returning banking to its neighborhood roots, institutions like South Shore Bank in Chicago attempt to resolve such tensions. It is now a nationwide model for community banking, along with BankBoston's First Community Bank.

Similarly, the fact that money can be counted means that financial measures can swamp other measures of performance and value and claim disproportionate time and attention—even when the counting is suspect. Sometimes, the financial measures are not the right ones for strategic decision making. CEOs can suffer from stock price addiction—losing sight of business purpose because of the seduction of following price movements.

Yet addiction to money is all too easy to understand. Just think about those ubiquitous lists of the world's richest companies and the world's richest people. How often do we see lists of the companies that have created the most jobs or done the most for the environment or trained the most employees to build future capabilities? Even those indicators of social value that are starting to appear (like the "most admired companies" lists) are published only once a year. Stock prices are available by the minute, every minute.

As community affiliations weaken—and the inducements to worship money mount—wealth threatens to replace other kinds of achievement as *the* basis of the global social pecking order. Perhaps the United States needs its own equivalent of the British knighthood to confer status and privilege on grounds other than wealth.

Still, money *is* connected to well-being. French philosopher Albert Camus reminded his countrypeople that "it's a kind of spiritual snobbery that makes people think they can be happy without money." In the industrialized world, money does seem to buy happiness. Using European Commission and university-based studies, political scientist Ronald Inglehart showed that reported happiness increases with family income in most countries (with Japan and Italy as glaring exceptions).

It will be interesting to see whether the association between money and happiness continues. By and large, today's rich are not a leisure class but a working class. In well-paid occupations in the

United States, for example, working hours have increased while leisure time has decreased. But working parents are unhappy when they have too little time to spend with their families. And perhaps the lesser happiness expressed by wealthier Japanese reflects the work absorption long associated with Japanese affluence.

At the same time, "*lack* of money is the root of all evil," as George Bernard Shaw paraphrased. A seemingly permanent underclass in the United States and Great Britain surrounds some of the most affluent cities. The juxtaposition of wealth and poverty, with appetites aroused but thwarted, contributes to growing urban violence. When legitimate opportunity is blocked but illegal means are close at hand, crime is rational. When the future holds no hope, people may seek illicit gratification now.

Lee Brown, former police commissioner of New York City, has recognized these correlations in his vision of community policing. But the challenges Brown faced underscores the money problem. While police officers can become social workers, drug counselors, and neighborhood problem solvers, they cannot provide jobs for or attract investment to the community.

Yet throwing money at problems will not solve them either. The experience of Chicago's South Shore Bank shows the difference between "charity" and "investment" in helping poor communities. Money by itself, without skill building or institutional change, can produce dependency, bureaucracy, and temptations to fraud. And charities have their own version of money addiction: a fundraising addiction that diverts their focus from doing good works to collecting money.

Too much money can also be associated with waste or lack of discipline. Adversity can breed innovation. Studies of entrepreneurship indicate that too much capital and too few checkpoints can harm fledgling enterprises. Even managers in Britain's National Health Service admit that tighter budgets have forced them to develop worthwhile innovations.

Money should never be separated from mission. It is an instrument, not an end. Detached from values, it may indeed be the root of all evil. Linked effectively to social purpose, it can be the root of opportunity.

25

The Long View

The issue of time horizons is complex. Long term is not automatically better than short term. Some businesses suffer from too little short-term thinking; for example, waiting for the future development project rather than innovating constantly today. Policies aimed at encouraging long-term investment that make it harder to break relationships, cancel commitments, or harvest proceeds in the short term also make it easier for unproductive, permanently failing organizations to limp along without changing.

More relevant are the connections between the short and the long term—that is, whether managers or investors consider the long-term consequences of their short-term actions. Institutions need both the flexibility to change quickly in shorter cycles and the focus to make dedicated long-term investments.

The ability to take the long view rests on social and political factors as much as it does on economic incentives. A complex system of relationships and interactions is involved in financial investment decisions. Rewriting the rules of this system requires political will. It requires simultaneous action on the part of many institutions, from government and the electorate to individual businesses and capital sources.

For long-term dedicated investment, interests must not only he aligned, they must be intertwined. It is not enough for people and institutions to march in the same direction; they must be willing to help each other along the way, seeing that their fate is shared. The direction the U.S. economy, or any economy, cannot be determined without a social consensus stemming from an awareness of interdependence.

Recent global political and economic upheavals have exposed the fault lines of history. Cracks in the sociopolitical consensus, widened by economic stagnation, can easily become earthquakes. Longstanding ethnic strains caused Yugoslavia to splinter violently, Czechoslovakia peacefully. The seemingly superefficient, unstoppable German economy faces labor strife and resentment of its burdens from the East. In the United States, decades of labor conflict died down in the 1980s, but stockholder conflict heated up. Today's political debate features the middle class versus the underclass. Yet commentators decry "special interest group politics" as though there were any other kind of politics!

Businesses operate through coalitions of stakeholders trying to maximize their own interests through their participation. Depending on national traditions and economic conditions, these coalitions can be highly unstable and conflict-ridden. Owners, employees, customers, or suppliers do not always want the same thing. Allies protect their own interests even while signing joint venture agreements. One partnership among European companies was being finalized on a lower floor of a German company's headquarters, while on the floor above, the company was buying the stock of its partners in preparation for a takeover attempt.

Whenever there is disagreement about organizational purpose, performance, or profit distribution, cooperation is replaced by conflict, and the ability of leaders to make long-term decisions is threatened. Those who met over power breakfasts to make deals in the 1980s are meeting in court in the 1990s. A recent parade of bankruptcies among U.S. retail chains was called "the lawyers' relief act" because of the multiple lawsuits stimulated by economic distress. Creditors sued the investment banks and accounting firms, vendors sued suppliers who were paid more, banks in lending consortia sued each other. In the meantime, management scrambled for capital for the long-term improvements to turn around the company and give stakeholders their share.

To gain the will to encourage long-term dedicated investment, human and organizational factors loom large. For example:

People take the long view when they have a deep understanding of system dynamics. They see the connections between actions in one place and consequences in another. They can therefore appreciate the need for indirect long-term investments (whether research and development experiments, infrastructure repairs, or education).

This understanding comes, in part, through valuing the past as a source of learning from experience. Examining history helps elicit root principles, cause-effect relationships, and insight into dynamics, trajectories, and consequences.

How easy it is, and how dangerous, to write-off or rewrite history! A financial services holding company pursuing an aggressive acquisition strategy discovered this too late, after it barely avoided bankruptcy. The CEO attributed the success of the company's initial purchases to its acquisition know-how, ignoring the many other factors involved, from a rising economy to selection of niches with weak competition. Despite repeated urging, he had no interest in careful assessment of the company's experience. Lacking understanding of the many variables involved in success, the company accelerated its acquisitions because of the "good deals" on the market. When financial performance deteriorated, the CEO commissioned a study that totally disconfirmed his preconceptions about selecting and managing acquisitions. Investing in the future was jeopardized by a failure to learn from the past.

Similarly, early leaders of many young Silicon Valley computer companies said their organizations were "different," a new model that would avoid the pitfalls other companies encountered as they grew. Therefore, they wanted only people who would invent new things; they thought experienced managers had nothing to teach them. When growth slowed and their products matured, they scrambled—often too late—to attract seasoned professional managers.

Knowledge is central to the new information-based economies. The strength of Japanese and German companies is derived from their ability to transmit knowledge in many directions across their organizations—a process that slows them down but enhances long-run competitiveness. Global managers are knowledge organizers and transmitters. While the value of business schools can be debated, the value of teaching and learning cannot.

Learning comes from a respect for experience and the desire to improve on it. Americans tend to overvalue new knowledge and undervalue experience. The United States is an example of what anthropologist Margaret Mead called "post-figurative cultures," in which children teach their parents the new skills needed to cope with the future. The Western belief in linear progress and the frontier experience of continual fresh starts in new locations reinforce the idea that the past is irrelevant. Yet some of the global economy's most formidable competitors come from Asian countries with cultural traditions of honoring age and the wisdom that comes from experience, countries whose religious beliefs stress cyclicality, holism, and repetition of timeless patterns.

People take the long view when they feel a commitment to those who come after them. They want to build enduring institutions and leave a legacy for the future. They care about posterity—their children and other people's children—and therefore see the need for actions to benefit the distant future, such as preserving the environment.

Who is "posterity"? Posterity does not vote, buy stock, supply products, or engage in any other form of immediate economic action. Yet people are sometimes motivated to sacrifice today's returns for the benefit of this invisible stakeholder. They save for their children and their children's children. They become philanthropists. They embrace ideals like national destiny, as America did in the nineteenth century and Japan did in the twentieth, that justify hard work and limit current consumption. Rekindling idealism involves a reminder that today is another step in history and an assurance that people's actions matter at the grass-roots as well as in the executive suite.

People care about their place in history when their own past is valued. If the past is obliterated, it is hard to care as much about continuity into the future—the reason black pride movements in the United States aimed at bringing blacks into the economic mainstream through rediscovering African roots. *An Orphan in History*—the title of a moving book by Paul Cowan about the search for roots—has a hard time finding sustaining values or believing in the future.

Chief executives of excellent companies known for long-term innovation, such as James Burke, retired chairman of Johnson & Johnson, are articulate about the many predecessors whose actions made today's achievements possible. They therefore want to pass on an institution of even more value to their successors. A grounding in history is a useful antidote to arrogance, and it enlarges a sense of responsibility for ensuring that assets do not deteriorate. Is it coincidental that students of history often become leaders? During the era when Yale College produced a large number of future CEOs of some of the top U.S. companies, the most popular major was history, not economics.

People take the long view when they believe the rules of the game are fair. They believe they will share equitably in the returns. They see that others play by the same rules.

It is hard to take the long view alone; why defer gains that might erode while others are cashing in? Those that might be willing to dedicate investment for the long-term common good are turned off by a system that they see as biased against them. American Airline's chief executive Robert Crandall was upset that bankrupt airlines can keep flying, thereby putting his company at a cost disadvantage, which makes it harder to generate capital for growth plans. A health care company is concerned about predatory pricing in a region with business practices that differ from those of its home base and, as a result, limits its investments to sure quick hits. Taxpayers' revolts are stimulated not just by concerns about government waste but also by concerns about whether others are paying their fair share.

People take the long view when they perceive leaders as trustworthy. They see that decisions take their needs into account, and therefore they feel included in plans. They believe that leaders mean what they say.

Trust is a matter of bets about future actions based on experience. A track record of keeping promises is a good predictor. Realigning interests and rebuilding commitment after traumatic restructuring events, for example, often consists of making short-term promises and keeping them, as a way to restore faith in leadership.

Chief executives who say they want to take the long view blame stakeholders with shorter time horizons for their companies' inability to invest in the future. Wall Street is not the only whipping boy. Bankers, venture partners, and unions are decried at board meetings for wanting to get more now, thereby forcing companies to cancel growth plans that would, executives claim, provide more for everyone later. But often these same complaining chief executives do not work hard enough on stakeholder involvement and consensus. They erode their credibility with stakeholders by violating agreements or squeezing them for more.

The future is inherently uncertain. Investment always requires faith as well as sacrifice. When actions demonstrate that leaders cannot be trusted to keep promises, the willingness to defer today's rewards is undermined. Skepticism that things will improve increases the desire for instant gratification. Gluttony is a logical corollary of loss of faith in the future. At many companies, well-paid young managers demand more compensation now because they see no point in waiting for a long climb up a crumbling corporate ladder.

Judging credibility, like assessing fairness, is a matter of viewing history. The long view stretches in two directions, backward as well as forward. Willingness to dedicate resources to secure the long-term future is grounded in values and experiences from the past.

Strengths derived from a company's home-base can be assets in global competition. Such regional strengths are historically rooted. The Japanese system of dedicated investment benefits from long institutional and familial relationships in dense, culturally homogeneous networks with shared values and a clear understanding of the contribution of each member to the success of the others—and the nation. In contrast, Americans, with short historical memories, a taste for fresh starts, and a diverse population of independent interests, face a significant challenge in crafting stable coalitions. Yet the opportunity provided by mobility and liquidity of capital and relationships has also helped the United States fuel entrepreneurship and avoid class warfare.

Preferring voluntary action over governmental restraint, Americans are not likely to rewrite the rules to favor longer term investment unless they also find a sense of common national purpose and common destiny. The emphasis for countries as well as companies should be on inclusion rather than exclusion. In a global economy, national pride should not be an excuse for protectionism but a call to respect and enhance the strengths of all constituents.

The lesson for today's leaders is clear. The long view must be a shared view. And it must reach in two directions, embodying wisdom and values from the past as well as hopes and dreams for the future.

Acknowledgments

The following colleagues and research associates deserve thanks for contributions through the years to research and consulting projects reported in this book, although any errors remain my responsibility: Kalman Applbaum, Janis Bowersox, Allan Cohen, Wendy D'Ambrose, Kenneth Farbstein, Henry Foley, William Fonvielle, Robert Gandossy, Lisa Richardson Henske, Myron Kellner-Rogers, Norman Klein, Martha Miller, Paul Myers, Jeffrey North, Todd Pitinsky, Gina Quinn, Rosanne Royer, Tobias Seggerman, William Simpson, Barry Stein, David Summers, Margaret Wheatley, Pamela Yatsko, Madelyn Yucht, and Joseph Zolner. Thanks are also due to John O'Connor for artwork and Nan Stone for many editorial contributions.

Research was conducted primarily through Harvard Business School, with the generous support of the Division of Research. Some projects were carried out at Yale University or Goodmeasure Inc., a Cambridge, Massachusetts, consulting firm. These organizations also deserve thanks for their support, as do numerous leaders in numerous companies around the world who provided opportunities and access.

The superb members of the team at HBS Press were outstanding collaborators in book preparation, including (but not confined to) Carol Franco, Sarah Merrigan, Nicola Sabin, and Gayle Treadwell.

Index

About the Author

Rosabeth Moss Kanter holds the Class of 1960 Chair as Professor of Business Administration at the Harvard Business School. Before joining the Harvard Business School faculty in 1986, Professor Kanter taught at Brandeis and Harvard Universities (1967–1977) and at Yale University (1977–1986). She was also a Fellow in Law and Social Sciences and a Visiting Scholar at Harvard Law School. She co-founded Goodmeasure, Inc., a consulting firm specializing in managing change, serving as chairman since 1977 and producing *A Tale of "O": On Being Different,* one of the world's best-selling videos on workplace diversity. From 1989–1992 Professor Kanter was also editor of the *Harvard Business Review,* a finalist for a National Magazine Award for General Excellence in 1991.

Professor Kanter has received numerous national honors, including a Guggenheim Fellowship, 18 honorary doctoral degrees, and several "Woman of the Year" awards. She has been a consultant to major corporations all over the world, including Bell Atlantic and BankBoston in the U.S., Northern Telecom in Canada, Volvo and Novartis in Europe, and San Miguel in Asia. She has served on government commissions on economic issues, including innovation and entrepreneurship, employee involvement, and takeover laws, and served on the Board of Overseers for the Malcolm Baldrige National Quality Award. She co-chairs the Massachusetts Governor's task force on international trade. She is also on the boards of public interest organizations such as City Year, the American Center for Quality and Productivity, and the Economic Policy Institute in Washington, and is a Fellow of the World Economic Forum and a member of the Council on Foreign Relations.

Professor Kanter was featured in the nationally broadcast American television special, "Quality or Else" (1991–1992), and was the subject of two prime-time television documentaries on the leadership of change by the British Broadcasting Corporation in 1988 and

1990. She hosts *Rosabeth Moss Kanter on Synergies, Alliances, and New Ventures* in the Harvard Business School Video Series and a new HBS Best Practices video series on partnering.

Professor Kanter is the author of *World Class: Thriving Locally in the Global Economy,* about the impact of globalization on businesses, workplaces, and communities. It shows how "collaborative advantage" produces success in the new economy. She also wrote *When Giants Learn to Dance: Mastering the Challenges of Strategy, Management and Careers in the 1990s* (1989), which received the Johnson, Smith & Knisely Award for New Perspectives on Executive Leadership and was translated into 10 languages. Other books include *The Challenge of Organizational Change* (1992), *The Change Masters: Innovation and Entrepreneurship in the American Corporation* (1983), and *Men and Women of the Corporation* (1977), winner of the C. Wright Mills Award for the year's best book on social issues. She has published 12 books and over 150 articles. "Best article" awards include a McKinsey Award from the *Harvard Business Review.*